MW00397146

The
LEGACY OF
LEADERSHIP

Leading with the End in Mind

**BIBLE STUDY
EDITION**

TOM OSBORNE

WITH CHAD BONHAM

Foreword by Dan Whitney, "Larry the Cable Guy"

THE LEGACY OF LEADERSHIP

Tom Osborne with Chad Bonham

ISBN 978-1-929478-35-4

Cross Training Publishing
www.crosstrainingpublishing.com
(308) 293-3891

Copyright © 2023 by Cross Training Publishing

Photo Credit: Joe Mixan and Gordon Thiessen

Cover Design: Seth Rexilus (WonderWild Co.)

All rights reserved. No part of this book may be reproduced
without written permission from the publisher, except by a
reviewer who may quote brief passages in a review; nor may any
part of this book be reproduced, stored in a retrieval system or
transmitted in any form or other without written permission from
the publisher.

TABLE OF CONTENTS

FOREWORD

I literally have nothing to do with Nebraska football other than I grew up in Pawnee City, Nebraska, as a huge fan of the Cornhuskers, and I'm now seven pounds shy of being a Husker left tackle. I do, however, feel like I'm qualified to write this foreword merely, because like every other Nebraska football fan that grew up in the Tom Osborne era, he was part of the soundtrack to our lives (that and the Eagles).

No matter what problems were going on in the world, we could always count on two things to keep everything balanced: the tractor pull at the fair and T.O. leading another Husker squad to a winning season. It was so automatic it got boring—like a 90-year-old hitting a driver 155 yards down the middle EVERY time. It was glorious.

I didn't meet Coach until 2005, and during that brief meeting, I could understand why his players and everyone associated with him loved him. Not only was I star-struck, but he was like a grandpa to me within the first 15 minutes. He did and said everything a loving grandpa would do and say, minus the phrase, "Pull my finger." It was the coolest thing ever to engage with my childhood hero.

As my relationship with him grew, and we got together a little more often, I not only began to love him as a legendary coach, but as a man who is unashamed to let people know of his love for Christ and how it molded everything in his life. I volunteer for the Fellowship of Christian Athletes and Coach Osborne, is the essence of FCA.

It's incredible to read this book and hear stories from former players and his impact on their lives—life lessons that extended way beyond the playing field but also resonated onto the field making people victorious in their spiritual and personal lives. I loved Tom Osborne as a kid because of football. Now that I have a family, I love him more for his faith walk and how he taught kids how to be champions in football as well as life. The proof is in this book and I'm honored to write the foreword.

Go Big Red! Love ya Coach!

~ Dan Whitney, aka Larry The Cable Guy

PROLOGUE

I will forever be thankful for Coach Osborne when he asked me if I had ever heard of FCA after practice. I recall thinking, "He knows I'm a Lincoln kid, so why is he asking me about the Farmers Coop of America?" He explained to me it was the Fellowship of Christian Athletes. He encouraged me to become involved and become one of the leaders. Several players in the 1960s were active, but there had been little activity in the 1970s. That changed my life as I later worked for FCA for 28 years and still serve as a volunteer.

As you will read in this book, former Husker Rod Yates and successful real estate developer states that Tom Osborne was a "wealth creator." I couldn't agree more. But we would both say that it was more than financial wealth. It was his example of faith, family, friends, and football. He always had a way of properly prioritizing these categories and helping other men do likewise. He left all of us a legacy of leadership.

When Coach Osborne asked me to publish this book, I was honored that he would ask me, and I appreciated him listening to my suggestion to add new content to his leadership teachings over the years. While you can find some of the principles in his previous books like *Mentoring Matters* or *Coaching Matters*, he has much more to teach me and many others about authentic leadership in a day when we badly need it. Tom also let me add interviews from former players, coaches, and others who validate the leadership principles in his book. Tom also let me add interviews from former players, coaches, and others who validate the leadership principles in his book which you will find at the end of each chapter "In Other Words."

As a former player and someone who has continued to be around the program, I knew many great stories about his leadership. Still, as Chad Bonham began to send me the interviews, I was so pleased with how well they illustrate what Coach Osborne has taught while he was coaching, serving in Congress, serving as Nebraska Athletic Director or leading a large non-profit like TeamMates Mentoring.

I'm thankful for all those who contributed stories to this book. You might find it interesting that I not only published this book as a former player, but the photos by Joe Mixan and cover design by Seth Rexilous were also by former Huskers.

Thanks to Tom Osborne, his family, and the organization he founded, TeamMates Mentoring, with their help to complete this book. Thank you to Monte Lange and Chris Anderson for your work on editing and proofing.

Finally, the one lesson Coach Osborne most helped me understand is to live with the end in mind. In other words, live life backward, by considering the one thing in the future that is certain—our death—and work back from that point. Him knowing his destination helped make sense of the journey. He coached like John Wooden by prioritizing the journey and not the scoreboard. The destination he has pointed his life toward is service to his Lord. He has let that end guide his priorities and goals.

~ **Gordon Thiessen**
Publisher (Husker 1975-79)

INTRODUCTION

It seems to me that some people are very concerned about leaving a legacy. For a politician, his or her legislative initiatives, peace accords, and economic proposals all play a part in the quest for a legacy. For authors, it's the number of books sold and the number of times they made it on the bestseller's list. In the same way, a coach's concern with legacy often focuses on their win-loss records.

Ron Brown, my longtime assistant coach at Nebraska, once told me, "Your legacy is not going to be about championships and wins and losses. It's going to be about things that have to do with the development of players, spiritual matters, how players are treated, and whether they grow personally or not."

I believe Ron spoke the truth. I've had many former players who are now successful in a variety of professions tell me that some of the most important years of their lives were the years they spent as a football player at Nebraska learning about perseverance and discipline and character. If there is any legacy, that is it.

You can live each day with your legacy in mind. You can make a difference in the lives around you, whether those who are under your direct leadership or those in your family, church, or community. When you strive to be a great leader, it's all about the journey, and the positive changes you have affected in the lives of those who need to be guided, mentored, or even given a glimmer of hope for the future.

Many people believe a legacy of leadership is measured in terms of success. So what is success? Is it just about winning? The acclaim? Trophies? Wealth? Personal happiness or satisfaction? I've been blessed to experience some of those things over the years, and I can answer that even though these things are nice at the time, they do not result in an enduring sense of meaning and purpose.

Accomplishments, applause, and awards are rewards that often come as a result of hard work and a determined spirit, but there is something bigger, something better, something that will outlast the winning season, the plushest corner office, the heftiest bonus, and a lot of cheers. That something can only be found when we look beyond the final score.

In your present leadership role or the one in which you will find yourself in the future, remember, it's not about numbers, how powerful you are, the number of championship titles you earned, or how well-liked you are. It's about how you lived your life and how you influenced the lives of others. I believe that is the true secret to great leadership.

What will you leave behind? How will others remember you? What is your legacy? Don't take leadership opportunities for granted. You only pass this way once, so make every opportunity to serve count.

As you read the rest of this book, keep that in mind. The true legacy of leadership is not about you. It's about honoring God through your leadership and serving those that you lead.

A note to readers. This book is based on the belief that each of us has a physical side, an intellectual capacity, and a spiritual nature. In my estimation, effective leadership involves nurturing all three facets of human capacity. Our culture has come to elevate physical and intellectual achievement, pushing spiritual matters aside.

The Greek philosophers Plato, Aristotle, and Socrates recognized the importance of these three dimensions in 300-400 B.C.

This book examines all three areas in relationship to leadership.

Many don't believe spirituality is part of effective leadership. This book is predicated on the idea that spirituality, is fundamental to leadership.

~ Tom Osborne

PART 1

~~~~~~

FOUNDATIONAL
ACTIONS

1

~~~~~~

CHAPTER ONE

ACCOUNTABILITY

THE LEGACY OF SUBMISSION

I was born in the late 1930s. My dad was a salesman, and he traveled the western part of Nebraska five days a week. The only time I saw him was on Saturday and Sunday. My mom spent a lot of time with me. She was a former teacher and taught me to read when I was a very young child.

On December 7, 1941, news that Pearl Harbor had been bombed came over the radio. I was only four years old, but I remember my dad's reaction. He jumped out of the chair and said, "I'm going to get into this thing," even though he was beyond draft age. My dad joined the Army, and we moved to St. Paul, Nebraska, to live with my grandparents.

When I was about six years old, I acquired a brick from somewhere in the neighborhood and, for some reason, decided I was going to throw the brick up on the roof of a neighbor's house.

To my consternation, the brick came down and went right through a window. I went home and told my mom about it. She marched me over there and had me knock on the door. The dad came to the door, and I was shaking in my boots.

I was amazed. He was very kind and said he had already put a pillow in the broken window. Our neighbor didn't say anything more about it. That was just one example of how my parents were never going to let me get away with doing something like that. At that moment, even though I had not yet learned the word accountability, I received an unforgettable lesson on exactly what that word meant.

Accountability is taking responsibility for your actions and performing the duties that you're to do as a parent, as a business leader, as a coach, as a pastor, as an employee, etc., and making sure that you live up to expectations that are placed upon you.

Being accountable as a leader, to yourself and to those you are serving, means telling the truth when, at times, it might be more advantageous to lie or distort the facts.

Accountable leaders don't use people like pawns on a chessboard. On the contrary, accountable leaders are more concerned with how they treat people and are willing to face the consequences of their actions.

All Day, Everyday

When people are accountable, it builds trust. People within the organization are going to know that they can trust the leader because the leader is going to hold himself to the same standard as everyone else.

Throughout my life, I was accountable to different people and groups at different stages. First of all, I was an assistant coach for 11 years. Bob Devaney was the head coach, and I was accountable to him. And then as head coach for 20 years, he was the Athletic Director so I was still accountable to Bob. We had more than 30 years together and I tried not to disappoint him.

When I was in the U.S. House of Representatives, I was accountable to my constituents in Nebraska's Third Congressional District, to my fellow congressmen and congresswomen, and ultimately to the U.S. Constitution.

Then, when I returned to Nebraska as the Athletic Director, I was accountable to the Board of Regents, the university's President, and to the many Nebraska alumni, fans, and supporters.

Those are just a few areas in my life where I needed to recognize and respect the concept of accountability. In fact, we all have multiple forms of accountability that we encounter on a daily basis. These include:

- Society: We are accountable to civil laws and moral codes that serve as guard rails, which are meant to encourage fair and respectful treatment of one another.
- Employers: No matter how high up the ladder, you are still accountable to a boss, whether that be in the form of a Board of Directors, Board of Trustees, or corporate shareholders.
- Work Peers: Similar to civil society, we are accountable for being part of a positive work environment in which the general well-being of each individual is a priority.
- Family: Parents are responsible for the physical, emotional, and spiritual care of their children. Family members are also often expected to promote accountability within the extended family unit (parents, siblings, etc.).

• God: We are ultimately accountable to a higher authority through biblical principles and even the natural order of creation.

In other words, accountability is an all-day, everyday proposition that, when lived out consistently, makes our world a much better place to live.

Off the Rails

On the other hand, there are many dangers for the leader with little sense of accountability. It's the metaphorical equivalent of hiking a mountain alone with no safety measures. There are many pitfalls and traps, and it's easy to lose one's way, or, even worse, go completely off the rails.

It seems that we see less accountability in many leaders today. Not having accountability can quickly give way to a leader's selfish ambitions and desires. So much modern-day leadership revolves around expediency and what looks good at the moment in exchange for higher salaries, higher profiles, and greater influence. True commitment and integrity are often tossed to the wayside.

We can be tempted to cut corners or slander someone else for personal gain. If there's no accountability for those looking to skirt the rules, not only do they eventually get hurt, but everyone around them also pays the price.

This sharp decline in accountability is pervasive throughout society, particularly in the political arena. It would be refreshing if somebody in the political arena would say, "I made a mistake," or, "We made the wrong decision," or, "This was my fault." You rarely hear that. Instead, most blame somebody else or circumstances to deflect personal responsibility when things go badly.

In God's Eyes

The principle of accountability has been around since the beginning of time. In the Book of Genesis, God instructed Adam and Eve not to eat from the tree of the knowledge of good and evil (Genesis 2:16-17). It was a guideline meant to protect them.

Unfortunately, as we read in Genesis 3, Eve fell prey to temptation and disobeyed God's command. She then shared the fruit with Adam, and both had to pay a severe price for their sin. That decision had a ripple effect of eternal proportions that we're still feeling today.

Later in biblical history, Jesus' teachings brought new light to the topic of accountability. In the Parable of the Talents (Matthew 25:14-30), Jesus talked about three servants who were given various financial resources to invest and steward in their master's absence. Two of them turned their talents into an increase, while the third hid his talent because he was afraid of losing it which angered his master. Two were rewarded for their efforts, while the third was severely punished.

In this story, accountability is referring to a responsibility for something one has been given (resources, relationships, etc.), and how those gifts make us accountable to God, to others, and even to ourselves. Power and position should have no impact on a leader's accountability.

Today, if often seems that the more authority a leader gets, the less accountability they display. In God's eyes, however, the more authority you have, the more accountable you are.

Our nation was founded on principles recognizing that we are accountable to God. When we remove those principles from the equation, self-interest emerges quickly. It seems we are drifting in that direction as a nation, which is very concerning.

None of us are perfect, and being human, we will fail at times. However, in the end, we can hope that the general trajectory of our lives and actions result in the accolade, "well done, good and faithful servant."

For we must all appear before the judgment seat of Christ, so that each one may receive what is due for what he has done in the body, whether good or evil. (2 Corinthians 5:10/ESV)

A Higher Standard

Accountability doesn't have to be a difficult endeavor, but there are some steps which make it an effective and enduring process. Here are a few things a leader can do in order to foster accountability for themselves and for those that they lead.

1. Be responsible to those you serve: Enter your leadership role from a posture of humility and service. As long as you are not being asked to compromise your beliefs, break the law, do something unbiblical or unethical, etc., be prepared to faithfully follow your governing authority and accept the consequences of your actions—good or bad.

2. Set guidelines: Be honest to your superiors about your strengths and weaknesses and put organizational and personal guardrails in place accordingly. This is also true for the guidelines set for employees, players, co-workers, etc. Make sure that those you lead have a clear understanding of what is acceptable and what is not.

3. Have clear consequences: There should be no question as to what will happen to you as a leader (or to followers) if guidelines are ignored or disobeyed.

4. Create strategic partnerships: Lock arms with older, more experienced mentors who will help you stay true to the guard rails and guidelines that have been set in place for your protection.

5. Lead by example: The best way to foster accountability among those you lead is to show them what accountability looks like at the top. Any hint of hypocrisy will result in a loss of trust which, in turn, fragments an organization.

6. Be transparent: Admit your mistakes. Don't create a false narrative. Leaders who lead with transparency and are clearly accountable will reap the benefits of loyalty, trust, and respect.

Somewhere along the way, hopefully, faith will come into play. We are called to a higher standard. Accountability may not necessarily mean that you're going to get paid more, or that you're given a promotion, or that you're going to get better press. Those things might be positive outcomes, but they should not be the motivation.

At the end of the day, an accountable leader should take the approach of a servant leader, where it's not all about you, but it's about trying to do the right thing and serving those you are leading the best you can.

In Other Words

I tried to be a very disciplined player throughout my years at Nebraska. That attitude paid off in more ways than one. I never fumbled in a game, penalties were rare, and I was never called for a personal foul.

But one day in practice during my senior season, a young player on the scout team was trying to get noticed and move up the depth chart by hitting me with a cheap shot. I exploded with anger, threw him to the ground, and engaged in some extracurricular activity.

Coach Osborne jogged down the field, yelling at me to get back in the huddle. He saw the cheap shot, but he was directing all his attention on me, the veteran player who should have known better. There was no way I would ever do that in a game, and I believe Coach Osborne knew that too, but his mantra was always, "If you do it in practice, you can do it in a game."

The next day in meetings, we were watching practice film, and we got to the part where I lost my cool. Coach Osborne stopped the tape and said, "Well, here's where Kenny possibly cost us the game by getting a 15-yard personal foul penalty."

He rewound the film and showed it again and kept going back and forth, back and forth. I couldn't believe it. I wasn't a troublemaker. I was a former walk-on that couldn't afford to mess up. I was always a rule follower and, at this point, a five-year veteran on the team.

And I think that was the point. Coach Osborne used me as an example—not just to point out that a 15-yard personal foul penalty could cost the team a game, but that all players would be held accountable for their actions. It's a lesson that served us well as we left the program and became leaders in our homes, in our churches, and in our communities.

~ **Ken Kaelin, Nebraska Football Player (1983-86)**

Coach Osborne felt a heavy responsibility to everyone involved in the football program—the players, the coaches, the staff, the university, the donors, and really the entire state of Nebraska. So, that probably explains some of the small things he did behind the scenes.

He knew the names of every player on the team, and he prayed for them before every game. I would say he also knew the names of 80 to 90 percent of the players' parents, and the ones he didn't know were the ones he didn't have the chance to meet. That was true for the scholarship players and the walk-ons alike.

Tom would spend one week with each coach on their recruiting trips. One thing I always noticed was how he took time to read and respond to every letter sent to him. And if someone thanked him for writing back, Coach would write back again—thanking each one for the thank you note!

Coach Osborne was also accountable to himself through an impressive life of self-discipline. He worked out almost every day of his life. We were in St. Louis one night and didn't get to our room until 11 o'clock. He was in the room next to me, and I heard his door close. I thought something was wrong, so I got up and looked down the hall. He was going out for a run.

Tom was also disciplined in how he ate. After his open-heart surgery, he had a very strict diet and never deviated from what he was supposed to do. Those things have become even more intense as he's gotten older, yet he has remained disciplined and accountable to himself and his doctors.

His commitment to the players, the coaches, the administration, and the fans, along with his personal discipline and accountability, rubbed off on everybody around him. Many people don't talk about those little things. But those little things really were big things and made a big difference in the success of Nebraska football.

~ Charlie McBride, Nebraska Assistant Football Coach (1977-81) and Defensive Coordinator (1982-99)

I played my final game for Nebraska at the 1984 Orange Bowl. I spent the next two years playing in the USFL with the Washington Federals and the Orlando Renegades. The first week I was in D.C., I picked up a drug addiction, and it followed me all the way to Atlanta, where the Falcons had signed me as a free agent in 1986.

By then, I was a full-blown addict. I really wasn't there to play football. I was just there. Before I played my first NFL game, cocaine convinced me that football was getting in the way of my use, so I walked away from the game and quit the NFL to become a full-time drug addict.

I was in prison four times and went to 10 treatment centers (I graduated from nine of them). I lost everything, including the two people who loved me unconditionally—my parents, who were both in Heaven.

In 2008, I was in prison for the fourth time, just kind of existing. I was in a very bad place mentally. I wasn't suicidal. I was closer to being homicidal. I wasn't going to hurt myself, but I had no problem hurting somebody else.

One day, the guard was picking on me, and I decided I was going to do something to him that would probably keep me locked up for the rest of my life. But the next time I saw him, he had a letter in his hand. He saw the look in my eyes and threw it on the floor before he could get too close.

For some reason, I picked up the letter and noticed the big red "N" on the corner of the envelope. It was from Nebraska's Athletic Department. I was immediately embarrassed. It took me a few minutes, but I finally got the courage to open it and read it. I have that letter memorized to this day:

"Dear Ricky, I know your parents believe in you. I believe in you. And upon your release, if there's anything I can do to help you, feel free to contact me."

The letter was from Tom Osborne, who was then the Athletic Director at Nebraska. At that moment, I fell on my knees in my prison cell and turned my life over to Christ.

When I got off my knees, my thinking started changing.

When I got released, I went to Memorial Stadium for the first time in over 20 years. It was a long walk up those stairs to his office. Coach Osborne greeted me with kindness. All I wanted to do was thank him for writing that letter because it kept me from making a decision that would have cost me my freedom for the rest of my life.

"Ricky, I just wrote a note," Coach said.

"Nah, Coach," I replied. "That letter came at the right time. It really meant a lot to know that somebody of importance in my life actually cares."

Ever since that day, I make sure to spend a few minutes with Coach once a week. I let him look me in the eye, and I look him in the eye. He's laid a foundation of accountability and shown me the importance of helping others. I will never let him forget what he's done for me. I became a licensed counselor and started the RCS Triumph Foundation. I go into treatment centers, prisons, churches, and schools—anywhere I can to help people.

Coach Osborne gave me the courage and inspiration to do something about my circumstances. It was all because of the leadership skills provided to me when I was a player for him, and the things he constantly repeated to me once I got my life turned around.

~ Ricky Simmons, Director of the RCS Triumph Foundation, Nebraska Football Player (1979-83), and USFL Player (1984-85)

2

CHAPTER TWO

~~~~~~~~

PRIORITIES

THE LEGACY OF ORDER

There are three dimensions of the human experience: the physical dimension, the intellectual dimension, and the spiritual dimension. An effective leader will be disciplined in all those areas, which will take shape in the form of priorities.

Priorities are simply an ordered list of your responsibilities to God, to others, and to yourself—all of which fit into one or more of the dimensions listed above.

In Stephen Covey's book *Seven Habits of Highly Successful People*, the second habit listed is entitled "Begin With the End in Mind." We should look at what we think will be important at the end of our lives and prioritize our time and effort accordingly.

Different leaders will have different priorities, but some core principles should play a factor in how those priorities are decided and acted upon. Let's take a look at how the three dimensions of the human experience factor into the prioritization process.

The Priority of Physical Discipline

Some people may prioritize physical health for vain purposes—to look good and attract attention. But keeping your body in good condition (both inside and out) has a much more impactful purpose.

If you've ever traveled on a plane, you've probably heard the flight attendant's instruction regarding oxygen masks: "Put your mask on first before helping someone else who needs assistance."

When you first hear those words, it might sound out of order or even self-serving. But you can't help others with their mask if you can't breathe. This is also true in our physical life. It's more difficult to help care for someone else's needs if you are impaired or physically struggling.

Physical discipline is even more important for those professions or personal endeavors that require physical health and strength. This is true for firefighters, police officers, construction workers, physical trainers, lifeguards, etc.

When I was a player and during my early years in coaching, organized physical training only occurred during the season. After two disappointing seasons in 1967 and 1968, things changed at the University of Nebraska. Boyd Epley was hired as the strength and conditioning coach. At that time, weightlifting was thought to cause athletes to be "muscle bound" and was discouraged by most coaches. Boyd was a pole vaulter who had gotten into weightlifting and told me that he thought strength training would help the football team.

Bob Devaney was the head football coach at that time, and he was willing to give Boyd a chance.

This transformed football at the University of Nebraska from three months of football in the fall and a month of spring football into a year-round training regimen involving weight lifting, flexibility, and agility workouts combined with good nutrition.

Over all those years, I saw that people who were most disciplined in their approach to conditioning were the most successful. If you weren't in the weight room and if you didn't practice hard, you had no chance.

It was interesting to see walk-on players, those who came without a scholarship, pass by the highly recruited scholarship athletes by out-working them.

We made sure that our team culture was a meritocracy. Everyone, scholarship or walk-on, was given an equal chance, and playing time was earned, not awarded due to reputation.

Carrying that over to my personal life, I've always tried to maintain a regular workout schedule. I still try to exercise each day for 30 to 45 minutes, whether cardiovascular activity or strength training.

Even though I jogged three to four miles a day and was in good condition, I was 48 years old, and I was having some chest pains. I thought it was just a chest cold, but I was having trouble keeping up with one of my coaches when we were jogging one day in San Diego.

I called a cardiologist in Lincoln that I knew and told him that I needed a checkup. I told him my symptoms, and he said he would be waiting to see me when my plane landed. I told him that I would see him when recruiting ended in two weeks. He was adamant that I come in as soon as possible. I did what he told me to do, and an angiogram showed 95 percent blockage of the left anterior descending artery, which was ominously known as "the widow maker." Surgery was performed the next morning. This came as a complete shock as I was not overweight, had never smoked, and exercised regularly. However, there was a history of heart disease in my family.

I was in a bit of a quandary because I wanted to continue coaching but I had two other arteries that were 30 percent blocked. The conventional wisdom at that time was that if you had blockage of an artery, it would probably re-block within six to seven years.

Dean Ornish was a nutritionist and cardiologist who wrote a book indicating his belief that atherosclerosis could be reversed. He advocated three things: group therapy, meditation, and diet.

I thought my diet had always been fairly good but I did make some changes. I also started to practice meditation every morning for about 20 minutes and then at noon for another 10 minutes. I combined that with prayer. Meditation was simply calming and focusing your mind. I found that was helpful, and I think that it was something that led to less stress. As a result of these changes to my physical discipline, I was able to coach for another 13 years, and I've not had a major recurrence of artery blockage. As a matter of fact, the bypassed arteries are still wide open 38 years later.

It also helped when I began delegating more responsibilities. I started to rotate the noon luncheon on Mondays and the early Friday morning breakfast in Omaha among our assistants. I prioritized what was important and took some of the extraneous non-essential things off my plate. I had to reorder my life to stay healthy with less stress so I could focus on the things that needed to be done.

I was still working 85 to 90 hour weeks, but the changes made a difference.

The Priority of Intellectual Discipline

We hear a lot about mental health these days, and there's a good reason for it. Our minds are collectively under attack from an onslaught of negative news, discouraging divisiveness, images of violence and depravity, and reports of war and chaos. Certainly, there are biological reasons for some of our world's mental health crises, but much of the depression and anxiety can be linked to factors that are more within our control than we might realize.

That's why it is vitally important for leaders, in particular, to protect their minds from destructive inputs and instead fortify their thoughts with constructive and positive ideas. We'll talk about the spiritual discipline of reading the Bible a little later, but there are other methods to making intellectual (or mental) discipline a priority.

One of the ways I've tried to stay mentally sharp is through reading. Even while in the throes of my coaching career, I stayed abreast of current events by reading the newspaper every day, but not the sports pages. Sometimes it was a fairly quick glance at certain things I was interested in, but it was that routine that brought balance to my day. I also read books on a regular basis, even if I just managed two or three pages per day.

Intellectual discipline can also mean actively improving your craft through workshops, classes, research, or receiving instruction from advisors or mentors. I know those professional advancements were always helpful throughout my career and helpful to my assistant coaches as well.

Making intellectual and mental discipline a priority will help you be a better leader in more ways than one. Keeping close tabs on what you allow into your thought life can help relieve stress and anxiety while simultaneously improving yourself intellectually and educationally, and it will increase your effectiveness within whatever specialized roles that are a part of your leadership position.

The Priority of Spiritual Discipline

Spiritual discipline is, in my opinion, a very important discipline and should always be high on any leader's priority list. Much like physical discipline, it isn't easy to handle challenging matters if you don't have a spiritual base.

A definition of spirituality that I like is this: Spirituality involves the recognition of a feeling or sense of belief that there is something greater than yourself. In other words, it is not all about me.

When I was coaching, I would get up at 5:30 in the morning and spend about 30 minutes in prayer and meditation. We started our coaches' meetings at 7 a.m., with a 10-minute devotional that included our trainers and strength staff. We read a Bible verse, discussed what it might mean for us, and then closed with a prayer. Around noon, I usually spent a few more minutes in prayer and meditation as a way to refocus for the rest of my day. And then in the evening, I would take some time to read a few verses of scripture before I went to bed.

Year round, I attended a weekly Bible study early on Friday morning (a Bible study I still attend), and our family went to church together on Sunday. This made a difference for me then, and it makes a difference for me now. Spiritual discipline might be different for you. However, steady discipline is required to improve in any area of endeavor, and this is true in spiritual matters as well.

Real Life Priorities

There is no one-size-fits-all priority list that can be applied to all leaders, but there are some core areas of life that should be near the top. Let's take a look at two important priorities that every leader will likely be committed to in order to be successful: family and team.

Family

It's nothing new, but as time passes, we see more instances where leaders put their careers and job responsibilities above family. Therefore, it should be no surprise that there is greater discontent in marriage than ever before, and our children are being drawn deeper into social media, virtual worlds, and in some cases, destructive behaviors.

That's why leaders should prioritize their family—caring for their spouse and children's well-being and strengthening that unique and lasting bond. After all, what's the point of having success if you've created a train wreck in your home and can't truly enjoy that success with the people you love the most?

Coaching is a difficult profession when it comes to priorities. Our staff worked 12 to 15 hours a day throughout the season and during recruiting, but I wanted to make sure that everyone made as much time as possible for their families. We worked until 10 p.m. on Sunday and Monday, when preparation for the next opponent was most intense. I expected each coach to have studied and graded the Saturday game film by noon on Sunday. Some graded the film late Saturday night, and some chose Sunday morning. I was up late Saturday, so our family could go to church on Sunday. We met at 7 a.m., Monday, Tuesday, Wednesday, and Thursday. Then after practice on Tuesday, Wednesday, and Thursday, we had dinner with our families and studied film at home once our children were in bed. I stayed with the team the Friday night before a Saturday game.

Recruiting was difficult as we lived in a sparsely populated state, so we recruited in every state. There was always one more phone call to make, one more film to watch, and one more plane to catch. This schedule sounds awful, but I talked to many coaches on other staffs who never saw their children for months. They left in the morning before their children were awake and got home after they had gone to bed for weeks on end.

During the offseason, life was more normal. I took a full month in July, mostly away from the job, to give the family my full, undivided attention.

So was I a good parent? My children knew I loved them and did the best I could, but I missed some important times with them and I regret that very much.

My kids have turned out to be really solid people and people of faith. I've been very proud of all of them, but most of that was due to my wife, Nancy. She went to every little league baseball game and every PTA meeting. She understood what needed to be done. She was there and she was very strong.

Parenting should always be a high priority, but there are many distractions in our country today. There is a lot of content on television, in movies, and on the Internet and social media that can lead people astray and distract them from their true priorities and values, which are found in the family.

There will also always be tough times in marriage. It's easy to cut and run and fall for the lie that the grass is greener on the other side of the fence, but that's not what we're called to do. We're called to be committed to our spouses and our children.

Team

Most leaders spend the bulk of their day at work. There are key relationships within that environment that might include peers and co-workers, employees, or, in the athletic sense, fellow coaches, athletes, and support staff. As leaders, we have an obligation to look out for the best interest and well-being of those we are working with and leading.

A few years ago, sportswriter Mike Babcock wrote a book called *The Heart of a Husker*. He interviewed 38 former players and asked them about the culture of our program. There was a common response from nearly all of them. There were 150 players on our teams. Nearly all noted that we knew their names, and they felt like the coaching staff cared for them and invested in them.

And it's true. We did care about them. We cared about their education. We cared about their character.

I always took time during fall camp to share my spiritual journey with the team. "If I'm going to be making decisions that affect you and you feel like I'm inconsistent with what I'm saying here about my spiritual walk and how I treat you, and how we run this football team, you are certainly free to call me on it."

Putting the needs of others at the forefront of leadership, whether that's your family or your team, will make you a better leader. It will also make for a much more pleasant (although never perfect) journey along the way.

An Ordered Life

Followers, employees, and team members often take on the characteristics of their leader. If a leader is willing to cut corners in his business or his personal life, you'll soon see that become pervasive throughout the organization or in his family. On the other hand, if the leader is disciplined and has a clear understanding of what matters most, you're more likely to see others follow his lead in that direction.

As a coach, I was responsible for many things like the Xs and Os, the organizational meetings, the practices, recruiting, and game management. It all had to be fairly detailed, and it required time and discipline.

There was a prioritized procedure that we went through every week. We would grade the film of our previous game and show it to our players. Then, we systematically prepared for opponents through an organized practice schedule, weightlifting, and all the things that we felt were necessary.

Systems and programs will look different for each leader, but there is a responsibility to lay those things out in a clear, orderly fashion. Otherwise, people will be going in a hundred different directions. Whether conscious or not, followers take on their leader's approach.

So, when you see dysfunction within an organization, it also usually starts at the top. However, if an organization is well structured and hits on all cylinders, it usually starts also at the top.

An Out of Order Life

Unfortunately, there are many supposedly successful people who later on have deep regrets about how they prioritized their life and put their self-interests over their families. Looking back, they can see a trail of broken relationships. Whether it's coaching or running a small business, it's far too easy to get caught up in the rat race. There's always one more phone call to make, one more piece of film to look at, or one more thing in the back of your mind.

Leaders tend to fall into two broad categories. The first group is those who are primarily self-serving and mostly interested in their economic benefits, their gratification, and their prestige. These leaders tend to do whatever it takes to be "successful," even if that means viewing their employees as nothing more than a means to accomplish their individual goals.

In that scenario, there's usually resentment, and often times the organization doesn't function very well.

The difficult thing to see today is how many people are abandoning their family responsibilities. Over half of our young people today are growing up without both biological parents. That is one of the most serious problems the United States faces today—the destruction of the nuclear family. I've mentored a lot of kids, and most of them have had some type of broken situation in their family. You see how much pain that causes and how much difficulty there is in those circumstances.

One of the ways ineffective leadership can be addressed is by understanding what requirements need to be in place before priorities are set—that is, a true understanding of the leader's roles and responsibilities balanced against the leader's values.

Leaders have professional responsibility but that can't take precedence over the individual's personal values. If you've decided that family will be a priority but the job requires you to consistently sacrifice personal time to work extra hours, a decision about whether or not that job is right for you will need to be made. This is a struggle I had in coaching and serving in Congress. I hoped there was enough balance there, but I am not sure I was a great example. The same is true if you've decided that personal integrity will be a priority but the job requires you to cut corners or creep into unethical behavior.

So, priorities aren't just about ordering your time and your effort, but priorities are also about deciding what your values are and what you aren't willing to compromise in exchange for job security or financial prosperity.

An Upside-Down Principle

So much of what we've discussed can be found within biblical principles. Here are a few examples:

On physical discipline: *Or do you not know that your body is a temple of the Holy Spirit within you, whom you have from God? You are not your own, for you were bought with a price. So glorify God in your body.* (1 Corinthians 6:19-20/ESV)

On intellectual discipline: *Finally, brothers, whatever is true, whatever is honorable, whatever is just, whatever is pure, whatever is lovely, whatever is commendable, if there is any excellence, if there is anything worthy of praise, think about these things. What you have learned, received, heard, and seen in me—practice these things, and the God of peace will be with you.* (Philippians 4:8-9/ESV)

On spiritual discipline: *Rejoice always, pray without ceasing, and give thanks in all circumstances; for this is the will of God in Christ Jesus for you.* (1 Thessalonians 5:16-18/ESV)

On family as a priority: *Train up a child in the way he should go; even when he is old he will not depart from it.* (Proverbs 22:6/ESV)

Ultimately, the best way to prioritize as a leader is to put God first and allow order to flow out of a commitment to Him first and to others second.

God's Kingdom is different from our world's system. The world says to take care of yourself first and then give others what is left over. But God says to take care of others first and then He will ensure you have what you need. That's an upside-down principle for sure, but there is much more joy, peace, and contentment to be found when you prioritize God and others ahead of your desires, goals, and dreams.

Finding Balance

Some leaders want to have their priorities in order but don't know how to balance spiritual, relational, physical, financial, and professional responsibilities. There is a great deal of potential wreckage if you don't pay attention to each of the important areas of your life.

If you're struggling to make a clear list of priorities, pray for guidance and ask a spiritual advisor for help. Once you've received clarity, write everything down, make a specific plan with time limits, and commit to sticking to the plan. Another thing that helps is limiting or eliminating any activities that might be time robbers or unnecessary distractions.

And most importantly, don't get so focused on tasks or long-term goals that you fail to take care of your spiritual, emotional, mental, intellectual, or physical needs. When those areas are strong, you are better equipped to serve the needs of those you are called to lead. Prioritizing our lives takes sacrifice, but it's always worth it in the end.

In Other Words

During the mid-1990s, Nebraska football dominated. I had the opportunity to interview head football coach, Tom Osborne, for an article in the Fellowship of Christian Athletes' *Sharing the Victory* magazine. Because of his success, there were plenty of reporter questions about his methods and leadership style. Still, I wanted to get to the heart of the matter—his faith. I played for him during the 1970s, so I knew he was a believer, but I wasn't aware of the specifics.

I asked him how often he prays and studies his Bible. Pretty simple. In a matter-a-fact manner, he said, "I usually spend time early each morning to pray and read the Bible for about an hour. Then again, I will try to find time during lunch if I can." Here was the busiest man I knew, telling me he regularly prioritized these two important spiritual disciplines. Many reporters were puzzled by Osborne's ability to handle stress and lead a national program. Not me. His character and leadership came from his daily relationship with his Lord.

**~ Gordon Thiessen, Cross Training Publishing, Co-Founder
of Kingdom Sports, and Nebraska Football Player (1975-79)**

I tragically lost my son when he was 15 years old. When Coach Osborne found out, he came to see how our family was doing. He brought me a devotional book and another book about Heaven. Although he had never lost a son, Coach did his best to empathize based on his experience of losing Brook Berringer, who was like a son to him.

It was truly incredible that he took the time to care about me and give me resources that he thought would help me in my time of mourning—even though I hadn't played for him in more than 20 years.

I run into Coach now and then, and he still knows my name and specific things about my life. That's not a surprise, really, because every Saturday morning on game days, he prayed through the depth chart and made sure to name every single player—from the starting lineup all the way down to the walk-ons and true freshmen.

Coach always prioritized his faith, his family, and his players and coaches—and that didn't stop after we were gone or after he stepped away from coaching. To this day, I know firsthand that Coach Osborne keeps God and all the special people in his life as a high priority. Every day I'm inspired to do my best to do the same.

> **~ Mike Anderson, Owner of Anderson Auto Group, NFL Europe Player (1993), and Nebraska Football Player (1990-93)**

3

CHAPTER THREE

~~~~~~

STRATEGY

THE LEGACY OF WISDOM

Strategy is the ability to see how things are going to play out. It's anticipating future events that you are going to have to deal with or overcome. Wisdom should be the core of any strategy, resulting in principles, preparation, planning, patience, and purposeful adjustments when necessary.

As a coach, I had to decide what we were going to hang our hat on. Were we going to be a team that primarily runs the ball or passes the ball? Would we run multiple defenses? What kind of quarterback were we going to recruit?

I can't say that I had a specific role model in the area of strategy, but I did like John Wooden's approach. I read his books and did get the opportunity to know him personally. He was intentional about putting a heavy emphasis on process. John was a coach and an English teacher. He was a very successful basketball coach at UCLA, winning ten national championships in 12 years.

I also had a variety of experiences with coaches in high school, college, and at the professional level. I saw many things that didn't work and decided early on I wasn't going to go down that path.

Going even further back, I played football, basketball, baseball, and ran track. I was able to take something away from every one of those situations. I could see what worked and what didn't work. Those experiences helped shape my view of strategy and planning—something that must always remain at the core of any effective leader's approach.

The Short and the Long

There are different plans and strategies you can have. There are short-term plans and strategies and long-term plans and strategies. Usually, you're going to have both operating at the same time.

For instance, in football, you have a long-term strategy for what you want your program or your team to look like over the course of a season or several seasons. The short-term strategies show up in training, conditioning, and practice, which ultimately show up during the next game. The long-term strategy involves big-picture goals and, more importantly, what culture you want surrounding your program or team.

Let's take a closer look at these two key components of strategy.

Short-Term Strategy

From a football perspective, you can't get much more short-term than what you are going to call the next play or the next defense. That, of course, is all situational, but in those moments, you look at what's happened in the past and how people lined up against you and what you've seen in the flow of the game or what you've seen on film, and you try to rely on that to anticipate what the best option would be in that moment.

In a business sense, you're talking about trying to make a sale and what you should say next or what you should do in the next few minutes. In that sense, strategy is about thinking on your feet and adjusting to meet the needs of the moment.

Short-term strategy can also equate to the daily routine. For a coach, that would be especially important during the season, with the practice schedule being a foundational part of a team's approach to success on a weekly basis. Our practices were intended to ensure there was as little idle time as possible and that everyone (not just the first and second-string players) would benefit. Here's what a typical practice schedule looked like during my time as the head coach at Nebraska:

```
                NEBRASKA FOOTBALL PRACTICE   GRASS
                WEDNESDAY OCTOBER 9,1991   FULL PADS
    2:00 - 3:15     MEET
    ----------------------------------
    3:30 - 3:40     STR
    3:40 - 3:45     SPEC
    3:45 - 4:50     GROUP
          - 4:05 - 4:15    TITE ENDS vs DLB's  [T]
          - 4:15 - 4:20    1 on 1   [T] both
          - 4:20 - 4:40    OFF SKEL [T]            4:20 - 4:50 DEF SKEL, BLITZ, RED ZONE [T]
          - 4:40 - 4:50    OFF FULL TEAM OPT [T]
    4:50 - 4:55     BREAK
    4:55 - 5:05     PUNTS (kicks) [T]
                    1 STA            SPD STA        DEFENSE
    5:05 - 5:20     1 -(3) [T]       2 -(4) [T]     5:05 - 5:15  GOAL LINE SHORT YD. [T]
    5:20 - 5:35     2 -(3) [T]       1 -(4) [T]     5:15 - 5:35  ALL TOGETHER    T
    5:35 - 5:50     RUN, STR, THROW, LIFT
```

During the summer leading up to Coach Matt Rhule's first season at Nebraska, I was pleased to hear him talk about how he had been implementing some of these practice methods back into the program.

"I've been very blessed that Coach Osborne has been willing to share some things with me," Rhule told reporters. "Really, practicing in the ways that Coach Devaney, Coach Osborne, and Coach (Frank) Solich did for 42 years of dominance...I'd be a fool if I didn't ask Coach Osborne what the blueprint is. He doesn't talk about plays; he talks about the way they practiced first and foremost."

In another press conference, Coach Rhule spoke about how it was already having an impact on the team: "The most important thing to me is reps. As I told the young guys at the end, a lot of places in the country, the freshmen showed up and they got five reps in practice today, but our guys all got 40. So it's just kind of what Coach Osborne told me, 'Make sure they all get reps.' It's a little bit of a strain on the coaches and the staff because you're having to be out there for a little bit longer. But it's fun. And it's good to see them (and) their personalities."

For leaders in all areas of life, short-term strategy may show up in the form of meeting schedules, daily checklists, monthly calendars, production schedules, productivity assessments, personnel reviews, activity agendas, work flow charts, etc.

All of these measuring sticks should include consistent routine and have a holistic approach. In other words, there shouldn't be much variation to the short-term strategy and it should ensure that everyone on your team is thoughtfully included in a way that maximizes the collective effort.

Long-Term Strategy

A long-term strategy is looking at what things will be critical and what values should be held on to and espoused, no matter how some details or short-term plans change over time.

One of our long-term strategies in coaching was how our players would be treated. We were going to try to bring the best out of them and care for them. We were going to be demanding, but at the same time, we wanted them to know that whatever we asked them to do was in their best interest. We were never going to denigrate or humiliate a player.

We also wanted to develop the spiritual side of our players, which is a little bit unusual. But we had chapel and mass before every game. I hired coaches like Ron Brown and Turner Gill, who were both strong spiritual leaders. Those kinds of things were more foundational in the long term but still played a very important part of my approach to coaching.

That was how we did things, but each leader must have foundational values and beliefs that will not change. We will address some of these ideals in the next section, but some, for example, may include love, integrity, humility, patience, self-control, and loyalty. These should be non-negotiable in order to provide a solid base from which an organization can be built for long-term success.

The Letter Box

In leadership, there will always be people who think you should do something different. Effective leaders need to have a certain frame of reference that will help them stay the course and keep them from being pushed and pulled off track.

This requires a certain core philosophy and core beliefs that are non-negotiable. That doesn't mean you're intractable and that you're not willing to change. Still, if you don't have a basic framework or a basic philosophy that's somewhat impervious to outside criticism, you'll find yourself being pulled in many different directions, which will make you ineffective.

This was especially important as the coach of a passionate fan base. When we lost a game, I would get a whole box full of letters. I would read them if they were signed, but I told my secretary to throw away any that weren't signed. One guy would want me to make this change to our offense. Another wanted me to try something else on defense. Some people would draw plays, and there would be 10 or 12 players on the field. Sometimes sportswriters would take me to task for not doing what they thought made sense. However, those folks did not know many of the things we were dealing with, such as minor injuries, personal problems of players, what we had seen in our opponent films, and what skills some had, and others didn't. They had a job to do, and I respected that, but I did not read the sports pages so I could keep my mind clear and be cordial to the writers irrespective of what they had written—favorable or unfavorable.

No matter how tempting it might have been to make changes just to appease restless fans, I had to remain disciplined and stay true to what our staff had committed to doing for that season. It's not to say we didn't make minor adjustments here and there, but remaining steady with the strategy we put in place during the offseason was ultimately the best decision.

At the end of the day, I tried to be consistent as to how I was going to approach things and how I was going to treat players and how I was going to deal with my family, and so on. That doesn't mean I was a perfect coach, father, or husband, but I always came back to the basic tenets of my faith, which were going to best serve everyone concerned.

Unsound Strategy

Sometimes a strategy can be based on things that are not sound. Winning at all costs, for instance, is not a sound strategy because bending the rules in the long term will eventually catch up to you. There are some coaches with very good win-loss records over a long period. They may have operated on unsound principles, but I wonder about the negative impact that likely had on their players. Some business owners make a lot of money through unscrupulous means, but what did that teach their employees about how to get ahead in life? Those might seem like effective long-term strategies, but they will ultimately be quite damaging.

Another dangerous approach to strategy can be taking a reactionary approach. Far too often, leaders lack the fortitude to stick with the plan when things get difficult or when they face outside (or even internal) challenges and adversity.

So much of today's leadership experience is about the "what have you done for me lately?" approach. In coaching, in politics, and much of the corporate world, the rope is pretty short. There aren't many coaches that will outlast two or three consecutive losing seasons. You have to deal with that reality.

It can be easy to go into panic mode and throw everything out after a bad season or a bad fiscal year and go in an entirely different direction. In the meantime, you might stray further than you intended and lose sight of where you were headed in the first place. Deciding when to make changes and how drastic those changes should be is a delicate balancing act and should only take place after significant research and advisement of wise counsel.

Situational Shifts

When it becomes clear that you need to readjust and make changes to your strategy, those changes should be well thought out, and they shouldn't change the more substantive principles that impact relationships, integrity, and spirituality.

In coaching, you might need to change some strategies when you realize that you will likely be fired if things don't get better. If you're in business and you're losing money, and the bank tells you that your credit is about to be exhausted, that's a time when you'd better rethink your plans and operations. If your marriage is suffering and it looks like things are about to fall apart, that's a good time to make some adjustments and get whatever help you need to take a different approach.

In all areas of life, there are those inflection points where the hard reality of the situation forces you to reevaluate to improve or salvage a situation. That was the case during my time at Nebraska, where we had three major resets of our coaching approach.

The first one was back in 1968. We lost to Oklahoma, 47-0, in the last game of the season. We finished 6-4 and didn't go to a bowl game. Bob Devaney's seat was getting pretty hot even though we had previously won four consecutive conference championships from 1963 to 1966.

Bob was willing to gamble on me and asked me to redesign the offense. He also put a lot of trust in Monte Kiffin and put Monte in charge of the defense. Monte had played at Nebraska and was only a few years out of college. And then, Bob allowed me to bring former pole-vaulter Boyd Epley in as the strength trainer even though he wasn't enamored with the idea. The conventional wisdom at the time was that weightlifting made the players muscle-bound and detracted from their natural athleticism.

Bob let me recruit some junior college players from California as we needed help in the offensive line. We had not recruited in California or junior colleges before.

Bob was willing to give all these ideas a shot, but if things didn't work out, we'd likely all be fired. So we made some major changes, and that resulted in two national championships (1970 and 1971), four conference championships, and four bowl victories (1969 to 1972).

Then, in the late 1970s, we were having a hard time beating Oklahoma. They had some excellent running quarterbacks that were difficult to contain. We also had some pretty good quarterbacks who went on to have good careers in the NFL, but we lost several consecutive games to Oklahoma.

Not stopping their option game was a major factor in those losses. We shifted to an offense that required quarterbacks who could run as well as throw. We also spent a twenty-minute period each Monday in which our defense worked against the wishbone offense Oklahoma ran. The changes helped us rattle off three straight victories in the series from 1981 to 1983.

Then again, in the early 1990s, we had some really solid nine and 10 seasons, but couldn't quite get over the hump. So we started the Unity Council and made many changes to our playbook. Everything was on the table. That resulted in three national championships.

So, in all major shifts, there were times of evaluation and resetting that were beneficial to the overall program. Still, in every case, we maintained our core principles of treating players well, staying within the rules, playing physical football with a good running game, and working very hard—players and coaches.

God's Game Plan

For many years, the Fellowship of Christian Athletes produced an annual Bible called "God's Game Plan." I can't think of a better way to describe His Holy Word. The Bible shows God's grand plan from the beginning, through the Old Testament, through the life of Christ, through the birth of the Church, and through the Revelation of the end times and eternity.

Within the many epic Old Testament stories, we can also read about some fascinating divinely inspired strategies for the heroes of the faith (e.g., Noah, Abraham, Joshua, Moses, Esther, etc.) and the great kings and military leaders.

Take, for instance, Gideon, an ordinary man whom God chose to lead the Israelite army against its tormenting enemy, the Midianites. The entire story is found in Judges 6-8 and is a fascinating example of how our plans can never compare to God's.

For Gideon, the first part of the plan seemed to be cut and dried: organize the 22,000 men available to join the army. But that wasn't God's plan. On two separate occasions, God gave Gideon instructions on how to downsize the army, which first dropped to 10,000 and ultimately down to 300.

Gideon also had to rely on God for a creative attack strategy against a much larger army; otherwise, defeat seemed inevitable. Each warrior carried a horn in one hand and torches in the other. While the enemy slept, the Israelites charged the camp, blew their horns, and shouted at the top of their lungs. The Midianites panicked and aimlessly attacked each other as they fled, never to return.

Later in the Old Testament, King Solomon (often considered the wisest man ever) wrote some advice for leaders on the subject of strategy that is still highly relevant today:

On principles: *Commit your work to the Lord, and your plans will be established.* (Proverbs 16:3 / ESV)

On preparation: *Prepare your work outside; get everything ready for yourself in the field, and after that build your house.* (Proverbs 24:27 / ESV)

On planning: *Without counsel, plans fail, but with many advisers, they succeed.* (Proverbs 15:22 / ESV)

On patience: *Trust in the Lord with all your heart, and do not lean on your own understanding. In all your ways acknowledge him, and he will make straight your paths.* (Proverbs 3:5-6 / ESV)

On purposeful adjustments: *For everything there is a season, and a time for every matter under heaven.* (Ecclesiastes 3:1/ESV)

We often create short-term strategies to fulfill a long-term goal or dream. We want those strategies to succeed, but our plans are meaningless at the end of the day if they're not based on sound biblical principles. Our ultimate call as leaders is to love God and love others. That is where true fulfillment can be found, and our short-term and long-term strategies should reflect that mission.

For we are his workmanship, created in Christ Jesus for good works, which God prepared beforehand, that we should walk in them. (Ephesians 2:10/ESV)

True North

Strategy is a necessary component in a leader's search for both short-term and long-term success, but there are some key elements that will increase effectiveness and impact:

1. Have a true north: When I was a pilot, everything was based on true north. There's magnetic north, and there's true north. Magnetic north is several degrees off. If you steer the airplane strictly on magnetic north, you're going to miss the North Pole by a thousand miles. So, you have to make an adjustment to your magnetic reading to get the true reading.

The push and pull of public opinion or what other people are thinking and saying is more like magnetic north. Following those voices will often take you way off course. That's why it's so important to steer your life in accordance with your true north.

That has to be principle centered. That has to be based on certain intractable beliefs that you hold. Those beliefs are not going to come and go. That standard is not going to shift based on public opinion or cultural and societal change.

We often hear people say that they "create their own truth." In other words, they are the sole arbiters of what is true and what is false. Self-interest can easily creep in, and "truth" may become significantly distorted.

2. Forge your strategy in thoughtful preparation: In coaching, the first thing we did after a game on Saturday was look at the film. We wanted to see what we did well and what we needed to improve on. Then, on Sunday and into Monday, we looked at our opponent's film and used what we saw to put together a game plan.

Within a game, there's also a situational strategy based on downs and yardage. We would prepare responses to certain situations we might face throughout the course of a game based on our personnel and the other team's tendencies.

All of that took somewhere between 90 and 100 hours a week. Some of that was on the practice field, and some of that was in meetings with players, but most of it was in staff meetings and film study. I spent about 35 hours a week watching films of our opponent's defense in many games and many situations. This often enabled me to anticipate what the opposing defensive coordinator was going to call next. Of course, I made mistakes, but those hours of film study enabled me to react intuitively without a play sheet and be right often enough to stay employed.

Preparation will look different depending on your professional field. Still, it is a key component that will help you be consistent, bring you accountability, and give you the ability to persevere when adverse circumstances come to challenge the plan that you know is the correct one that is consistent with scriptural tenets.

3. Rely on trusted advisors: The average FBS coach stays in one place for only about three years. Maybe it's because they were fired, or perhaps it's because they got a better opportunity elsewhere. But one of the strengths we had here at Nebraska was that we didn't have a lot of coaches coming and going.

As a result, a great deal of institutional knowledge built up over the years. If a team used a defense or offense we hadn't prepared for, we could still recall how we handled that situation. I was very fortunate to have coaches who stayed around for a long time and became those trusted advisors that every leader desires to have on their side.

The same is true for all leaders who will undoubtedly need to rely on others with expertise and knowledge in certain areas that aren't their strong suit.

4. Be patient: We'll spend more time discussing this principle in Chapter 8, but it's important to ensure patience is an intentional part of both your short-term and long-term strategies. Giving up too quickly or being easily swayed by outside voices often derails good plans that just need extra time and effort to produce tangible results.

5. Be flexible: Good leaders will always have a long-term plan, but they also need to be able to think on their feet and adjust on the run. Life often throws you some curves that you haven't anticipated. In coaching, injuries may sideline key players. In business, markets shift or key employees leave.

But even when working with a flexible mindset, you still need a basic approach and core values that you're not going to violate.

Divine Alignment

The long-term goal for the Christian leader should be that, at the end of your life on judgment day, you're able to say, "Lord, I did my best to honor You." Then, whatever plans you had along the way will end up lining up with what God had planned for you.

When you desire to honor and serve God, He will guide you to the right places at the right time and give you the foundations for a long-term strategy. And then, through prayer, wise advisers, and personal attention to research and detail, God will help you lay out the short-term strategies in between that will end up getting you where you're supposed to be.

How do you know what God would have you do? I am often leery of those who say, "God told me to do this." This may be true, but it is often easy to confuse what you want to do with God's will. What job you take, which person you marry, and what school you attend are very important, but what God would have us do is not always clear.

If your decisions are consistent with scripture, if choices are advocated by people of faith who know you well, and if prayer nudges you in a specific direction, you can have some clarity. Having said that, my personal experience has often been that I see God's working in my life more clearly in retrospect than I could at the time a decision was made.

I thought about going into the ministry and attended seminary for a short time before choosing to play pro football. I was planning a career in college administration but ended up coaching and marrying Nancy. All those decisions were for the best and seemed, from my current perspective, to have been consistent with what God would have me do.

In Other Words

In 1995, we played Michigan State in East Lansing. Lawrence Phillips had 206 yards, and it ended up being the worst defeat in Nick Saban's career, 50-10. After the game, Tom put his arm around Nick's and said, "Keep your chin up. You're pretty good."

That following January, I gave a private clinic for Nick's defensive staff, and he sat in on the interview. Nick had me over to the house for dinner that evening with him and his wife and son, and we talked in greater depth about Coach Osborne's practice methods, which he would implement at Michigan State and later on at Alabama.

Nick, like so many others back then, wondered why Nebraska developed so many elite athletes and had a "next man up" approach. It all comes back to practice. We had snotty-nosed freshmen lining up every day against future NFL players. There was never a moment where everyone wasn't working on something or learning something of great value to themselves and the team.

Coach Osborne's practice methods proved invaluable many times but can best be highlighted when we played Kansas State in 1994. Coach wasn't sure if we could beat them. Tommie Frazier was our starting quarterback, but Brook Berringer was getting as many practice reps from the backup position. The only problem was that Frazier got knocked out for several games, and Brook was injured during the previous game. So, we gave the start to Matt Turman.

On game day in Manhattan, our defense played well, and Matt didn't make any mistakes. Coach Osborne didn't ask too much of Matt that day. He just needed to stay within himself and run the plays he'd learned in practice. Brook came in for one series late in the first half, but he was still nursing a collapsed lung, and Matt finished the game.

Because of Coach's practice methods that gave all players reps, Matt was more prepared than the average third-string quarterback, and we won the game, 17-6.

You look at Alabama now, and they have the same mentality. Nick Saban learned that from Coach Osborne, and more programs could benefit if they would embrace the kind of strategy that sees equal value in every member of the team.

~ **George Darlington, Nebraska Assistant Football Coach (1973-2002)**

Coach Osborne had a pulse beat on everybody on the team. During my playing days, we had a freshman team with about 110 players. I was listed as third or fourth string cornerback going into fall camp. The varsity started a half hour before the freshman practice.

On the third day of camp, I was walking out of the north stadium locker room door early, and the varsity was just about ready to start. Coach came running by, saw me, called me by my first name, and jogged away. He took about ten steps and, to my surprise, stopped and came back to talk to me.

"Jim, I see they have you listed at cornerback," Coach said. "You go to Coach Fisher and tell him I want him to move you to monster back because I think that's a better fit for you."

It's amazing how he synthesized that thought in 10 steps. He had an entire varsity roster and another 110 freshmen, yet he knew me and had the foresight to empower me to facilitate a change that would impact my career in a big way.

~ **Jim Pillen, 41st Governor of Nebraska and Nebraska Football Player (1975-78)**

During my time at Nebraska, Coach Osborne served as the offensive coordinator, but when we were game planning, he would spend time with us in the defensive room. Without question, he was the brightest, smartest guy there, but he had a way of convincing you that you were the smartest guy, and he always could always bring out your best.

Coach Osborne was always three steps ahead of everyone else. He had a secret recipe for success. If Harvard Business School would have studied how we operated as a coaching staff, I think they would have described it as "organized chaos." But how it unfolded was truly a masterpiece. He was the professor, instructing us on what to do, but he always allowed us to be creative and operate in our strengths.

During my years at North Dakota State, we won three consecutive FCS Championships with an overall record of 104-32. People would always ask how we were doing it, and I would pull out a file called "Osborne 101." A big part of that was utilizing a similar practice schedule that Coach Osborne used at Nebraska, although that wasn't implemented right away.

When I started at North Dakota State, the program was Division II for one season before moving to the FCS and the Great West Conference. We were doing pretty well, including back-to-back 10-1 seasons, but then we moved up to FCS, got into the Missouri Valley Conference, and went 6-5 and 3-8. I met with the staff, and they wanted us to come up with some inspirational slogans on a t-shirt and different things like that. But I was sitting there thinking, "How in the world were we so successful at Nebraska?"

My immediate thoughts went back to the way we practiced. So I met with the coaches and mandated that we were going to practice like we did at Nebraska. I got pushback like you wouldn't believe, but I looked them all straight in the eye and told him it was non-negotiable. Everyone down to the deep snapper was going to get those repetitions. And that was the start of our climb.

After I took the Wyoming job, I hired a trainer from Alabama to join our staff. I asked him how Coach Nick Saban structured his practices, and he told me it was almost identical to what we were doing at Wyoming. I wasn't surprised.

In 1994, we soundly defeated Coach Nick Saban's Michigan State team, 50-10. During the offseason, Coach George Darlington did a clinic for Coach Saban's defensive coaches and shared how Coach Osborne practiced with him. He adopted that strategy at Michigan State and later at Alabama.

The secret was giving all of the players practice reps. No one was standing around. Everyone, including the true freshmen and walk-ons, had something to do and something they could learn while the guys on the two-deep prepared for the upcoming game.

Again, that was the genius of Coach Osborne. He was a master strategist who wasn't as concerned about winning as we were about putting his players and coaches in the best position for success. The winning was simply a byproduct of his true love and care for those under his leadership.

> **~ Craig Bohl, Wyoming Head Football Coach (2014-pres.), North Dakota State Head Football Coach (2003-13), Nebraska Defensive Coordinator (2000-02), Nebraska Assistant Coach (1995-99), and Nebraska Player (1977-79)**

PART II

FOUNDATIONAL
VALUES

4

~~~~~

CHAPTER FOUR

VALUES AND VISION

THE LEGACY OF CONVICTION

Everyone is called to be a leader in one way or another. We all have different gifts and varying areas of influence. How and who we lead will change throughout our lives, but one thing never changes. We will always need a solid foundation upon which to build that leadership, and the firmness of that foundation will determine how effective we ultimately will be.

With that in mind, let's take a look at two key building blocks for being a successful, transformational leader: values and vision.

Values

You can't have a solid foundation for leadership if you don't have solid values. Even worse is when you don't know what your values are and you don't have an understanding of why you need them.

I was blessed to have parents that taught me sound values at a very young age. Throughout my life I had others who reinforced those values through my experiences in church, school, and sports. Those values served me well as an athlete, as a student, and eventually as an aspiring football coach.

As my time in coaching progressed I became more aware of the fact that many of the concepts I was trying to communicate to our players did not resonate with them. To many of them, the term "honesty" had more to do with not getting caught than with telling the truth and keeping one's word. They understood what courage meant when it came to physical bravery but had little understanding of what moral courage was—the courage to endure ridicule or ostracism for doing the right thing. Similarly, the meaning of words such as loyalty, generosity, self-sacrifice and accountability were not very clear to many of my players.

I had gotten to know Marty Shottenheimer, former coach of the Kansas City Chiefs, and he told me he had been presenting his players with a "theme of the week," a concept he wanted to emphasize during the week's preparation for an upcoming opponent. I thought this approach would work well in presenting different character traits I wanted my team to understand more clearly.

So each week we introduced a character trait on Monday during our team meeting. We would have it written prominently in the weekly scouting report on our upcoming opponent. We would have two or three quotes from well-known people referring to the character trait, and then I would make some mention of the trait each day during our team meeting, which would further explain what the trait might mean to each player and our team.

For example, the theme for a week might be "courage." We included a quote attributed to former Green Bay Packer Coach Vince Lombardi, "fatigue makes cowards of us all." His quote referred to the fact that when a player was exhausted he could no longer do the brave thing— pursue the football on defense or block down-field on offense.

We also included a quote from Confucius, which said, "to see what is right and not do it is a lack of courage." This quote obviously referred to moral courage, a willingness to do the right thing even though it might be unpopular. We then gave examples of what physical courage and moral courage might look like in their daily lives and what those concepts might mean to our team.

In the course of a 13 or 14-week season, our players were presented with a thorough explanation of several different character traits and what those traits might mean to them personally and to our team. In short, they took a character education course, even though we didn't label it as such.

I think it made a difference. Occasionally I would see a player quoted in the newspaper or overhear a conversation between players in which they would relate something which had been presented in reference to a character trait. I think it also helped our team chemistry, as it caused players to be more conscious of values which bind people together and made them more willing to sacrifice personal objectives in order to serve others.

In many cases today's family unit has been compromised by a lack of parenting. For some players the coach is the only one who is best positioned to impart sound teaching on matters related to character. Many times, the coach is the one authority figure who commands respect and is also involved in something so important to athletes, their sport, that they will pay close attention.

Legendary coach John Wooden was fond of pointing out that his father gave him a creed when he graduated from the eighth grade, which provided him a compass by which to live his life, and guided him through the challenges of coaching. The creed is as follows:

- Be true to yourself.
- Help others.
- Make friendship a fine art.
- Drink deeply from good books, especially the Bible.
- Make each day your masterpiece.
- Build a shelter against a rainy day by the life that you live.
- Give thanks for your blessings and pray for guidance every day.

Fortunately, John didn't lose the handwritten note his father gave him containing the seven principles but rather incorporated them into his daily life and based his life on the wisdom they contained.

Somewhere I have a signed copy of John's "Pyramid For Success," a pyramid of 15 principles, which build upon each other until one arrives at the apex of the pyramid and the final principle—competitive greatness. Through a lifetime of coaching, John developed, revised, and perfected the pyramid, which stated clearly his philosophy of striving for excellence as a coach.

As a result of much reflection and experience, he came to know what he believed was important as a coach, both in coaching basketball and in helping his players grow and mature as young men. I was only in his presence a handful of times, but I was greatly influenced by the principles with which he coached and conducted his personal life. My wife Nancy and I visited John when he was in his late nineties, just a few months before he died.

One of those principles, which made a huge difference in the way I coached, was that John never mentioned winning to his teams. This seemed paradoxical in that John was possibly the most successful coach of all time in terms of winning basketball games, yet he never mentioned the importance of winning to his players. Instead he talked about the process or the journey that leads to competitive excellence.

He began each season by showing players how to put their socks on so they would not develop blisters, how to bend their knees on free throws, and how to pass the ball—fundamentals. He thought practicing the basics often enough, along with playing well with the right intensity, would bring positive results. Talking about winning was unnecessary.

It made more sense to teach ball carriers to carry the ball high and tight and tacklers to keep their heads up than to preach winning. So, the process was what we emphasized, not the final results.

In any endeavor, business, medicine, or education, an emphasis on final results without proper processes and procedures often ends badly. Getting the process right will lead to better outcomes.

Values are a key building block for leadership because without knowing what you truly believe, there's a good chance you will lack the confidence and consistency needed to inspire your team to follow you. And if you are always changing your mind, it's probably because you haven't fully defined your values and wholeheartedly embraced them.

Earlier I mentioned how I was blessed to have parents and mentors that taught me the values that I have held throughout my life. For me, those values are rooted in moral truth from the Bible. Some of those core values include:

- Faith
- Love
- Hope
- Peace
- Humility
- Honesty
- Generosity
- Kindness
- Forgiveness
- Justice
- Courage
- Respect

You can easily imagine what might happen if you were to waver on any one of the items on that list. For instance, if your trust in God is shaken, you might start to look for other people or things to depend upon. Or, if you stray from an attitude of love for the people you are leading, you will inevitably veer into using fear, anger, and manipulation, which are unsustainable and ultimately ineffective methods.

In the New Testament, Jesus shared a brief but powerful parable about the importance of having (and living by) biblical values.

"Therefore, everyone who hears these words of Mine, and acts on them, will be like a wise man who built his house on the rock. And the rain fell and the floods came, and the winds blew and slammed against that house; and yet it did not fall, for it had been founded on the rock. And everyone who hears these words of Mine, and does not act on them, will be like a foolish man who built his house on the sand. And the rain fell and the floods came, and the winds blew and slammed against that house; and it fell—and its collapse was great." (Matthew 7:24-27/NASB)

Throughout history, there are many examples of leaders who have risen and fallen because they either had no values to begin with or they had values but abandoned them in exchange for convenience, acceptance, or personal gain. But the leaders that stand the test of time are the ones that know their values, base those values on biblical truth, and stand on those values no matter what is happening around them.

Vision

As you begin to feel more secure in your core values and beliefs, the next step in your leadership journey should be casting a vision for what kind of leader you want to be and how you want your leadership to impact others.

Proverbs 29:18 states: *"Where there is no vision the people perish."* Without a proper vision of what the team needs to look like in the future, it is difficult to mold a team, business, organization, or family into what it needs to be, so vision is an important aspect of leadership. Vision is a picture of the future, which produces passion. The prospect of the end product causes you to want to get out of bed in the morning and get started.

It is critical for the coach to not only have a clear vision of what the team should become, but the coach also needs to have the ability to communicate that vision to assistants and players in such a way that they understand and are motivated to attain what is envisioned. This is true not just for a football team, but for any organization.

Each summer before the football season began we would start our preparation for the season by having our coaching staff construct a vision statement of our coaching philosophy. It was important that the coaches all had input and buy-in, so it was not seen as something, which was only my vision but was a shared vision.

We would then have a meeting with all of the people in the Athletic Department who interacted with our players on a regular basis and review the vision statement with them, particularly the parts, which addressed how players were to be treated. It was important that the players saw consistency in how each person dealt with them in the training room, the academic center, the training table, the weight room, as well as on the practice field.

Another important part of creating a vision was to outline an offensive, defensive, and special teams philosophy. It is critical that a team has an identity, a shared understanding of what the team is going to emphasize and be known for. I realize I am using football terms here, but that is what I know best and hopefully coaches who are reading this and coaching other sports will be able to extrapolate to their sport as well as those in other areas of leadership.

Nebraska weather varies a great deal. The football season starts with very hot weather and ends with the possibility of snow. There is often very windy weather as well. Therefore we emphasized the running game, play action passes, and controlling the football on offense. We believed that a strong running game would prevail no matter what the weather was, whereas a strong reliance on passing would not do as well in a strong wind and cold weather. We would nearly always have three or four games in weather like that. This does not mean that passing was unimportant. We often led our conference in touchdown passes because opponents were usually more vulnerable to passes as they tried to stop our running game.

I tried to envision an offense through the eyes of defensive coaches—what would be hardest to stop. Oklahoma used to run the wishbone, and I saw how hard it was to defend because the wishbone is predicated on running the option. You had to have people assigned to stopping the fullback dive, the quarterback keeps, and the pitch going wide. To stop the quarterback and the pitch you had to involve your defensive backs, particularly the safeties, and this left you very vulnerable to the play action pass. So, like Oklahoma, we ran several different kinds of options along with power football.

We had a play action pass related to every basic running play. We ran many different sets with a rapid tempo, and the quarterback controlled the play selection by calling audibles at the line of scrimmage. I wanted the quarterbacks to recognize defenses and get us into the correct play immediately, not through signals from the sidelines, which is often done today. The sideline signals slow the tempo and enable the opposing defense to change alignment. In short, the quarterback was to see the defense as I would and adjust accordingly.

We went through a similar process in envisioning our defensive identity. We evolved from a reading "bend but don't break" philosophy using mostly zone coverages in the 70s to an attacking defense and much man-to-man coverage in the 90s. We practiced our kicking game in the middle of practice rather than at the end of practice, which so many teams do, almost as an afterthought. We wanted to make sure players realized that kicking was as important as offense and defense and we put our best players on the kicking teams, not back-ups as is often practiced.

It is extremely important that coaches and players have a shared understanding of what is going to be emphasized. For example, our quarterbacks, receivers, and their respective coaches understood we would only throw about 20 passes a game on average, less than most other teams.

Our receivers were also going to have to be good downfield blockers because of our emphasis on the running game. Since players knew what was expected before the season started and why we were doing what we were doing, we had little unhappiness concerning fewer passes and the emphasis on the running game.

Vision is important beyond the playing field. As previously mentioned in Chapter 2, Stephen Covey wrote a book entitled *The Seven Habits of Highly Effective People*, in which the second habit is "Begin With The End In Mind." Covey recognizes the fact that all of us face one common experience, our mortality. He advocates that each of us takes the time to write what we would like a family member, a friend, and a business associate to say about us at our funeral. He then says we should contemplate what we have written because those things will be of greatest importance to us at the end of our lives.

We are forced to look at our lives from an end perspective, which is not a bad idea as many of us spend great amounts of time focusing on things that aren't important in the long run and often ignore the most valuable things. Each of us only has so much time; it is our most important commodity, so spending it unwisely is a tragedy. To realize at the end of one's life that it was largely a life filled with regrets is very sad.

Coaching is very demanding and time-consuming and coaches, like everyone else, can lose track of what is most important. The coach who gave me my first coaching opportunity was Bob Devaney, a very successful coach at the University of Wyoming and then at the University of Nebraska, where he won eight conference championships and two National Championships in a span of only eleven years. Bob was Athletic Director at Nebraska as well as head football coach and hired me to replace him as football coach when he decided to become full-time Athletic Director.

I worked for and with Bob for 30 years until he retired. I got word that he was in the hospital and was not doing well, so I went to visit him. He had decided his situation was hopeless, and he had pulled out all the tubes, which had supported his life so I knew this would be our last visit.

The interesting thing about that visit was that we didn't communicate about the things you might think we would: the national championships, the wins and losses, the awards, financial success. Bob had accomplished about all you could in coaching, and yet that was unimportant now.

Rather it became obvious that what was important was his family. His wife and two children were there; it is hard to die alone, yet many do. Relationships were also important such our relationship and relationships with former players and coaches.

At the end of our visit, I asked him if it would be all right if I said a prayer and he nodded, and a tear rolled down his cheek, so I knew his relationship with God was important at that time as well. When we face the immediate prospect of moving beyond the veil, what is next assumes a prominent place of importance for most.

I treasure that memory, that last interaction, as Bob had been such a big part of my life and I knew I would miss his friendship, yet I had hope he would end up in a better place.

In keeping with the idea of looking at our lives from the end of life perspective, it is important to look closely at our present priorities, what we spend our time and energy on and what gets ignored. Many coaches lose their marriage, their children, and sometimes their soul to the unending quest to win games. The more you win, the higher the expectations, and a coach can get caught up in a never-ending quest for "success," which is very elusive. This is true not only in coaching, but also in other demanding jobs.

I recall sitting on a team bus outside the Orange Bowl stadium in Miami in January of 1971 following the win over LSU, which gave us the National Championship. It was 2 a.m., I was an assistant coach, and this was supposed to be the ultimate experience a coach could have. I thought, "Is this all that there is to this?" At that moment I realized the journey was more important than the destination. If a coach can learn to enjoy the journey, the relationships, his family, and his relationship with God, coaching can be a healthy and fulfilling profession. It doesn't mean the coach is not competitive and does not seek excellence, but rather that he can balance the demands of coaching with those things which will be of ultimate importance at the end of life.

Grantland Rice, a famous sportswriter in the middle of the last century, once wrote, "For when the One Great Scorer comes to write against your name, it matters not that you won or lost, but how you played the game."

This may seem hopelessly idealistic to a coach fighting to win enough games to keep his job. However, it seems to me that coaching in accordance with sound spiritual principles provides a sense of meaning and purpose beyond winning. A coach's greatest legacy is not written in his win-loss record, but rather in the lives of those he coached. That influence will ripple down through many generations.

Values and Vision: A Powerful Combination

As a foundation for leadership, there is no getting around the need for unshakable core values and a vision for how you intend to lead. It's impossible, however, to lead effectively if you have one but not the other.

You can have values but won't go very far without vision. Conversely, you can have a big, bold vision, but having no values or having values that easily shift and change will shortchange that vision at some point along the way.

Even more importantly, successful leadership requires that your values and vision align. For instance, if one of your values is respect, then your vision for leadership must include an outcome in which those you lead not only respect each other, but also respect others outside of the group, team, or organization. Sometimes coaches try to motivate their team by generating hatred for the next opponent. I remember an opposing coach who took that to an extreme, but often hatred turns to fear and confusion when events turn against that team.

We taught our players to respect opponents, help them up, and not talk trash, yet we were a very physical team. Before each game, I spent time praying for each of our players' safety and performance. I also prayed for our opponents and that the game would be played in a way that would honor God. We had almost no ugly incidents in the games we played. I never prayed for victory, as I doubt that God favors one team more than another.

Sometimes the answer to prayer is unexpected. One such game was the 1984 Orange Bowl game against Miami. We fell behind by 17 points and climbed slowly back into the game despite losing our great running back, Mike Rozier, to injury. We tried to win the game in the final seconds by attempting a two-point conversion instead of kicking an extra point and tying the game. We lost the National Championship that night, and it was devastating to our players, coaches, and fans, yet that game was played in a way consistent with what our faith would want. It is remembered better than any game we played in the 1980s. Even though we lost the National Championship that night, I was proud of how our team competed at a national championship level.

If one of your values is generosity, your vision for leadership must include specific goals regarding giving and sharing resources with others in need.

It makes no sense, for example, to claim values such as integrity and justice while having a vision that allows for cheating, shortcuts, and cutthroat, win-at-all-costs tactics. When values and vision don't align, hypocrisy becomes the norm, which invites scrutiny, criticism, and in many cases, destructive outcomes.

Having aligned values and vision is important in every aspect of leadership. It starts with how you lead yourself and carries over into how you lead within your family, your workplace, your friend groups, your community, and your church. Make sure to take time at various times along your journey to reassess both.

As long as your values are based on moral truth, they should never change. On the other hand, your short-term vision and plans may shift based on circumstances, but your long-term vision of being a transformational leader, like your values, should remain constant.

Over time, you will see the benefits of values and vision. They will provide the rock solid foundation upon which all other building blocks of leadership can grow and thrive.

In Other Words

The greatest leader who ever walked the earth lived 2,000 years ago and has billions of followers today. He spent time with and influenced only 12 close followers. The ripple effects from His life have emanated and expanded outward for generations and across the globe. My dad understands this principle that the good we can do and the positive influence we can provide for just one person may return 100 or even 1,000-fold in the years beyond our own lifespans. That faith-based principle has guided his mindset, heart, and actions since he accepted Christ as a twenty-year-old. I believe the choices he's made with his time, talent, and treasure are explained and understood through the lens of that driving principle.

My dad chose Christianity and to be a follower of Christ as a young man. And it's funny how when you become a follower of Christ, it seems you inevitably become a leader. In my younger days, when I was questioning faith and life, my dad said to me, "Even if it weren't true, it is still the best way to live." My dad's life is evidence that it is, in fact, true. The fruits of the Spirit and the fruits of a well-lived life are evidence of God's power and His desire to work through us to make this world a little more like Heaven.

We each have the ability to make the same choice for Christ as my dad and to see the fruits in our own lives. My dad isn't perfect, but he picked up his cross and did what he felt God called him to do throughout his life. He overcame his fears, self-doubts, and also the resistance and criticism of others to fulfill much of his calling. He is more than just a coach. He is a father figure to many, an inspiration, a role model, a modest servant, and a humble follower of Christ, and as a culmination of those things, a leader too.

~ **Mike Osborne, Son of Tom Osborne**

Coach Osborne can see things that other people don't see. He put Nebraska football on the map with innovative ideas, such as his training camp methods, the strength and conditioning program, and the Hewit Academic Center. No one else in the country was doing things like Nebraska, although many have since caught up to his original vision for excellence within a college football program.

I was fortunate to save enough money to attend Nebraska's football camp the summer going into my senior year. All I knew was that you gave a hundred percent. You work hard. You finish the drill. I believed this camp would teach me something that might help me get recruited by a smaller Division I school or a larger Division II school.

On the last day of camp, Coach Osborne pulled me aside and asked me questions about my background and where I was from. He noticed my speed, my quickness, and the effort I had been giving throughout the week. I couldn't believe he would pick me out of all those players for that one-on-one conversation.

I returned to Pine Bluff, Arkansas, motivated to improve my grades and work even harder on the field. Lo and behold, I had a great senior year. I got the ACT score I needed, and schools started recruiting me. But when Coach Osborne called me in November and offered me a scholarship, it was a no-brainer for me to accept and play for the Huskers. Unfortunately, Coach Osborne retired at the end of the season, but I still count it a privilege to have been a member of his final recruiting class.

I came to Nebraska as an undersized defensive end. It would have been easy to get discouraged and not believe this was the place for me, but I continued to believe in what Coach Osborne could see. I knew he had brought me to Nebraska for a reason. I started three seasons and led the team in sacks. I was also a three-time First-Team Academic All-Big 12 and was part of back-to-back Big 12 championships.

Now, I've come full circle because Coach Osborne selected me to serve his non-profit—TeamMates Mentoring, his other favorite team, as CEO. I'm sure many people were more qualified and had more experience, but Coach has that ability to see things other people can't see. I'm fortunate that he saw my leadership potential. He also saw my heart, passion, and work ethic, which caught his eye at that football camp.

Now, I get to work with Coach Osborne every single day. His vision for my life motivates me to work even harder to help carry on his legacy and help thousands of students reach their full potential.

Coach Osborne will forever be a mentor and a role model. His true legacy is not what he accomplished on the field but his impact on thousands of people's lives, including me.

**~ Demoine Adams, CEO of TeamMates Mentoring
and Nebraska Football Player (1998-2002)**

When I think about Coach Osborne, one of the first things that comes to mind is his faith. To be honest, I wasn't paying nearly enough attention as a young player, but when I returned as an assistant coach, his willingness to openly share his beliefs with others had a big impact on my life.

It wasn't just his words but also his actions that displayed what it looks like to be a follower of Christ while walking in an intense spotlight. He had personal values that he wasn't going to get away from, no matter what the circumstances were or what other people might have been tempted to do in the same situation.

I saw Coach Osborne grow in his faith, and he passed his knowledge and wisdom along to us. During our staff Bible studies, He would explain why belief in Christ was important and share scriptures that we needed to have in our minds and hearts to help us along the way. Coach also reminded us of the importance of spending time with God.

As I became a head coach, his example of faith became especially important. I could truly understand why I needed to include those biblical principles in my life as the leadership responsibilities intensified. Even more impressive was how Coach showed that it's possible to lead this way at a public school, which I had the chance to also do at Buffalo and Kansas and later on at Liberty, a private school.

Coach's values gave him the ability to plan for the future and the solid foundation to act on that plan. I too, want to lead with biblical values so that everything I do is meaningful and spiritually impactful.

~ **Turner Gill, Former Liberty Head Football Coach (2012-18), Kansas Head Coach (2010-11), Buffalo Head Football Coach (2006-09), Green Bay Packers Director of Player Development & Assistant Wide Receiver Coach (2005), Nebraska Assistant Football Coach (1992-2004), CFL Player (1984-85), and Nebraska Football Player (1980-83)**

When I was playing football at Hastings College, my roommate and I took a senior-level differential equations class from a professor named Jim Standley, who had been teaching there for a long time. As football players, the previous week's game was a topic of a brief classroom discussion with a comparative chat regarding how Nebraska's game that same weekend ended up. During NU losses, we always gave him a bit of a hard time because he was a huge Tom Osborne supporter.

Of course, we knew who Coach Osborne was, and we knew he was a former Hastings Bronco and all the things he'd accomplished as a student-athlete there. In fact, Professor Standley had been there so long that he actually had Coach Osborne as a student. But we would crack jokes about how Nebraska consistently lost to Oklahoma, and he always got a little angry when we brought it up.

One day, Professor Standley stopped class and told us a story that took place during the winter on the HC campus. He had slipped and fallen on the ice and was lying there with what would turn out to be a broken hip. Somehow, Coach Osborne, a student-athlete at the time, wandered along and saw him desperately needing help. Coach Osborne picked him up and carried him to the infirmary. And that was the hill Professor Standley proudly "stood on" for Coach Osborne.

I wouldn't meet Coach until several years later, but that story always left an indelible mark in my mind—that a college athlete would help his professor the way he did. I always hoped I would do the same if I ever found myself in a similar circumstance.

I later learned about Coach Osborne's unshakeable commitment to his faith and fairness. I've heard him speak many times, had a few opportunities to talk to him privately, and read all his books. I've always been impressed with his willingness to speak his mind when he was part of the U.S. House of Representatives and when he ran for Governor of Nebraska.

In 2012, Texas Congressman Ron Paul resigned from the U.S. House to run for President. A group of politically involved individuals in Houston, Texas, approached me about running for his open seat. I was still an active astronaut with NASA then, so I reached out to anyone I knew who had anything to do with politics to accurately assess what I might be getting into.

So, I took a shot in the dark and called Coach Osborne. I was honored that I could actually reach him; it was an amazing one-hour conversation. It was like I was talking to my father.

"Well, Clayton," he said (and I paraphrase here). "You're the kind of person that Washington D.C. needs, but you've gotta love that lifestyle."

I didn't fully understand what he meant, so he explained by telling me a story about his time on Capitol Hill. One day, his staff told him they were coming back to the office at 7 o'clock to craft some legislation. He said, "Okay," went to dinner, and came back to the office. His staff couldn't believe he had shown up.

"You said we were going to craft some legislation at 7 o'clock," he replied. "But the Congressmen never show up," his staff explained.

Coach Osborne didn't tell me what I should do, but that story about his experience spoke volumes and helped me understand that at that time, Washington D.C. wasn't the place for me.

People always ask me who my inspirations and my idols were growing up. They expect me to say someone like Neil Armstrong, but I always tell them this: I had two idols, one was my father, and the other was Tom Osborne. I'm forever grateful for having met him and for all of the wisdom he has imparted into my life.

~ **Clay Anderson, Retired NASA Astronaut**

5

CHAPTER FIVE

~~~~~

LOVE

THE LEGACY OF HEART

" People don't care how much you know until they know how much you care."

That popular quote is often used to talk about the importance of showing love and compassion for people first before sharing instructions or personal beliefs.

But it's also very true when it comes to leadership. It's much easier to lead others when they know you actually care about them as individuals—and that is only possible when you truly love the people you have been called to lead.

The word love has many connotations. The Greeks recognized this long ago and used several different words to express the many facets of "love."

Eros meant erotic love or romantic love. Unfortunately our entertainment industry has emphasized erotic "love" to such a degree that our culture often thinks of the physical expression of love as the only dimension of the concept.

The Greek word *storge* was most commonly used to describe a parent's love for a child and a child's love for a parent. It represented a strong natural family affection.

Filia is love for a friend, a long-standing devotion to one who has shared interests and experiences.

Agape is unconditional, selfless love for another. It is willing the best for another. It is having unconditional positive regard and wanting a positive outcome for another. *Agape* certainly can have a strong emotional component.

Jesus was referring to an *agape* kind of love when He was commanding people to "love your enemies." It is possible to will the best for another even though that person is not your friend, is unlovely, or may even antagonistic. The neighbor who is unfriendly and doesn't speak, has leaves blow from his yard to yours, or is not a good citizen, can still be the recipient of your unconditional positive regard if you make up your mind that you will display a supportive, positive attitude toward that person no matter what he does.

Agape is a form of love, which is primarily an act of will, a supportive attitude toward another irrespective of circumstance. This type of love is crucial in leadership.

So, the leader wills the best and wants the best possible outcome for the person being led. There will be days where things seem to click and both people are in sync and they share a time of strong positive emotion and support. And then there will be those times when one or the other is having a bad day, or is distracted, and the good feeling isn't there. However, if the one being led understands that the leader is there to serve their best interests and truly cares about his or her well-being, the relationship will survive and thrive even though there will be occasional rough spots.

Sometimes a person's experiences with leaders in the past have been hurtful. If the leader continuously demonstrates love for the person being led, regardless of the response in return, the relationship will usually blossom.

There are many ways to show that you truly love the people that you have been called to lead. Let's take a look at some tangible ways this can effectively be done.

The Power of Affirmation

Used as a verb, affirmation may be defined as "a declaration that something is true." Used as a noun, affirmation is used to mean "emotional support or encouragement." We often carry perceptions about ourselves, which have been implanted in our psyches when we were very young.

Affirmation is a powerful thing. A child who has been told that he or she is intelligent will often carry that perception throughout their lifetime. On the other hand someone who has been repeatedly put down for their lack of understanding as a youngster will often internalize the notion that they are inherently stupid. This will become part of the self-image they will carry with them into the future.

I saw the importance of affirmation during my years in coaching. If we told a player that we believed in him, that he would one day be an outstanding player if he continued to work hard, we would often see a considerable improvement in performance and demeanor.

Sometimes a player, energized by words of affirmation, would grow into the player he had no idea that he was capable of becoming. We tried not to discourage players but a look of disgust or a negative comment would often trigger self-doubt and a decline in performance. Even large, strong football players have fragile egos and can be impacted significantly by what coaches think of them.

Lou Holtz once visited our practices and sat in our meetings with players. Lou visited while he was the head football coach at Arkansas. Before he left he told me the thing that most impressed him about his visit to Nebraska was how positive our coaches were. He had never observed that amount of positive feedback in the coaching world before.

Coaches often see their jobs as finding fault, criticizing. We thought that it was important to catch a player doing something right and to praise and reinforce the desired action rather than constantly criticizing them. If a player made a mistake it was important to not personally attack him by questioning his intelligence, courage, or commitment, but rather to explain clearly what he had done wrong and what we wanted him to do the next time in a way that was supportive and reflected confidence in his ability to get it right.

Often when some of our freshmen arrived on campus, we could see that they were a long way from being major college football players and once in a while we would hear a coach say that a young man would "never play here." That type of labeling was discouraged. We continually saw young people make tremendous improvement as they matured, worked in the weight room, and perfected their skills. Many of those who were thought to be unlikely to ever play became some of our best players in their third or fourth years.

Henry Ford once said, "Whether you think you can or think you can't—you are right." Those who think they can are usually people who have had parents or a teacher, a coach or a mentor who has given them the idea that they can achieve significant things in their lives. Those who think they can't are often people who have received negative messages about their abilities at critical junctures in their lives, usually when they are quite young.

Affirmation statements such as "I believe in you," "I know you can do it," "You have unusual talent," and "You always come through in a tight situation" are powerful, but they must be rooted in reality. To tell someone who has little or no musical talent that they will one day become a great concert pianist is not only inaccurate, it is also cruel. It builds up a false expectation, which will almost certainly be dashed when the person one day realizes that he or she will never achieve the success, which he or she had been led to believe that he or she would one day experience.

All of us have talents, things that we do better than other things. Yet, surprisingly, many people aren't aware of their talents. Talents, or strengths, usually come easily to us. They are natural and are often taken for granted, so we don't really identify them as strengths. We assume that nearly everyone else can do the same thing and has the same strengths, yet each person is unique and has special gifts.

During my years in graduate school at the University of Nebraska in the early 1960s, I came in contact with a professor who was starting to think about the importance of strengths. Dr. Don Clifton taught in the Educational Psychology Department and his work deviated markedly from the standard areas of psychological study at that time.

Much research was devoted to the study of animals during that period, mostly mice and rats, but sometimes chimpanzees, dogs and other animals. It was believed that if we could begin to understand why a rat would turn right or left in a maze, or why a mouse would hit a lever for a certain number of times in order to get a pellet of food, or why a monkey would perform a task to get a banana, then we could eventually move up the phylogenetic scale in our research and be able to determine what made human beings tick.

If psychologists weren't studying animals, most of the research concerning people at that time had to do with the study of abnormal behavior and mental illness. Don Clifton quoted psychologist Martin Seligman who said: "Psychology is half-baked, literally half-baked. We have baked the part about mental illness. We have baked the part about repair and damage. But the other side is unbaked. The side of strengths, the side of what we are good at, the side…of what makes life worth living."

Clifton was fascinated by exceptional performance and by the unique talents and strengths of people. In his book, *Now Discover Your Strengths*, he set forth two primary premises:

1. Each person's talents are unique and enduring.

2. Each person's greatest room for growth is in the area of his greatest strength.

He stated "our research into human strengths does not support the extreme, and extremely misleading, assertion that 'you can play any role you set your mind to,' but it does lead us to this truth: whatever you set your mind to, you will be most successful when you craft the role you play to your signature talents most of the time."

He stated that "Rapid learning, yearning to engage in a task or activity again being absorbed in an activity to the point where one loses track of time, deriving satisfaction from the activity completion, is a sign that strengths are in play."

We have come to believe that identifying the strengths of young people and then affirming those strengths accomplishes several things:

1. Most young people are not aware of their strengths. Discovering the fact that they have areas of unique talent is exciting to them.

2. Gallup research has shown that discovering and exploring the strengths of a young person through the mentoring experience causes the mentee to look forward to seeing the mentor to an even greater degree than before.

3. Research has also shown that discovering one's strengths leads to an increased level of hope in the mentee. Knowing that one has special talents makes a young person more hopeful about the future and about their ability to accomplish great things with their life.

When an individual is made aware of his or her strengths and thinks about how those strengths can be utilized, the future often appears brighter and possibilities open up, which at one time appeared to be beyond reach.

The Power of Commitment

Another key word in leadership is commitment. We often think of love being a feeling, however a major part of truly loving another person doesn't have to do with emotion nearly so much as being committed to that person.

Commitment implies a steadfast dedication to the wellbeing of another through thick and thin, for better or for worse, in sickness or in health (to paraphrase marriage vows), no matter what the circumstance. Commitment is a decision and a promise.

There are two different ways that commitment can be exhibited: unconditional love and tough love. Sometimes we think of these aspects of love as being very different. Unconditional love is usually thought of as full of grace and acceptance while tough love is thought of as a little less compassionate and perhaps not so forgiving.

But really, unconditional love and tough love are two sides of the same coin. Both types of love are attached to the commitment you have for someone that you truly care about and want to see experience the best outcomes in life.

Unconditional love is a prerequisite for successful leadership. This is true for the parent, the coach, the pastor, and the CEO. This doesn't mean putting up with nonsense or harmful behavior. It does mean, however, showing as much mercy as possible, giving second and third (or more) chances, and being there to assist, guide, and advise as much as you are able.

Tough love, on the other hand, is equally important. In some ways, you could say tough love is an extension of unconditional love. Because, if you truly love someone, you will tell them some hard truths, you will dole out some uncomfortable discipline and correction, and you will even cut ties at some point if their behavior does not change and is harmful for themselves and others.

I certainly had plenty of opportunities to show my commitment as leader through both unconditional and tough love to my kids, to my coaches, and to my players. Being committed as a leader often means making difficult choices, but as the Apostle Paul wrote to church members in ancient Greece, you should always be prepared to speak truth in love.

No Greater Love

Earlier in this chapter, I referenced the words of Christ in which He commanded His followers to love their enemies (Matthew 5:44). In

Matthew 22:39, He also taught that the second greatest commandment (after loving God with all your heart) was to love your neighbors as yourself.

Jesus takes the conversation even deeper when He describes what the most intense outpouring of love should look like:

"Greater love has no one than that, that someone lay down his life for his friends." (John 15:13/ESV)

Jesus didn't just talk the talk. He walked the walk. Jesus loved everyone, even His enemies, just as a true servant leader should. That love brought Him to earth and led Him to give His life as the ultimate example. He sacrificed His life for our sins so we could be reconciled with God.

But God shows His love for us in that while we were still sinners, Christ died for us. (Romans 5:8/ESV)

After Jesus was raised from the dead, He commissioned His followers to spread the gospel and His message of love to the world. The disciples became Apostles and the Christian church was born. Paul, the most well known of the Apostles, wrote some divinely-inspired teachings about love, including this powerful passage that is fittingly quoted at many weddings:

Love is patient and kind; love does not envy or boast; it is not arrogant or rude. It does not insist on its own way; it is not irritable or resentful; it does not rejoice at wrongdoing, but rejoices with the truth. Love bears all things, believes all things, hopes all things, endures all things.

So now faith, hope, and love abide, these three; but the greatest of these is love. (1 Corinthians 13:4-7, 13/ESV)

It is impossible to be a transformational leader without true love for those whom you are leading. Looking to Jesus' words, His example, and the way His love continued through His followers is the best way to see that kind of love manifest itself in your leadership at home, in the office, at the church, and in the community. Love changes everything.

In Other Words

Coach Osborne's strongest motivation was love. That's unusual in college football where coaches have traditionally used fear to get the most out of their players. That was never the case with Coach. He never used fear. He always led with love.

I had a few opportunities to pursue other jobs and improve my financial situation, but Coach would tell me, "Well, money isn't everything."

"Well, that's easy for him to say," I would think to myself. "He's making a lot more money than me."

But then Coach followed with this: "The greatest investment you can make is in people."

Coach was really good at investing in people. Even when I was a student trainer, he always made me feel like my role was really important and that he truly cared about me. That feeling of being loved and needed had a profound effect on so many of us in the program. We didn't want to let Coach down. We were going to work harder and get better.

He loved people in ways that really mattered. When Coach asked players about their families, he often knew their parents' names and details about individual circumstances. That's how he invested in people—not just while they were on the team but also even after they had left the program.

Coach didn't invent the phrase "What Would Jesus Do?" but he certainly lived it out long before it was made popular. He did what Jesus would do. He loved people well and treated them all with kindness, dignity, and respect.

~ Doak Ostergard, Nebraska Football Alumni Relations, Nebraska Head Athletic Trainer (1997-2006), and Nebraska Assistant Athletic Trainer (1989-96)

I started with FCA in 1994 as the area campus representative at Nebraska. I stepped into an amazing time when Coach Osborne led the Huskers to national championships in 1994, 1995, and 1997. Every Friday night before a home game, the team would stay at a hotel nearby campus. The next morning, we would have a team chapel service with a guest speaker that assistant coach Ron Brown and I would line up.

On one particular Saturday morning, I arrived to help prepare for chapel and I noticed Coach Osborne sitting alone with his Bible open. We started a conversation and I asked him what he was doing. There were two things, actually, that he did every Saturday morning. First, he was preparing for the Sunday School class he was going to be teaching the next day. That was how much he loved God's Word and sharing it with others.

Coach Osborne also used that time to pray for every player on the roster. Most people would probably print up a list and read through the list—especially at Nebraska, where sometimes there might be 180 guys, including all of the walk-ons. But Coach Osborne didn't need the roster. He knew each and every player by name.

Ask any big-time college football coach what they do on game day morning, and most, if not all of them, will talk about game prep, meetings, and anything else related to what needs to be done to secure a victory. Coach Osborne was very different. His deep love for God's Word made studying it and teaching it a priority. And his deep love for his players made praying for them a consistent routine. That love and compassion is what made him a great coach and an even greater man.

~ Chris Bubak, FCA Regional Director of Donor and Board Advancement, FCA State Director (2008-23), FCA Assistant State Director (2004-07), and FCA Area Representative (1993-2003)

Coach Osborne cared deeply about all of his players, and that has influenced their desire to want to be just like him. That was certainly true of my son Brook who played quarterback at Nebraska from 1992 to 1995. I saw firsthand evidence of Coach Osborne's genuine love as he grieved at the time of Brook's accident.

Two days after the accident, I went to Nebraska intending to talk to the local TV stations, radio stations, and newspapers, so I could thank everyone for their outpouring of support. But the football department offered to call a press conference so I could speak to everyone at the same time.

My youngest daughter Drue, sat next to me as I read a prepared statement to the reporters. As I looked up from my paper, I could see Coach Osborne standing against the wall behind them—tears were rolling down his face. I knew how much he cared about Brook as he does all of his players. His heart was truly broken.

Over the years, Coach Osborne has kept in touch. He has often shared through his own books and speeches the impact that Brook had on the program and on him personally. I will always be grateful for the love and leadership Coach Osborne showed Brook and how he continues to honor him to this day.

~ **Jan Berringer, Mother of Brook Berringer**

Tom Osborne is one of those people who many feel they know because of his position and success as the Husker football coach. I feel very grateful to have known him personally as my coach, mentor, leader, and, today, my friend.

I remember the first time I met Coach. He seemed larger than life. You can't be in his presence very long without being struck by his confident stature and quiet solidarity of personhood. One of the attributes that most impacted me was his deep concern and wholehearted love for everyone under his umbrella.

I first experienced it in the spring of my freshman year. What is now named Tom Osborne Field in Memorial Stadium was packed with athletes, freshmen through seniors, all vying for a place on the team. I had just come off a knee injury from playing in the Shrine Bowl the summer before. When Coach walked by, he leaned over and asked, "Stan, how's your knee?" As a young athlete, I was moved that with hundreds of young men to oversee, he not only remembered my name but also the nature of my injury. And he cared enough to stop and ask me how I was doing as a person, not merely as a player.

The longer I was around the program, the clearer it was that Coach saw his players holistically as young men with a life to live, challenges to navigate, and opportunities to seize: the good, the bad, and the ugly.

One semester, when I got a little off scholastically, Coach Osborne called a group of us who were struggling with classes. I remember him communicating his concern for our future as men. He told us that he was not and we should not be content with just getting by as athletes but to excel to our fullest potential with everything we have and do in life. His love for all of us was abundantly clear to me.

Years later, after I was done playing football, Coach Osborne was in the headlines for standing by one of his players. Former running back Lawrence Phillips made some poor choices and got into legal trouble, which became national news. Some in the media grilled Coach for giving him a second chance, accusing him of compromising because of Lawrence's incredible talent. It was a difficult circumstance for sure, but anyone who questioned Tom Osborne's motives for his loyalty and the investment he made in Lawrence's life did not know Tom Osborne. There was never a question in my mind that Coach would have responded the same and given that same level of support to any of his players, at any skill level.

Today, some 40 years later, when I reflect on the unique opportunity I had to play for Tom Osborne, the world may know him as a legend, but I know him for his love.

~ Stan Parker, Team Lead at My Bridge Radio (1998-pres.), Co-Pastor of Student Ministries at First Evangelical Free Church (1994-98), FCA Area Representative (1987-94), and Nebraska Football Player (1983-86)

6

~~~~~~~

CHAPTER SIX

INTEGRITY

THE LEGACY OF CHARACTER

I n the chapter on accountability, I told the story about how I foolishly tried to throw a brick onto my neighbor's roof and instead threw it through a window. My mother made me confess my actions, which was one of my first lessons on being held accountable by a higher authority.

But there was another lesson that I learned that day. It was an exercise in the concept of integrity. My mother could have been too embarrassed to confront her mischievous son's behavior and the potential ramifications such as having to pay for the broken window. Instead, she showed integrity and did the right thing.

Over the years, my parents continued to instill in me that concept of integrity. As I matured, I gained a deeper understanding of the word. Integrity, quite simply, means that you're not one person one day and someone else the next day. It means you're principle-centered and not driven by the bottom line—whether you win or lose, whether you make money, whatever people think of you.

Integrity is multi-faceted. It has to do with telling the truth. It has to do with keeping promises. It has to do with a certain level of consistency. When you live with integrity, you're driven by an adherence to the principle of honesty and fixed to a sense of moral clarity.

For leaders, integrity is a vital part of their working relationships because integrity produces trust. When leaders are honest and keep their promises, others will inherently trust them and be more comfortable and follow their lead.

Steven Covey's son (also named Steven) wrote a book called *The Speed of Trust* He opines that organizations with a high level of trust, where followers trust the leadership, are very agile. They can move quickly. They don't have to worry about looking over their shoulders to see who is out to get them because they know everyone is working toward the same goals.

I think that's true of almost any organization, whether in business, a family, or an athletic team. You must have a high level of trust in order to really be effective. Trust isn't going to be there without honesty. People won't be able to take you at your word.

A Different Principle

Back in the '60s, and particularly in the '70s and '80s, many aspects of college football got out of control. I wouldn't say everybody was doing it, but there was quite a bit of cheating—enough to make it an unhealthy environment. Long before the National Image and Likeness (NIL) rule was in place, players were offered clothes, cars, and cash. At one point, most of the teams in the old Southwest Conference were on probation, which primarily led to its demise.

The NCAA enforcement staff was not very big, and there were many things going on that weren't appropriate. Some of them were just downright unethical. Some of the teams we were competing against were not offering the same scholarship we were. One of my coaches told me, "If we can't beat 'em, maybe we should join 'em."

I'm pretty sure he was mostly joking, but just in case there was any seriousness to his comment, I made sure to be perfectly clear in my response. "No, we're going to adhere to a different principle. We might get fired if we can't keep up, but we'll never do something outside the rules."

That was a decision we made. We couldn't control what other people were doing, but we could at least control our behavior. And thankfully, we survived and were able to stand the test of time.

Integrity and Trust

Sometimes we think dishonesty is cheating on your income taxes or offering illegal inducements in recruiting. Still, in the athletic world, one thing that is fairly rampant is making promises that can't be kept—like promising a 17-year-old high school athlete that he'll come in and start for you immediately or that you will change your whole offense for him. One thing we never wanted to do was to give anybody the idea that it was going to be quick and easy or that there was any promise as to playing time.

In Chapter 2, I mentioned the book *The Heart of a Husker* in which a sportswriter in Lincoln interviewed 38 former players and eight assistant coaches.. The most common thing mentioned was the issue of honesty and the fact that our program stood for integrity. The players shared stories about how they had been promised playing time, starting positions, and, in a few cases, some illegal inducements by other programs. But at Nebraska, they were talked to about an opportunity. They would have to prove themselves. There were no deals, no promises.

For many of those players, our approach had the ring of authenticity. They sensed that some of the things they had been told elsewhere would be hard to deliver. We lost some players. There's no question that some players didn't come here because we didn't tell them what they wanted to hear. But at the end of the day, integrity and honesty were always an important part of the culture, and because of that, there was a high level of trust in the organization.

Crisis of Confidence

In 2007, I spent a year teaching at the College of Business before becoming Nebraska Athletic Director. Ethics was one of the prominent topics of discussion. A few years earlier, around 2001, several corporate scandals involved companies such as Enron, World Com, Tyco, and Arthur Anderson. The people who were supposed to be watchdogs and doing auditing were implicated in those scandals.

It doesn't seem like much has changed. We have a crisis of confidence throughout the nation and within our government. Congressional approval continues to be low, and trust has eroded in the business world, in sports, and sometimes even in the clergy. Recently the FBI, once considered the gold standard of law enforcement, has been called into question.

That's why it's so important that we continue to teach the principle of integrity through churches, ministries like the Fellowship of Christian Athletes, and organizations like Character Counts.

If you don't have integrity, it's very hard to make democracy work because we're so interdependent in a democracy. We have to be able to trust our leadership. When you cease to have that level of trust, your foundational beliefs begin to disintegrate. When that happens, there certainly may be legal consequences—such as penalties for not paying your taxes or breaking NCAA rules—but perhaps the worst personal consequence is when people no longer trust you, and it becomes difficult to maintain healthy relationships. On a national level, our very foundation as a country is shaken if we lose trust in our institutions.

Improving Integrity

Warren Buffett said something one time that resonated with me. He said, "Character is a choice." We think about physical traits like the color of our eyes. There's not much you can do about that. Sometimes there are talents like musical or athletic ability, which might give us a leg up in those endeavors if we have them. But character isn't a trait. It's not a talent. It's a choice. That's good, and it's bad because what it means is that everyone can have sound character. Everyone can be a person of integrity. And yet everyone is capable of very poor character and very bad integrity.

You create sound character and integrity by individual choices over time. Every day, people have several opportunities to either tell the truth, or spin and twist the truth, or tell an outright lie to make them look better than they really are. Eventually, that becomes ingrained. It becomes part of your very being. In order to improve your integrity, there has to be a certain level of intentionality.

So, character is a choice. If someone chooses to tell the truth on a regular basis, it becomes a habit. Dishonesty also can be habitual. If an employee, a leader, or a marriage partner is dishonest, trust is broken. We have a great deal of brokenness in our country today as a result.

The Biblical Approach

When Jesus was recasting and reinterpreting the Ten Commandments, He said, "Let your yes be yes and your no be no." In essence, Jesus was telling us that you shouldn't heap empty phrases to cast yourself in a different light. Yet, today we have advertising agencies and public relations firms that specialize in trying to make things look better than they really are. We also have social media platforms that allow us to only show others our best parts and hide our flaws.

Western culture is caught up in the notion that you'd better put a different twist on things than reality. Jesus told us to do otherwise. He taught us to lay everything out there and live with the consequences. Your life will be much easier. Jesus looked at the heart and the intent of the individual. Therefore, it's very important that integrity comes from your heart. Integrity should ultimately become an inseparable part of your being.

Jesus didn't just teach about integrity. He lived it out every day for the world to see. There were several times when He talked to the Aristocracy, the temple leaders, the scribes, and the Pharisees, and He was very honest with them. He pointed out their hypocrisy and their lack of caring for other people. The result of His honesty enabled Him to be authentic and allowed Him to be true to His mission,

When He was before the Sanhedrin, they wanted Him to renounce that He was the Son of God and the Messiah. He refused to do so, which essentially led to Him giving up His life. He could have saved His life by renouncing or recanting and saying He wasn't whom He said He was. In a way, integrity cost Him His very life.

When He was lifted up, all men were drawn to Him. Through the crucifixion and resurrection, Jesus has powerfully and eternally impacted millions over the last 2,000 years.

I am one of those whose life has been changed because of Christ's integrity. I am by no means a perfect person, and I am fallible, just like everyone else. My prayer is that I'm better now at living like Jesus than when I first became a Christian.

John Wooden once wrote that he never talked about winning with his players. He quoted Cervantes, who said, "The journey is more important than the end." The important thing was how you practiced, how you did the drills, how you competed, and how you went through the process. The wins and losses would take care of themselves.

In competition and life, we tend to focus on the final score, the profit-loss statements, and the tangible rewards, but Jesus emphasized the process or the journey. It's not about the outcome. It's about how we play the game. It's about how we live our lives. If you keep your eyes fixed on Jesus, those things work out as He sees fit. As the Apostle Paul wrote in Hebrews 12:2, Jesus is the "author and perfecter of our faith."

The Benefits of Integrity

Our primary motivation for living with integrity should be to obey Christ's commands and be more like Him. But there are many benefits as well.

When you tell the truth, you don't have to have a long memory. You don't have to remember what you said the last time when you misled somebody. Life is much simpler. It's not as complicated. That's a great benefit. You have a better chance to sleep at night. You can look at yourself in the mirror.

Living with integrity is freeing. You're not looking over your shoulder much. Your relationships improve because when people see you as a person of integrity, they will gravitate toward you. They'll have more confidence in you and confide in you. This is true within families, friendships, businesses, and sports teams. Integrity is at the core of everything.

Imagine what our world would look like if the majority of its people were intentional about living with integrity. There would be less divorce. There would be fewer corporate scandals. There would be less political division. There would be less war. More integrity would push our culture toward biblical principles such as trust, unity, peace, and love.

In Other Words

Every athletic program puts its best foot forward when recruiting for its future. That part of the college game will never change. In fact, winning in the margins becomes even more important with NIL, transfer portals, and the like.

I recalled visiting Nebraska in 1981 and was struck by the transparency and honesty of an academic counselor named Ursula Walsh. We were brainstorming about what path could be taken to obtain what at the time was called a PLM degree (Petroleum Land Management) at Nebraska. Nebraska didn't have a program by that title. I recall Ms. Walsh acknowledging what I was already aware of. The University of Oklahoma has the best PLM program in the nation. It was important to me because our family inherited land in East Texas, and it had several active wells from which our family received royalties. I'd make trips down to Panola County, Texas, from Oklahoma with my dad and brothers, and I'd learn about how the land went back to the Emancipation Proclamation.

So, it was sentimental and historically important stuff. But Ursula looked me straight in the eyes and said. "If your heart is set on being a petroleum engineer, you should go to Oklahoma. They have the best program." I went home thinking, "I can trust these people."

I was amazed at how honest she was. She pitched alternatives, but never once did she present anything other than what was the truth. That resonated with me. I'm a son of a missionary. I went to church three times a week. It was normal to me. We learned an awful lot about what integrity looks like through narratives of scripture. Ursula reminded me of Lois, the grandmother of the great Apostle and philosopher Timothy. She had an ability and willingness to see into my heart. Once she knew what my core values were, she pointed me in the direction I should go. That is an atypical trait in the zero-sum world of elite college recruiting.

The late Ursula Walsh remains one of my favorite people for her integrity. In the times since I've seen Coach Tom Osborne, that story usually comes up in conversation. Ursula was an extension of the integrity that he was known for during his legendary tenure at Nebraska. They were both stalwart examples of what it looks like to do the right thing no matter what. You might lose something in the short term, but in the end, you'll always end up coming out ahead.

~ Spencer Tillman, Senior Analyst at Fox Sports, President & CEO of Axiom Sports Products Inc., NFL Player (1988-93), Super Bowl Champion (1985), and Oklahoma Football Player (1983-86)

After playing tight end for two years at Ventura College, I had several choices for where to play at the next level including USC, UCLA, Oklahoma, and Nebraska. My football friends and I always felt like

Nebraska was a mythical powerhouse—even more so than the Trojans and the Bruins, which were in our backyard.

In December 1975, Coach Osborne came to my parent's home in Ventura to make a final recruiting push. He sat in our living room as my five sisters and three brothers gathered around the highly esteemed head coach. It took just a few words for me to know where I was going to go:

"Mark, we like how you play," Coach said. "You're a Husker-type player, and after watching film and talking to coaches who coached with and against you, we think you can play here. But just so you know, we have lots of very good tight ends, and you'll need to beat them out in order to get playing time. I can't make a promise you'll play. The only promise I can make is that, no matter where you are on the depth chart in your career here, you will retain your scholarship through graduation regardless."

That is the mark of a true leader. Other coaches had made vacuous promises, but even as a 20-year-old kid, I knew Coach Osborne spoke the truth, had integrity, and wouldn't tell me something he thought I wanted to hear. I committed that day. It was one of the best decisions of my life, and Coach Osborne will always be in my highest regard.

**~ Mark Dufresne, NFL Draft Pick (1978) and
Nebraska Football Player (1976-77)**

Coach Osborne always tried his best to do the right thing for the right reason. He didn't have an agenda. I don't think Coach would look back on his life and say he never made mistakes, but his intentions were pure, and he made decisions based on the knowledge and information he had at the time—despite the intense opposition.

As a leader, when you make decisions that way, your team ultimately emerges stronger and more unified. That won't preclude you from dealing with significant challenges because almost everyone else has an agenda.

So many times, I sit around the table and look at people and know exactly the conflict they have. It's that struggle to want to do the right thing but understanding that doing so might cost you something personally and might not line up with your agenda. But that was never a struggle for Coach.

A coach can't always communicate everything to the media or the public. I watched many times when he went out front and took the arrows, even though he could have passed the blame on to someone else who might have actually deserved it.

I was part of the Unity Council, and he made some decisions based on what the seniors had requested on behalf of the team. Some of those decisions weren't popular with the national media, and he took the heat when the media was berating and criticizing him.

On the flip side, when there was all kinds of praise, and everybody was celebrating, Coach slowly moved to the back of the room and allowed others to enjoy the moment. In all things, he did what I'm trying to do today—make sound decisions that are in the best long-term interest of the University of Nebraska.

Honestly, I don't think Coach could care less about what other people thought. In many respects, he wasn't trying to impress or please man. He was trying to please the only person he truly served—his Maker.

~ Trev Alberts, Nebraska Athletic Director, NFL Player (1994-96), and Nebraska Football Player (1990-93)

7

CHAPTER SEVEN

~~~~~~~

HUMILITY

THE LEGACY OF SELF-ASSESSMENT

Woody Varner was the president of Nebraska during my time as an assistant coach and my early years as the head coach. Woody always tried to make things work the best they could without much fanfare. He had a good sense of humor. He was somewhat self-effacing, and he certainly wasn't abrasive. Woody wasn't a top-down guy. He wasn't going to impose his will on everybody else, and I always appreciated that.

Those first few years as head coach, it was a one-game season, and that one game was Oklahoma. We usually played OU at the end of the year; most of the time, it was for the conference championship. We lost the first five times we played Oklahoma. As the head coach, I wasn't very popular with the fans. After those losses, I'd often be at home with the shades drawn and the phone off the hook. At some point later that night, there'd be a knock on the door, and it was Woody Varner with his wife Paula.

His sense of humor lightened the atmosphere even when it felt like a wake. I'm sure he had many places to be and many things to do, but he took the time to visit a 30-something-year-old coach and his family when he needed some encouragement.

Woody's example in that story and many other instances provides a clear picture of humility, simply being aware that it isn't all about you. Someone who is humble likely wants to do their best for the team or the organization and cares about those around them. In other words, a humble leader is a servant leader.

My time in coaching enabled me to look at the big picture. That's just the nature of athletics. It's not always going to be accolades or great feelings. There are going to be some tough times. So humility is naturally built into our lives. We're going to be humbled one way or another. Life has a way of slapping you down. That doesn't seem to faze some people who will still be self-centered, but the more trials you experience, the more you realize that everyone is vulnerable and there are no maladies known to man that can't happen to anyone at some point.

Sometimes, however, we have the wrong impression of humility. A humble person can often be perceived as blowing in the wind and doesn't have much of a backbone. He just goes with the flow and has no particular thoughts on what he wants to accomplish. But in all truth, humble people do care and often care passionately. The difference is that they care more about others and the overall organization's success (whether that be within a company, an athletic team, a church, a non-profit, or a family).

Modeling Humility

As the head coach, I tried to become more sensitive as time passed. I tried to be aware of when a player's parent was sick, if there had been a tragedy in their family, or if they were struggling in school. I wanted them to know that I was available and that they could come and see me. But I didn't just wait for them to come and see me. I would try to reach out to them to discuss their problems, and I still try to do that today.

It was always important to do my best to treat my players in a way consistent with the scriptures and my values. I think they knew I cared about them, and not just because they could perform well on the field. It didn't matter if they were a starter or a fourth-string walk-on. I knew their names and did my best to be in touch with every individual.

Some of the most important times of my week were the 20 or 30 minutes after practice in the weight room. I'd go in and walk around, maybe lift a weight or two. But during that short period, I talked to five or six guys each day. I was on their turf instead of them being called into my office. We usually talked about their high school football team, their parents, a test they had coming up, or things that were important in their life. Over the course of the season, I probably talked to each player on our team five or six times on a fairly personal and informal level.

I don't want anyone to read this and think I was perfect and always said the right things at the right time. I'm sure there have been times I could have or should have done more. But the general thrust of how I conducted myself with my players was that they knew that I cared about them—even when I was asking them to do hard things or when

I needed to discipline them. I did those things because I valued them and wanted the best for them.

Uncommonly Unselfish

Some players seek to honor God with the way they play. They are unselfish, treat opponents respectfully, don't trash-talk, and give maximum effort. Many fans might say that nobody plays the game of football this way. However, I have known many who did, and they were among our best players. They were great contributors.

One such player was Brook Berringer from Goodland, Kansas. When Brook arrived in Lincoln, we were using dual-threat quarterbacks who could both run and throw. But after his redshirt season in 1991, we recruited Tommie Frazier. When senior Mike Grant struggled early in the 1992 season, Tommie was inserted to revive the offense and ultimately won the starting job. Brook spent the next two years as the backup.

Brook would get his chance, however, during the 1994 season. After a 3-0 start, Tommie left the game against Pacific with blood clots in his leg. Brook took over for his fallen teammate in the 70-21 blowout and led us to a 42-32 victory against Wyoming in his first career start. But in that contest, Brook took a vicious helmet to the ribs. Although in considerable pain, he finished the game, not realizing that he had sustained five cracked ribs and a punctured lung.

The physicians ran a tube between two of his ribs to deflate the outer cavity of the lung so it could inflate again. They drained the blood and fluids into a bag as his mother watched in disbelief.

Brook started the next game against Oklahoma State with a flack jacket to protect his ribs and lungs. A doctor stayed on the sidelines for the express purpose of monitoring his physical well-being. However, he took another hard hit in the ribs, and the lung deflated again. The doctors inserted a needle in his ribcage and inflated his lung again. The doctors told me that if he deflated the lung again, he would be done for the rest of the season. Walk-on Matt Turman started the next game against Kansas State, although Brook found his way back on the field in a tough 17-6 road win.

Through all of the adversity, we entered the homecoming game against No. 2-ranked Colorado with an 8-0 record. By most accounts, this matchup would likely determine the Big Eight championship and play a major factor in the national championship picture. Still not 100 percent healthy, Brook was determined to make the start.

It turned out to be Brook's defining moment. Our defense kept the Buffalo offense in check, and we vaulted to No. 1 in the rankings with a dominant 24-7 win.

Brook started the final three regular season games and led the Huskers to a 12-0 record and a marquee matchup with Miami in the Orange Bowl that would serve as the National Championship game. By then, however, Tommie had recovered from his injury. We had a scrimmage before the bowl game and Tommie graded best over Brook, but we told Brook he would play too. Tommie got off to a shaky start and threw an interception on Nebraska's second series.

As Miami jumped out to a 10-0 first-quarter lead, we replaced Tommie with Brook, who promptly got us on the board with a 19-yard touchdown pass to Mark Gilman. But we put Tommie back in the game when the offense stalled throughout the third quarter. He recovered from his earlier woes to orchestrate a pair of touchdown drives. We won the game 24-17 and won our first National Championship while I was the head coach.

While Tommie's triumphant return was a key to victory, it's no secret that Brook was one of the primary reasons we made it to the Orange Bowl undefeated.

Brook approached the 1995 season wanting to win the top spot on the depth chart. After a spirited competition between him and Tommie during spring ball, I waited until the following August to announce a starting quarterback.

That summer, Brook accepted Christ and grew quickly and firmly in his newfound faith. Although he was already a very loyal player, I believe his trust in God helped him overcome the disappointment of starting the season, once again, as Tommie's backup. Brook worked hard and did everything he was asked to do. He didn't complain, didn't cause disruption, did the right things, and said the right things.

The way he handled things was exemplary and noticeable to others on the team. Brook spoke at elementary schools, visited people in hospitals, and used his influence unselfishly.

We dominated the 1995 season and ultimately won the National Championship after defeating No. 2-ranked Florida in the Fiesta Bowl. Despite not playing much, Brook was considered a likely NFL Draft pick. He was also becoming an avid aviator who routinely flew small planes. On April 18, 1996, Brook took a 1946 Piper Cub over Raymond, Nebraska, with Tobey Lake, his girlfriend's brother. It was two days before the draft and the same day as the annual FCA banquet, where he was scheduled to speak.

Around 3:30 p.m., word got to Ron Brown that there had been a crash. It was a windy day and the plane's engine had quit. Ron and I quickly drove to the crash site, where it was confirmed. Brook and Tobey were gone. The FCA banquet took place as scheduled. Brook's funeral was broadcast on local radio a few days later, and many people across Nebraska accepted Christ after hearing Brook's testimony and Ron Brown share the gospel message. Our whole team drove three hundred miles to the funeral in Goodland, Kansas. People lined the highway displaying signs dedicated to Brook.

Several years later, I was approached about erecting a personal statue outside Memorial Stadium. I wasn't interested in that. But when one designer showed me an idea that included Brook, that concept was something I could get behind.

Some have wondered why it wasn't a generic player, and I can understand that reasoning. But in a sense, Brook's spirit epitomizes the sacrifices that so many small-town kids have made to make Nebraska's program great. He was not a walk-on, but he symbolized the efforts of so many of those players. His impact was great. He embodied many of the things we tried to do here. He was a good student with unimpeachable character. He was well-liked, well-respected, and a good leader. As a result, Brook made his mark here like so many others before him and after him. He represented the very best in all of us.

The Ripple Effect of Humility

When people with a little bit of ego get around somebody who has some humility, it can challenge their way of thinking about how they treat others. This often creates a ripple effect throughout whatever organization they might represent.

In a day and age where it's so easy for players to leave one team for another, Brook showed the world what true loyalty could and should look like in college athletics and beyond. And the foundation for that loyalty was based on a Christ-like humility that can't otherwise be explained.

After Brook's death, many players began to put team welfare before personal goals and aspirations. Many gave great effort on the scout team for as long as four years, with very little playing time. Some of these players were people of faith, and others were not, but they seemed to find added meaning and purpose in their lives by contributing to the team's welfare, even if, like Brook, they had to sacrifice to make the team stronger.

This willingness to serve others became very powerful. It was woven into our culture and was almost palpable in its effect on the program. Having our players perform community service was part of our Life Skills program. Players were encouraged to serve others by visiting hospitals, speaking at schools, or mentoring children.

A team bound together by mutual love and concern will have greater team unity and a willingness to sacrifice for each other. Great teams are usually set apart by exceptional team chemistry; talent carries a team only so far, and there are many talented teams. Great team chemistry based on love, respect, and a willingness to serve comes from the spirit.

The Pitfalls of Pride

The opposite of humility is pride. It is perhaps the most dangerous trait for any leader. When leaders believe it's about them, they try to grab the limelight and take credit for things they haven't done. That hurts camaraderie, mutual respect, and teamwork.

People trying to follow a prideful leader realize that they're expendable and that they're really not that important to the leader. They're more like pawns on a chessboard. They are disposable.

Unfortunately, we see a lot of egocentric behavior in politics, athletics, and the corporate world. From an athletic standpoint, I always discouraged trash-talking, whether before the game, in the press, or on the field, because generally, that leads to dysfunction somewhere during the game. We taught our players to respect their opponents.

We played very physical football, but if I saw a player trying to win the game with his mouth, I'd get him out of there as soon as possible. Sooner or later, trash-talking usually escalates into a penalty, and it could come at a key time in the game.

The same is true when pride rears its ugly head in other areas of leadership. At some point, a puffed-up approach will lead to self-serving and overconfidence, leading to mistakes that will ultimately lead to a downfall.

Sober Self-Assessment

My grandfather was a minister, and my folks always took me to Sunday School and church. But my faith at that time was probably, in large part, the faith of my family. It was more traditional and something I grew up with.

Then, during the summer of 1957, between my sophomore and junior year in college, I went to an FCA Camp at Estes Park, Colorado. It was the organization's second conference. Most of the people attending were college athletes, along with several professional athletes.

I was in a huddle group led by Clendon Thomas, an All-American running back at Oklahoma. There were probably 20 to 25 Oklahoma football players there. Strangely enough, I got to know many of them, and some of those friendships endured for many years.

One of the Bible verses I read during the conference was in Matthew 16:24-25:

Then Jesus told his disciples, "If anyone would come after me, let him deny himself and take up his cross and follow me. For whoever would save his life will lose it, but whoever loses his life for my sake will find it. (ESV)

The part about denying yourself really grabbed my attention. A Christian walk wouldn't be easy; it could require personal sacrifice and even giving up your life. And then the second part of that scripture grabbed my attention. I realized that athletics had occupied most of my time, energy, and attention. From eighth grade to high school and my first two years of college, I played them all: football, basketball, track, and baseball. The scripture made me realize that being a good athlete had been so primary in my life that it was as though I was trying to save my life through athletics.

The Scripture indicated athletic success, wealth, and influence would eventually end. Losing one's life for Christ's sake had eternal consequences. That FCA conference was a turning point for me.

Losing your life means that your purpose is to serve others and honor God, and put Him first. Then, the pieces of your life will begin to fit together. That was the path I chose, and that passage in Matthew had a lot to do with the choice I made. Hopefully, I've gotten a little better at following Him and serving Him as time passed.

The Bible has so much more to say about pride and humility. One powerful story takes place in Matthew 10:35-45. James and John, two disciples that were also brothers, had gone to see Jesus and asked if they would each be seated on His right hand and His left hand in the Kingdom of Heaven. The other disciples heard about it and there were some hard feelings. Even in His own group, Jesus saw examples of people trying to exalt themselves at the expense of others.

That's when Jesus taught them a lesson about servant leadership:

"But it shall not be so among you. But whoever would be great among you must be your servant, and whoever would be first among you must be slave of all. For even the Son of Man came not to be served but to serve, and to give his life as a ransom for many." (vv. 43-45/ESV)

Jesus didn't just teach about humility. He modeled it in the most powerful display of sacrificial love known to humankind. Jesus was born as a human child in unglamorous circumstances. Jesus then lived an ordinary life before spending three hard years ministering to an audience that often included people who hated Him and wanted to kill Him for His teachings.

Ultimately, Jesus allowed Himself to be falsely accused and tried for crimes He didn't commit. He was stripped, beaten, whipped, spat upon, cursed, mocked, humiliated, nailed to a cross, and hung between two common thieves until His eventual death. If anyone had the right to be prideful and reject that kind of treatment, it was the Son of God. Yet He resisted that temptation and set an example for us.

Do nothing from selfish ambition or conceit, but in humility count others more significant than yourselves. Let each of you look not only to his own interests, but also to the interests of others. Have this mind among yourselves, which is yours in Christ Jesus, who, though he was in the form of God, did not count equality with God a thing to be grasped, but emptied himself, by taking the form of a servant, being born in the likeness of men. And being found in human form, he humbled himself by becoming obedient to the point of death, even death on a cross. (Philippians 2:3-8/ESV)

The Apostle Paul, once an arrogant man who hated Christians and vowed to snuff them out, wrote that powerful passage. His life changed when he encountered Christ in a miraculous vision (Acts 9). Paul's writings are among the most preached scriptures in Church history. He added some more cogent advice for anyone who finds themselves getting caught up in prideful thoughts, attitudes, or behaviors:

For by the grace given to me I say to everyone among you not to think of himself more highly than he ought to think, but to think with sober judgment, each according to the measure of faith that God has assigned. (Romans 12:3/ESV)

In other words, pride goes before a fall. We should recognize our weaknesses and acknowledge that our strengths come from God and God alone.

Leadership Worth Following

If you are struggling with pride, join the club. We all do. If you want to reject pride and embrace godly humility, which we all should, it's not easy, but it can be done with God's help. Here are a few ways to remove pride as a leader (and from all areas of your life) and begin making a real difference with humility and selflessness:

1. Know your purpose: You can't kill pride if you don't understand that your call to leadership isn't about you but a much larger divine plan to serve God and others.

2. Know your role: You can't do it all, and you shouldn't want to try to do it all. There's a reason you have your particular position, and allowing others to operate within their roles will create an atmosphere of mutual reliance and help ward off prideful attitudes.

3. Know your strengths: It's okay to recognize what you're good at, but never forget that your gifts came from God, and you likely had people along the way that helped you hone and improve them.

4. Know your weaknesses: We all have them, and that's a good thing. Your weaknesses force you to rely on God and others. Recognizing that need for help can strip our pride and keep us humble.

5. Know your future: You can't know the specific details of what your life has in store, but you can know that there is an expiration date to this life, and what you did with it will matter more than you can ever imagine.

Just as prideful leaders can damage camaraderie, mutual respect, teamwork, confidence, and self-worth, a humble servant leader can increase productivity, develop team cohesion, encourage creativity, build confidence, and foster an environment of loyalty and trust. That's the kind of leadership worth following.

In Other Words

Coach Osborne has been an active supporter of the Fellowship of Christian Athletes since he first attended an FCA Camp at Estes, Colorado, in 1957. There's a reason he is in the FCA Hall of Champions. I would put him up there with Tom Landry as one of the icons who has given so much of his life to the ministry of reaching athletes and coaches for Christ.

I've personally watched him travel all over the state of Nebraska and across the country, speaking free of charge for conferences, camps, banquets, and fundraisers. It didn't matter if it was a group of thousands or a small handful. He's always generously given his time and his best.

In 2021, there was a banquet in Wichita for which he accepted an invitation to be the keynote speaker. Coach Osborne had a lot going on back in Lincoln, including a board meeting for TeamMates, his mentoring organization. It was a month out from the event when I told him it would be okay if he had to back out from the event, but there was no way he was going to do that. Coach Osborne, like always, was going to do everything he could to keep his commitment.

"FCA has done a lot for me," he told me. "FCA is the reason why I'm walking with the Lord. I want to go and share that with other people."

His commitment to FCA throughout the years says a lot about his faithfulness, his loyalty, and his consistency, but more than anything; it says so much more about his humility and his willingness to selflessly put others first—even at great risk to his own well-being—so he can speak on, first and foremost, behalf of Jesus Christ, but also on behalf of FCA.

~ Chris Bubak, FCA Regional Director of Donor and Board Advancement, FCA State Director (2008-23), FCA Assistant State Director (2004-07), and FCA Area Representative (1993-2003)

It was right after we won the 1994 National Championship Game against Miami. Celebrations had broken out on the field. Coach Osborne had taken his Gatorade bath. There were lots of hugs and high-fives as everyone headed to the locker room.

That's when I received one of the worst calls in my life.

My wife, Molvina was seven months pregnant with our first child and had experienced some serious problems during the game. Unbeknownst to me, she was rushed back to our hotel in downtown Miami with a police escort.

I received that information quietly and didn't tell anyone else. All I could do was pray and hope that my wife and the baby were okay. There was nothing more I could do but get on the team bus and take the long, slow ride through massive traffic back to the hotel.

Coach Osborne was sitting up in the front, a few rows ahead of me. I knew the media would be waiting for us, and he would be mobbed. But instead of getting off the bus as expected, Coach pulled a fast one. He snuck out the back entrance of the bus and somehow made his way to a remote entrance and up a back stairway.

The average head coach would have gladly jumped into the arms of the media to celebrate his first National Championship—not Coach Osborne. I was also looking to escape the mob so I followed him from a distance. He never turned back.

I finally got to the hotel room where thankfully, my wife was resting comfortably. She had talked to her doctor, and everything was good with her and the baby.

At about two o'clock in the morning, I got a call from Coach Osborne. He had heard about Molvina and wanted to make sure everything was okay and if there was anything he could do to help. Here was this man who had won his first national title, and he was concerned about his young receivers coach and his family.

"Coach, why didn't you get out there in front of the media," I asked.

"I'm getting up early," he responded. "I'm flying to Haiti tomorrow with a buddy to do some mission work."

Coach Osborne never let the left hand know what the right hand was doing. He could've made a big deal about going on that trip, but he had the humility to keep it private and serve others out of pure motives. There are many more stories like that where Coach helped people, and no one knew. I was blessed to see a few of those scenarios play out and learn firsthand what it looks like to love God and love others.

~ Ron Brown, Nebraska Football Director of Player Support and Outreach, Nebraska Football Senior Offensive Analyst (2021-22), Nebraska Football Director of Player Development (2018-20), Liberty Football Associate Head Coach (2014-17), and Nebraska Football Assistant Coach (1987-2003, 2008-14)

During my time as an assistant coach at Nebraska, there were many times I saw Coach Osborne take time to thank people for their contributions to the program. It didn't matter what their role might have been. He wanted them to know they were valued and had an important part to play.

One example was when he told the people cleaning the offices why their job made a difference. He would show appreciation to them because so many people came through those doors, and the outward appearance was a reflection of the program as a whole. These conversations happened regularly with equipment managers, trainers, academic staff, media relations staff, Life Skills staff, football support staff, landscapers, janitors, maintenance crews, painters, and so on.

Head football coaches are very busy. They have a lot of things pulling on them and competing for their time. But Coach always had a genuine humility that drove his intentional actions. He wanted to make everyone feel valued.

When I became a head coach, I remembered that about Coach and wanted to emulate his appreciation for those who do the small things behind the scenes—the small things that are actually big things and really make a big difference.

~ Turner Gill, Liberty Head Football Coach (2012-18), Kansas Head Football Coach (2010-11), Buffalo Head Football Coach (2006-09), Green Bay Packers Director of Player Development and Assistant Wide Receiver Coach (2005), Nebraska Assistant Football Coach (1992-2004), CFL Player (1984-85), and Nebraska Football Player (1980-83)

8

CHAPTER EIGHT

~~~~~

PATIENCE

THE LEGACY OF THE LONG VIEW

Patience is the ability to take the long view and to realize that, sometimes, effective conclusions take time.

My first example of patience was through the example of my parents. Early on, my mom showed incredible patience with my younger brother and me when our dad spent five years overseas during World War II. She was under a lot of stress, but she hung in there.

Many years later, my mom had a stroke while in her 70s. My dad wasn't in the best health either, but he stood by her and did everything he could for her, which also required great care and patience.

So I saw how both of them lived out their lives and were devoted to each other with love and patience. That made a big impact on me.

Early in my coaching career, I was blessed to serve as a head coach under Nebraska Athletic Director Bob Devaney. In today's microwave culture, it's very likely I wouldn't have survived those first few seasons, but Bob had an ability to take the long view. He saw something in me that I probably didn't see in myself, giving me time to develop into a better head coach.

Those examples of patience impacted the way I coached my players. So often, when a player messes up on or off the field, there's a temptation to light into them. As time passed, I realized that sometimes the best thing I could do was listen. I developed more patience, and instead of immediately correcting a player by having them run up the stadium steps or another form of discipline, I learned that it is more effective to sit down with them and find out what's really going on.

Years after my coaching career, I had a unique opportunity to do some mentoring within the Creighton Athletic Department. There was a basketball player on the team who was talented but very inconsistent. One night he'd play great, and the next night he was not very good at all. The coach at that time was Dana Altman. He expressed concern and frustration and wanted to know if I could work with this young athlete.

The first time we met, I sat down and asked him to tell me about himself. His grandmother had raised him in Los Angeles. She had cancer and didn't have much time left to live. It had been weighing on his mind. We met several times regularly, and after a while, he started playing better and was more consistent. As it turned out, he simply needed someone who understood his situation, cared about him, and was patient enough to make a difference.

The Best Thing

Impatience looks for the next thing, but patience waits for the best thing. I can certainly attest to that truth in my life.

After college, there was a young lady I was dating, and that led to our engagement. But then, I was cut by the San Francisco 49ers and sent across the country to play for the Washington Redskins. Eventually, our relationship fell apart. It seemed like a tragic thing at the time, but looking back on it, I can see that it was the best outcome. Some of the clearest understanding of God's purpose came from reflecting on past events.

During that time with the Redskins, I pulled a hamstring, and they wanted to ensure I could play. They gave me a shot of Novocain every week and put me out there, but I developed some scar tissue over time. At the end of the season, I realized I was physically unable to perform. Every time I tried to accelerate, my hamstring knotted up. For a receiver, that was career-ending. I wasn't a great player, but I was good enough to play several more years if I could run, but I couldn't.

So I went back to Nebraska and enrolled in graduate school, and met my wife Nancy—an unexpected blessing that likely wouldn't have occurred had my football career been extended.

I didn't really have any intention of going into coaching. In fact, my graduate work was leading me toward a career in college administration. During that time, Bob Devaney arrived in Lincoln to take the head football position. I missed athletics and wanted to ease my way out of a life of athletic competition. I went to see Bob about a graduate assistant position, but he already had the coaches he needed.

Bob said, "You know, I've got some guys over in one of the dorms that are really causing trouble. They've thrown the dorm counselor out, and they're running their own show."

Bob wanted to know if I'd move in with them and get things straightened out. If I could do that, he would allow me to eat meals at the training table. So I accepted the challenge

I had to break up a few fights and make a few appearances before various student tribunals for discipline, but eventually, things eased up. Once spring ball came around, Bob offered me a position as a graduate assistant. I didn't actually intend to go into a coaching career, but that situation, which required a lot of patience, was the catalyst for what was to come.

One Step Closer

When Thomas Edison worked on the light bulb, he experienced nearly a thousand failures. Rather than being discouraged, he always said, "Well, I'm one step closer to the right answer."

Edison's story is a testament to the importance of valuing process over short-term results. During my coaching career, sometimes fans would be very impatient because we ran the football a lot. We played in a part of the country where you're going to have some windy days, which made it hard to throw the ball. And some days, it was really cold—sometimes even with snow. That's why we were so committed to running the ball, even though we did have an effective passing game.

Whenever we lost a game, there was a tendency for people to say, "Well, if you had just thrown the ball more, you would've won." But we committed to a certain process and felt it was the most effective plan over the long haul.

It's not just important to be patient with yourself and with the plan. It's also important to be patient with other people, especially those you're leading, whether that's your family members, players, employees, or staff.

One way to be more patient with others is to take advantage of their strengths. With my assistant coaches, for example, there were several demands on their time. There was recruiting, X's and O's, internal communication (amongst the staff), and external communication (to the players), among other responsibilities. I never had a coach who was perfect in all of those areas, including myself. For instance, if someone was a really great recruiter but not the best at field strategy, I would give that person more recruiting responsibilities.

In 25 years, I only fired two coaches and today, those coaches are still friends of mine. A lot of that can be attributed to patience, but it's easier to be patient when you've put your coaches in the best position for success. However, even when there were mistakes, I always tried not to fly off the handle. The same was true with players. I was slow to kick players off the team for disciplinary reasons unless they intentionally violated our discipline code.

That doesn't mean we didn't have standards and a strict team policies. But we weren't just going to discard people to look better in the newspaper.

After I was done coaching, Frank Solich, one of my assistants, took over and did an excellent job. Then another coach was hired. His background was in the NFL. Nebraska still had a lot of players when he arrived, and many of them were walk-ons. In his first meeting, he told the players there were too many of them and that he would get rid of many of them. I'm sure some of those players could have been really good with time, but you have to have the patience to develop as many as you can.

General managers and athletic directors, unfortunately, often have the same mindset. They are quick to hire and fire in a quest for the perfect fit. But if you're patient, perhaps someone who wasn't terribly effective initially could become a really good coach or, in the corporate world, a really good employee. Every day you show patience for those you are leading, like Thomas Edison, might bring them one step closer to becoming the best they can be.

A great example of the importance of patience is my friend, Coach Bill Snyder, who was hired at Kansas State in 1989. Kansas State football was in bad shape when he arrived. In his first four seasons, things were difficult, with only one winning season. His administration stayed with him, and he turned Kansas State into a national power, being ranked in the top 10 many times. Bill had a great work ethic and did one of the best coaching jobs in the country over his 27-year career.

The Dangers of Impatience

It's incredible how impatient we are when we don't see the long view. We miss great opportunities when we lose patience with people who might need a little more time to figure things out and work through challenging circumstances.

Impatience can lead to destabilization. In the athletic world, for instance, the pattern of having a new coach every three or four years can create a downward spiral that is hard to recover from.

Most of our fans at Nebraska now might realize that firing Frank Solich after a 9-3 season in 2003 was probably not the best choice. He played for a National Championship. He won a Big 12 Championship. He went to a bowl game every year. He won 75 percent of his games. Most people in the College Football Hall of Fame don't have a record that good.

We're seeing the dangers of impatience show up in today's athletic world even more, which is a far cry from how things were in the early days of my coaching career.

Nebraska, like most programs, had a freshman team, and there was a time when freshmen were not eligible to play. Even when they became eligible, we still maintained a freshman team. The idea was that players would spend a year on the freshman team and would then redshirt the next year. Hopefully, by their third year, they would develop enough to see some playing time. The goal was that they would be very productive during their last two or three years of eligibility. For most Nebraska players, that was the general pattern.

I remember Andy Means, a walk-on from Holdrege, Nebraska, who arrived on campus weighing 160 pounds and running a 4.9 40-yard dash, slow for a defensive back. With time and hard work, Andy weighed 180 pounds and ran a very solid 4.5. He started for us for two years and was an All-Conference player.

Mitch Krenk walked on from Nebraska City as a 190-pound tight end with very average speed. Mitch started for us and went on to play several years in the NFL.

Now, many freshmen leave if they don't see enough playing time during their first year. But some initial data is coming out that indicates that the majority of players that enter the transfer portal don't really improve their situations. Some might make a lateral move. Some might move up in the ranks but see even less playing time. Some might increase their playing time but have to go to a smaller program or lower division.

That's why taking a long view is so important. Good things take time and often come with adverse circumstances. Shortcuts often lead to further delay and outcomes that aren't necessarily better than what would have happened with a more patient mindset.

A Matter of Trust

The Bible is lined with stories of patience, impatience, and the ramifications of both, not to mention all of the universally relevant advice, encouragement, and instruction given in Psalms, the Proverbs, the Gospels, and the apostolic letters. In all of these writings, the common denominator is trust:

The Story of Joseph

One of the most inspiring stories of patience can be found in Exodus 37 to 50. Joseph, one of Jacob's younger sons, received two dreams from God but spent decades going through his brother's betrayal, slavery in Egypt, a false sexual assault accusation, and several years in prison before seeing those dreams come true.

Finally, because of his patience and perseverance, Joseph became Egypt's second most powerful man and made divinely inspired decisions that saved the entire region from a seven-year famine. His story remains one of those powerful examples of being patient and trusting God's plan.

The Story of Jesus and Peter

In the New Testament, there is an inspiring example of a patient leader. The story of Jesus and His disciple Peter can be found scattered throughout the four Gospels. Still, the theme is consistent: an impetuous, zealous, quick-tempered, but incredibly passionate and loyal follower asks all the wrong questions, makes all kinds of bold claims and promises, and then cowardly denies his teacher when his own life is in danger.

After Jesus' crucifixion, He didn't give up on Peter but instead showed the same kind of patience and compassion He'd shown for the previous three years. Peter grew into one of the most powerful evangelists history has ever known. His leadership was a key aspect of the Early Church's unprecedented growth. Peter's teachings in the Book of Acts and apostolic letters became a part of the biblical New Testament that we have today. That only happened because of Jesus' patient leadership over Peter.

Leadership often results in dealing with trying situations and difficult people. Oftentimes our patience grows thin. Seeking God's help at such times provides the proper perspective.

Even youths shall faint and be weary, and young men shall fall exhausted; but they who wait for the Lord shall renew their strength; they shall mount up with wings like eagles; they shall run and not be weary; they shall walk and not faint. (Isaiah 40:30-31/ESV)

Taking the Long View

Leadership can be a long, difficult journey. That's true for your job. That's true for your family. That's true for every area in your life where you serve in a leadership role.

For instance, parents go through a period, especially when their kids are going through adolescence and some periods of rebellion, when they have to keep the mindset that this too will pass.

The same is true in marriage. There are times when things don't go as smoothly as you'd hoped. But if you stay with it and exercise as much love and patience as you can, things can work themselves out.

In all cases, taking the long view or keeping the end in mind will help you get through those difficult times and those moments when you don't think you can wait much longer. Here are a few things that you can do as a leader to maintain the long view and stay patient until the work is done:

1. Trust the promise: If God has called you into a leadership position, then that comes with the promise that He will use you for a purpose whether or not you immediately see the big picture.

2. Trust the plan: With purpose comes a plan. If it comes from God through divine inspiration or trusted, wise friends and advisors, you can walk that plan out in confidence and remain steadfast and patient even when the outcome you are seeking isn't immediately visible.

3. Trust the process: Sometimes things take longer than expected or desired because there is an important lesson to be learned or an invaluable character trait that needs to be obtained. Soak it in, and don't rush past those things that are meant for your long-term benefit.

4. Trust for the best: Don't let impatience take you off course or force you into making decisions that may have far-reaching ramifications.

Patience may be one of a leader's least favorite words, but in the long run, it is one of a leader's most important tools for true success.

There will be times when changes are necessary for the welfare of the organization, but restraint and seeking God's wisdom often saves us from impulsive action, which can be destructive.

In Other Words

I was raised in a Christian home but didn't come to know Jesus until my freshman year at Nebraska. I stopped attending church with my parents when I was a junior in high school, and it was my choice. When I got to Nebraska, Tom Sorley was my roommate. I was just trying to be accepted and find my way after living away from home for the first time.

That same year, I got involved with the party scene. At the same time, Tom began to share what it looked like to have a personal relationship with Christ. He was going through the same issues, but he was handling things in a totally different way.

One night, I was at a party where pot was being smoked. Someone reported it to campus security, who showed up at the dorm room and took us down to the police stations. That was the thing that God used to save my life.

The next day, I was back in my room, reflecting on how I needed to change my life. I thought about what Tom had taught me and what Coach Osborne had modeled when I first met him when he was recruiting me in my home. That's when I prayed and made the decision to truly follow Christ and start my new life with Him.

Coach Osborne obviously found out about the incident. There was a chance I could be kicked off the team and lose my scholarship even though all charges had been dropped. But instead, Coach Osborne was kind enough to give me a second chance. He showed great patience with an insecure kid and allowed me to show him I could do better and conform to his high expectations.

I often think about what my life would have looked like had Coach Osborne not modeled mercy and grace to me. I easily could have lost my chance to play in the NFL or to meet my wife.

Coach Osborne was sometimes criticized throughout his coaching career for giving so many second chances. Not every recipient of his patience honored him for that. Still, there are a lot of us out there whose lives were changed because he refused to give up so easily. Coach Osborne understood what we were going through and did everything he could to help us become the men we were created to be.

> **~ George Andrews, Senior Financial Advisor with
> Ronald Blue Trust, NFL Player (1978-84), and Nebraska
> Football Player (1975-78)**

9

~~~~~~

CHAPTER NINE

SELF-CONTROL

THE LEGACY OF TEMPERANCE

Most of the time when I was coaching, I did my best not to come unglued. There may have been a time or two, but it wasn't very often. John Wooden was one of the people I admired from a distance in the area of self-control. I only watched him coach on television, but I did know him personally. Coach Wooden always seemed to be in control of his emotions. That doesn't mean he wasn't passionate, and that doesn't mean he wasn't demanding and exacting.

One way that Coach Wooden stood out was in his language, which is often reflective of self-control. Some of his players have said that the most emotive language he used was "goodness gracious sakes alive."

That's quite a contrast to what the stereotypical coaches have been known to communicate. Akin to drill sergeants, "old school" coaches can become very profane and will attack others personally when they get angry—questioning their intelligence or disparaging their ancestry. It's not always the case, but a lack of self-control often comes out in those kinds of negative verbal expressions.

This is easier said than done when an official makes a bad call, when a child misbehaves, or an employee is insubordinate.

So what is self-control? Also referred to as temperance, self-control is the ability to manage your emotions and your actions in such a way that you are not disruptive or harmful to other people. It means that you can be thoughtful in any given situation and not fly off the handle.

Unfortunately, self-control is not something we're naturally born with. We don't come out of the womb and automatically have the ability to manage our thoughts, emotions, words, and actions. But the good news is, having composure even in the most difficult circumstances is a trait that every leader can learn to exhibit.

It's All Connected

As already mentioned, there are three key areas where self-control takes place: in the mind (your thought life), in the soul (your emotions), and in the body (your words and actions). Simply put, thoughts become emotions, and emotions turn into actions.

Science has proven the correlation between these three areas through something called "galvanic skin response," which indicates perspiration and stress in the body. In other words, your physical response to thoughts and emotions doesn't just show up in your actions. It might not be overt, but it affects your whole system if you're highly distressed. It's all connected. Lie detector tests involve measurements of physical responses to specific questions.

I called nearly every play of Bob Devaney's final years as head coach at Nebraska, (1969 to 1972), and continued to do so for the next 25 years as head coach. Sometimes those calls came in situations where the game's outcome was on the line, or we needed a critical first down. Losing emotional control at those times would have been disastrous.

So, what enhanced the likelihood of having emotional control?

1. Preparation: As I have mentioned, our hours were very long. I spent 30 to 40 hours per week studying each opponent on film. It was important to have a sense of what defense we were most likely to see in each situation. If our opponent gave something unusual, I spent many hours preparing our quarterbacks to audible to the right play. I also devoted time to listing each play we had from each formation, so I would not need to take time to read a play sheet before calling a play. We ensured that assistants would get the right personnel for the formation called, and coaches in the press box were prepared to let me know if they saw something unusual or if a player was not performing well.

Preparation is important for the trial lawyer, first responders, salespeople, performers, or even a parent dealing with a difficult child. It is an important part of the process.

2. Maintaining a clear mind: There was always some hate mail, negative press, and occasional angry phone calls. I read only signed mail and answered it, did not read the sports page, and took the phone off the hook after a loss (I had a listed number).

If a knowledgeable person had something constructive to say, I listened. Filling your mind with negativity does not help.

Social media was just getting started toward the end of my coaching career, but it was very much alive during my time in Congress and as

Athletic Director. I have never engaged in social media, which is probably a sign of old age, but it does not seem to serve a good purpose.

3. Meditation: I mentioned that after open heart surgery in 1985 that I began practicing meditation early in the morning and again for a short time at noon. This led to better focus and a quiet mind. I have continued to meditate each morning.

Sometimes meditation conjures up the image of a monk sitting in a cave reciting a mantra. For me, meditation was paying attention to breathing and dismissing random thoughts, staying in the moment, and being focused and relaxed. Having meditated with regularity promoted the ability to call up the relaxation response at times of stress and pressure.

4. Prayer: Prayer was similar to meditation, and one often followed the other. I prayed for family members. The morning of the game, I prayed for each player who would be playing that day by name. I prayed that opponents would be protected from injury and that the game would be played in a way that would honor God. I prayed for those with whom I had a difficult relationship. Scripture says to pray for our enemies. It is hard to hate someone when you pray for them, and hatred is more harmful to the person doing the hating than to the object of the hatred.

It is important to lift up things we are grateful for and not exclusively use prayer as a wish list of personal needs, although that is part of prayer also. Prayer seems to help the individual praying to see things God's way rather than to maneuver God to conform to our desires. The short devotional and prayer we had before starting our staff meetings helped set the tone for the day and seemed to be a good influence on how we treated our players and each other.

We live in a fast-paced world with a great deal of information coming at us from all angles and high levels of stress. I don't want to give the impression that I was a saint. I am as flawed as most people. The practices listed above were helpful in coping with a demanding occupation. We see many people dealing with stress in self-defeating ways, such as alcohol abuse, drugs, and promiscuous lifestyles. Such escapism results in more distress. It is better to face adversity head-on and learn to move through it rather than to deny its existence by escaping into harmful behaviors.

That's why a leader should not make decisions based on emotions but on logic and truth. You can't allow fear, hate, anger, depression, or even immense happiness to rule your actions. Emotion-based leadership will eventually hurt yourself and those that you are leading.

Furthermore, an organization is often reflective of the leader's actions. If the leader is volatile and sometimes out of control, then obviously, it's going to create a rather anxious environment because people are not going to know what's coming next. Is the leader going to explode? Is the leader going to be unreasonable? That makes for a very uneasy working arrangement. That is true in a business, on a team, or in a family. I recall hearing about the owner of a professional sports team whose employees talked business with him only first thing in the mornings. This person had a drinking problem and became more volatile and unreasonable as the day went on.

On the other hand, having a measured approach and the ability to handle your emotions is an important part of leadership. Generally speaking, a self-controlled leader's actions will be commensurate with the situation. They won't be over-reactive, they won't be overly harsh, and they won't fly off the handle at the first sign of adversity.

Unnatural Rivalry

There was a team that, at one point, decided they were going to make Nebraska their rival. Nebraska and Oklahoma had been a rivalry based primarily on the fact that 29 out of 30 years, the winner of that game won the conference championship. It was a very natural rivalry, but it was always respectful and never evolved into a hateful thing.

But this one particular team decided that creating a rivalry with Nebraska would make them better. That decision led to a lot of interaction in the press, where people from that state would take shots at Nebraska and tell jokes about our team and our state that, as a result, pushed things to an emotionally fevered pitch.

During one game against this team, we were behind 14 to nothing. They ran the opening kickoff back for a touchdown, and we fumbled, and they ran that in for a touchdown. I don't think there were two min-utes off the clock, and we were down two touchdowns.

We just kept playing, and eventually, the game shifted. The other team, which was motivated a great deal by anger and hatred, quickly became somewhat disorganized. The final score was 50-something to 14. Our athletes were able to maintain composure and execute what they were trained to do without getting overly emotionally involved. That's always the best way to perform.

A Different Approach

When something disturbing happens, you can follow one of two paths. One is to make yourself feel better, at least temporarily, by exploding or turning to some sort of coping mechanism. The other is to immediately focus on how to make things better and resist the temptation to make things worse. There's quite a difference between those two responses.

Still, when we feel like we've been treated unfairly or treated badly, our first impulse is to retaliate, cheat back, or defend ourselves. As a coach, there were many occasions when that was the case.

I'm reminded of the 1995 Orange Bowl when we played Miami on their home field for the National Championship. There was a lot of trash-talking, primarily from the other team. For that game and any game, if I saw a player getting involved in verbal exchanges with the opponent, I would take him out of the game because those verbal inter-changes often led to a physical response that would result in a penalty.

I also told our players to help their opponents up after each play. We were a physical football team. We tackled hard. We blocked hard. But we were going to do our best to show proper respect to our opponents.

At halftime of that game, I told the players that I felt that something was going to blow up in the second half—something that would be harmful to the team. I told our players that if an opposing player took a swing at them, they were to drop their hands and not even take a defensive posture. So often, a player will get his hands up. The mere action of it will result in offsetting penalties.

In the second half, Miami had the ball, and they were driving into our territory. At the end of the play, one of their players was on top of our defensive tackle Christian Peter, punching him. Christian immediately dropped his hands straight down at his side. Sure enough, Miami got a 15-yard penalty. It killed their drive at a critical time in the fourth quarter. We won the game, 24-17, and the National Championship.

A Battle of Biblical Proportions

Self-control has been an ongoing battle for humankind since the beginning of recorded history. From a biblical standpoint, it all started in Genesis 3 with Adam and Eve, the first man and woman, who lived in the Garden of Eden. God gave them authority over the land and only one rule to follow—they were not permitted to eat the fruit from the tree of the knowledge of good and evil.

Satan was a fallen archangel who tried to overthrow God's heavenly kingdom. Banished to the earth, he appeared to Eve as a snake lurking on the forbidden tree. He made three appeals, which later would be defined as the lust of the eyes (an appeal to our thoughts), the pride of life (an appeal to our emotions), and the lust of the flesh (an appeal to our body through our actions). The fruit looked good; it would make her like God, and, even better, it tasted good.

Eve's lack of self-control caused her to sin against God. She ate the fruit and gave some to Adam, who also lacked self-control and partook. Satan understood their weakness and took advantage with three big lies that ushered sin and death into our world.

There are many other examples of otherwise strong leaders whose self-control problems caused a lot of trouble:

• Samson's pride in his strength and heroism paved the way for destructive behavior with problematic women.

• David's desire for another man's wife caused great heartbreak and a sad ending to his otherwise triumphant reign.

• Solomon's pride in his riches, among other personal idols and vices, led to a decline in his kingdom and the ultimate realization that everything was meaningless.

In all three cases, not only did those and other flawed biblical leaders suffer from their actions, but so did the people that they were responsible for leading. But Jesus gave us the script for how to overcome those temptations and how to exercise self-control.

To prepare for His ministry, Jesus spent 40 days in the wilderness fasting and praying (Matthew 4:1-11). When He was physically at His weakest, Satan tempted Him with the same three appeals he made to Adam and Eve. He tempted Jesus to turn the rocks into bread (an appeal to His body through His actions), he tempted Him to throw Himself down from the temple and be rescued by the angels (an appeal to His soul through His emotions), and he tempted Him to bow down and reject God in exchange for the worldly kingdom (an appeal to His eyes through His thoughts).

But even though Jesus was weak in His body, He was strong in spirit and was able to have self-control and resist temptation because of consistent prayer and a disciplined mind. Through that 40-day process, Jesus had laid everything down and had already made the decision to trust and follow God fully.

A Perfect Model of Self-Control

Through the life of Jesus, we see a sinless man who was the perfect model of self-control. That doesn't mean He was emotionless or passionless. Quite the contrary, in one famous instance, Jesus expressed His anger at the money changers who were using the temple as a place to sell goods instead of honoring it as a place of prayer and worship. He turned over the tables and chased them out with a whip made out of cords (John 2:14-17).

But Jesus did not sin because His actions were justified, and His anger was righteous. Many years later, the Apostle Paul wrote this warning about anger and self-control:

Be angry and do not sin; do not let the sun go down on your anger, and give no opportunity to the devil. (Ephesians 4:26-27 / ESV)

At the end of Jesus' ministry, however, we see a very different scenario. Jesus had been falsely accused and was hanging on the cross for the sins of the world. Even as the soldiers were mocking Him from below, He said, *"Father, forgive them, for they know not what they do."* (Luke 23:34 / ESV)

That's a pretty big step for someone being actively crucified. It's something we should all aspire to do, yet we often find it difficult to forgive people who have said hurtful things or caused injurious and damaging harm. What Jesus modeled at that moment was an incredible act, not just of love but also of self-control.

The Power of Death and Life

I've always realized the power of the spoken word. From my experience with former coaches and authority figures, I've seen how harmful the spoken word can be. I don't think enough coaches realize how powerful their words are in shaping a young person's confidence and how they feel about themselves. I remember my son had a coach who said some things to him that were very hurtful and derogatory. He remembers those words to this day. I recall criticism I received from a coach in the eighth grade. I made sure I played in a way that belied the criticism from then on.

But I've also seen how uplifting the spoken word can be when someone tells you they believe in you, that they see your talent, that they appreciate what you've done, or that they value your opinion. It is very uplifting.

As Solomon wisely wrote: *"Death and life are in the power of the tongue, and those who love it will eat its fruits."* (Proverbs 18:21/ESV)

Another powerful scripture in 1 John 1:1 says, *"In the beginning was the Word. And the Word was God. And the Word was with God."* John was in exile on the island of Patmos, and legend has it that he was the only disciple who was not martyred. John was old and had many years to contemplate who Jesus was. In explaining Jesus to the gentile world, he seized upon the Greek belief that the spoken word had a life of its own, a power of its own.

Sometimes we lose track of the words that come out of our mouths. They really are very powerful and have a significant impact on other people—the words parents say to children, the words spouses say to each other, the words bosses say to an employee, and the words a coach says to a player.

I have had many conversations with former players in which they ask, "Do you remember when you said..." I seldom remember the occasion or the quote, but for some reason, it resonated with the player for years.

We live in a world where we're pushed and pulled in a lot of different ways, and things come up unexpectedly. To maintain that mindset sometimes is difficult, and it takes practice. You have to work at controlling your emotions and being reflective about how your words and actions impact another person.

For the Christian, self-control is possible through knowing God's Word, believing what it says about us, following what it tells us to do, and allowing the Spirit to give us the strength and guidance to live it out, resist the temptation to give into temptations that appeal to our thoughts, our emotions, and our flesh.

But again, as mentioned earlier in this chapter, it all starts in the mind, and the Bible has a prescription for how to fight off those things that can cause our self-control to spiral into some dark, destructive places:

Finally, brothers, whatever is true, whatever is honorable, whatever is just, whatever is pure, whatever is lovely, whatever is commendable, if there is any excellence, if there is anything worthy of praise, think about these things. (Philippians 4:8/ESV)

The Exercise of Self-Control

Self-control might be the most important of the biblical Fruits of the Spirit. So much good can be done when we control our thoughts, emotions, actions, and words. But so much bad can happen when we lose control of just one of those areas of our personhood.

Here are some things to consider as you work to shore up your self-control in whatever leadership role you are called to fill:

1. Guard your eyes and ears: We can't control everything we hear and see. We're going to hear negative things. We're going to see disturbing things that we don't want to see. The key is capturing those thoughts and replacing them with good thoughts before they turn into negative emotions. I follow the news, but sometimes two straight hours of cable news can get depressing. Most of the major news is depressing.

2. Flush out negative thoughts: It's easy to ruminate on ugly words that have been said to you or even something you said that you wish you could take back. You can dwell on it and replay it in your mind, or you can consciously turn those thoughts into something positive—thoughts of thankfulness, gratitude, love, hope, and forgiveness. It does make a difference.

3. Keep your emotions in check: Redirect negative emotions such as anger, sadness, or fear and turn them into something positive. Speak truth over those emotions. Anger can turn to either hate or grace. Sadness can turn to either depression or compassion. Natural desire and physical needs can take us toward lust and overindulgence, or we can have faith and trust that God's way is best for us.

4. Watch your words: It takes a conscious awareness that there are certain things that you're not going to say—certain curse words or themes that you're not going to express verbally. Eventually, that becomes a habit. The more you exercise control in your words, the more it becomes second nature.

5. Control your actions: If you're depressed, that could lead to drinking, drugs, or overeating. If you've been convinced you're not good enough, you might cut corners or cheat—like an athlete using performance-enhancing drugs. These actions come from a place of fear. Your physical reactions always start in your mind and in your heart.

6. Practice consistent routine: Some tools to help with self-control include the practice of scripture reading, prayer, and meditation. Also, know what things you should avoid (entertainment and news outlets or places where you might easily fall prey to temptations, for example) that can make maintaining self-control especially difficult.

7. Take time to reflect: Ask yourself probing questions before deciding what you watch or listen to or how to respond to adverse situations. Will this help make things better or worse? Will this harm me or someone else? Will this make me feel good or bad later on?

Self-control is a vital character trait for a leader who wants to leave a lasting legacy. It's not only valuable for the leader but also important for those being led and will determine just how effective that leadership will ultimately be.

In Other Words

One day during my first year at Nebraska, the freshman team was having a scrimmage, and Coach Osborne just happened to walk over to watch. I was playing on the defensive side of the ball when another freshman clipped me. As far as I was concerned, it was an illegal block and a pretty cheap shot. The guy was an offensive lineman and much bigger than me. It felt like I'd been chopped in half. I was very frustrated and angry.

As I came off the field, I took my helmet off and tossed it on the ground as hard as I could. It was an older-style helmet with ear pads on the side. It was like an explosion. The helmet started bouncing, and the momentum took it right in front of Coach Osborne. He had seen the whole scene unfold, and I was immediately embarrassed about my actions. Coach Osborne very calmly picked the helmet up and handed it to me.

"We don't treat our equipment that way," he said. "That's not how we do things around here. If you've got an issue with Mark, you need to talk to him about that, but we don't tolerate this kind of behavior."

That was the end of it. I was thankful he didn't make me run stairs or something worse. But it was clear that I had done wrong and would need to make sure never to do anything like that again. That was my only warning.

Coach Osborne was always fair and treated his players with respect and love. He was never abusive and never lost his temper or used bad language. He was always a model of self-control for his assistant coaches, the players, his staff, our fans, and our opponents.

~ Gordon Thiessen, Cross Training Publishing, Co-Founder of Kingdom Sports, and Nebraska Football Player (1975-79)

10

CHAPTER TEN

~~~~~~~

LOYALTY I

THE LEGACY OF SACRIFICE

One of the great memories I have of my father was the loyalty and devotion he showed toward my mother. As I mentioned in a previous chapter, my mother had a severe stroke at age 72, which rendered her speechless and partially paralyzed. Despite health problems associated with his heart disease, my father cared for and assisted her, attending to her needs.

The effort expended in getting her in and out of a wheelchair and in and out of bed hastened his death four years later. He stood by her, however, and did everything he could to make her comfortable. That picture of loyalty has stayed with me ever since.

Loyalty became a major factor at the conclusion of my senior year in high school. I had some success as a high school athlete and was offered football scholarships to several universities. I also was offered basketball scholarships by several schools. However, since age ten, I had lived across the street from Hastings College, a small liberal arts school located in my hometown, Hastings, Nebraska.

As I grew up, I spent every spare moment at the college football field or basketball gymnasium. Tom McLaughlin, the football and track coach, had developed a good relationship with me. I liked Tom and trusted him. My father, grandfather, and two uncles had played football at Hastings College, so I heard many stories about past athletic teams. I knew every player, every coach, watched every athletic contest, and grew up with a strong loyalty to Hastings College.

The football coach at Nebraska offered a scholarship but said I could not also play basketball. The basketball coach at the University offered a scholarship but told me I could not play football.

I considered several schools, but when decision time came, I found that my allegiance to Hastings College was stronger than the attraction of playing football or basketball at a major university. I enrolled at Hastings with no scholarship aid. I paid my way through school and played football and basketball and ran track. I even surprised myself when I found that I could not turn my back on the school that had meant so much to me during my formative years.

Staying with people and institutions that were somehow influential and important to me has remained a persistent pattern. I coached football at Nebraska for 36 years as an assistant and then head coach. I can honestly say that I have not regretted any decision I have made based on loyalty—some of which are detailed throughout the rest of this chapter.

The Devaney Effect

As I think back over 36 years of involvement with Nebraska football, I realize that loyalty has been a dominant factor throughout that period of time. On April 25, 1998, my "retirement" banquet, involving 700 players and coaches who had been part of Nebraska football since 1962, was held at the Bob Devaney Sports Center on the University of Nebraska campus.

It was surprising that so many former players and coaches attended, and it seemed that there was a very strong common bond among all of those who were present. Their devotion and loyalty to the University of Nebraska, and the football program in particular, were very apparent. There was a powerful bond that drew us together.

This common bond was not a random event, but rather came directly from a strong sense of loyalty instilled by Bob Devaney, who was the head football coach at the University of Nebraska from 1962 through the 1972 season and continued as athletic director until 1992.

Bob was one of those old school coaches who believed that if you played for him or coached for him, you were one of his. He would always take time to show that he remembered you, cared about you, and was interested in what you were doing. He had a knack for making people feel at ease. Through his sense of humor and personal charisma, he created a strong sense of devotion among his players.

Bob had a temper and at times could be fairly volatile, but these periods of anger never lasted long. He was quick to forgive and always made the object of his wrath feel accepted and comfortable within a short period of time. Bob stood behind his players and coaches through thick and thin.

When Bob first came to Nebraska, he was immediately successful. He was 9-2 his first season and won nine or 10 games each of the next four years. Bob also led Nebraska to four straight Big 8 championships.

But in 1967 and 1968, Nebraska had a couple of "bad" years—both ending 6-4, the only two seasons in 37 years (1962 to 98) in which Nebraska did not go to a bowl game. The 1968 season ended with a 47-0 thumping by Oklahoma in Norman. Nebraska fans were not happy and there was a good deal of grumbling.

It is fairly common when things are not going well for a team for the head coach to fire either the offensive assistants or the defensive staff. This decision deflects blame and responsibility from the head coach. The wolves want sacrificial lambs when you lose. Bob had pressure to get rid of some coaches after the second 6-4 season, but at that time, he said very publicly, "If one person goes, we all go. We're in this together."

Bob refused to blame any assistant or player. He maintained a steady resolve and was supportive of all of those he worked with. Everyone on Bob's staff felt needed and appreciated. This loyalty was rewarded by two national championship seasons in 1970 and 1971. Somehow our coaches had gotten a lot smarter in only two years, as there was suddenly no longer any talk of getting rid of coaches. This attitude of "we're all in this together" persisted for many years. Each coach on Bob's staff and my staff knew that he would not become a scapegoat if things got tough.

At that point, I was about 30 years old and had a wife and three kids. His indication of loyalty meant a lot to me and meant a lot to our staff. Bob commanded a great deal of loyalty from his staff and from his players because he was loyal.

Later on, when I became head coach and Bob was the athletic director, our contracts were mostly done on a handshake. I don't think I ever had anything more than just a sheet of paper saying what my salary was. It was just strictly a handshake between Bob and myself, and I never had an agent. I appreciated doing business that way. I trusted Bob and he trusted me.

Leading by Example

I have always believed that if one area of a football team is not performing well, it is the head coach's responsibility to see that the necessary adjustments are made to produce the desired performance. Most assistant coaches are willing to learn, and I believe this is true for people in all kinds of jobs. If they won't follow instructions or make an effort to improve, then a change may be required. It was my job as head coach to make sure people knew what was expected of them and to recommend areas for improvement.

In my 25 years as a head coach, I dismissed only two coaches. Had I been more specific concerning what I expected earlier in those coaches' careers at Nebraska, both might have been saved. Our coaching staff was remarkably stable. The average tenure of our assistant coaches was 14 years, compared to an NCAA Division I average of about three years. Several of the assistant coaches who were there at or near the beginning of my career as head coach were with me at the end.

I can't emphasize enough how important staff continuity was to the success of our program. When a coach leaves a staff, it is usually at the end of the football season and right in the middle of the recruiting season. When the assistant coach who is recruiting a young man leaves a university, the athlete loses his most important contact with that school. Unless the player has no other options available, it is very unusual to have the player eventually sign with the school from which the assistant left. Since schools lose approximately three out of nine football assistants in an average year, about one-third of those schools' recruiting capacity is seriously impaired.

The benefits of staff continuity extend beyond recruiting. We had to spend very little time "coaching the coaches." When a new coach joins the staff, he must learn terminology, personnel, and a whole new culture. Since our coaches were together for so long, we seldom had to slow the learning process so new coaches could be brought up to speed.

Even though I was never a particularly hot commodity in the coaching profession, there were a few opportunities to go into professional football or to other major universities for a higher salary. But any coaching offer that was of interest to me became a staff decision, rather than a personal decision.

The only offer I took seriously was from the University of Colorado following my sixth year as head coach. Early in my career, we had a hard time beating Oklahoma—losing the first five times we played. We finally won in 1978 over a top-ranked Oklahoma team, 17-14. We were so emotionally spent that we lost to Missouri the next week and were told we had to play Oklahoma again in the Orange Bowl.

Playing Oklahoma a second time in only six weeks after finally beating them was a hard thing to swallow. In the rematch, we out gained Oklahoma in total yardage but lost, 31–24. I was discouraged and frustrated. Some fans had been fairly negative, as we hadn't been as dominant as they had hoped.

So, when the Colorado job was offered, I talked the situation over with my coaching staff. We agreed that Colorado appeared to be an easier recruiting situation and the coaches shared some of my disappointment concerning fan reaction. So it was decided that I would go to Boulder and take a look.

When my wife, Nancy, and I made the trip, I thought that we would take the job. The facilities were good and the location was as nice as we had thought, yet on the return trip to Lincoln, I thought about how I would break the news to the Nebraska players that I was leaving. The more I tried to construct that speech in my mind, the more I realized I couldn't make it. I had told those players that Nebraska was the best place for them, and I didn't know how I could now tell them that someplace else was better for me.

I sat down with the staff and told them I couldn't leave. I never took a serious look at another job. Even when I was still considering the move, however, the staff knew that we were a package. If I went, all those who wanted to go could join me. It is not uncommon for a head coach to take a job and leave most of his previous staff stranded. If the assistants don't go with the head coach, the new head coach coming in often doesn't hire them either.

It's important to realize that the consequences of your actions often reach far beyond your personal interests.

Next Level Loyalty

Many Nebraska coaches came up through the ranks. Most started out as graduate assistants and then progressed to full-time coaches. When a vacancy on the coaching staff occurred, both Bob Devaney and I gave first consideration to people already associated with the program. Bob named me head coach in 1973 after I had been a graduate assistant and assistant for 11 years. Milt Tenopir, offensive line coach; Dan Young, offensive line and kicking coach; Turner Gill, quarterback coach; Craig Bohl, linebacker coach; and Frank Solich, head coach from 1998 to 2003, all started at Nebraska as graduate assistants. Through patience, hard work, and loyalty, they became outstanding coaches.

It seems that many organizations are fearful of internal hiring. This is particularly true of institutions of higher learning, where there is often much concern about "inbreeding." This hiring process often results in poor personnel choices. It is very difficult to know about a person's character, work habits, and ability to relate to others simply by looking at a resume or conducting an interview.

In working with people for a period of years, you can know exactly what they can do and how they will react in pressure situations. My observation has been that people from within an organization are much more apt to stay and work hard for that organization. They are more likely to be motivated by a desire to see the organization they have helped build do well than by a desire for personal gain.

Bill Walsh, former San Francisco 49ers coach and executive, says, "The best way to maintain the continuity of an already winning profile, however, is to hire from within."

Loyalty demonstrated at the top often results in loyalty from within the ranks.

A Forgotten Attribute

Loyalty is not valued as much as it once was in our culture. In professional athletics, we see continual movement of players and coaches as they look for more pay, a better contract, and more security. Professional teams often move from city to city to pursue a better financial situation. College coaches have joined the parade of those seeking a higher bidder. Contracts are often not honored and promises to players are quickly forgotten.

A well-known television personality indicated that this was "the American way" as she moved from one network to another for a higher salary. This lack of stability and loyalty is certainly wearing thin with many fans.

I am often concerned when I hear coaches and players say, "I have to do what's best for me and my family," as they leave their present team for a better deal. There is very little concern for their teammates, coaches, organizations, and fans, and these decisions to jump ship are often not right for them and their families in the long run, with the turmoil caused by moving around frequently outweighing certain financial benefits.

There are times when career moves are warranted; however, such moves should be made for the right reasons. It seems that too few decisions are made in our culture out of a concern for the common good. Too often money and self-interest are the only factors given much weight. Loyalty has become an almost forgotten attribute.

The Dangers of Disloyalty

On the other side of loyalty is the dangerous characteristic of disloyalty. When we are disloyal, we compromise our character. Disloyalty often has to do with a self-serving attitude. Essentially, disloyalty is a betrayal of friendship or a betrayal of a gesture of good will. Our society is very self-absorbed. As a result, sometimes we repay those who have done good things for us with disloyal acts because it might advance our cause or make things easier for us.

Disloyalty is especially devastating to a team. This can take place when one player talks behind another player's back or when players undercut the coach. You have to have a great deal of loyalty and mutual trust and genuine caring and love for the people you're playing with in order to have a great team. Disloyalty can destroy all of those things in short order.

The public has lost a certain amount of trust in many of our leaders whether they are politicians or coaches or business leaders. Sometimes people don't really see things through. They make a commitment to do something and if they think they've got a better deal somewhere, all of the sudden they're gone. Contracts don't mean what they once did. Disloyalty is far too common today and we can see its negative impact in every aspect of our society.

The Blueprint for Loyalty

The Bible gives us some great examples of what loyalty should look like and how it can benefit our lives. In the Old Testament, for example, we see how Noah's family stuck with him while everyone was mocking him for obeying God's command to build the ark. We see other instances of intense loyalty within Joshua's commitment to serving Moses throughout the Israelite's difficult trek to the Promised Land, David and Jonathan's undying friendship amid King Saul's treacherous hatred and jealousy, Ruth's dedication to her mother-in-law Naomi, and Queen Esther's courageous devotion to the Jewish people.

But one of the best blueprints for loyalty, especially within the team context, can be found in the New Testament Gospels. There were many people who followed Jesus but 12 men became His most loyal and committed disciples. After facing adversity and intense opposition, the disciples' loyalty was put to the test:

After this many of his disciples turned back and no longer walked with him. So Jesus said to the twelve, "Do you want to go away as well?" Simon Peter answered him, "Lord, to whom shall we go? You have the words of eternal life." – John 6:66-68

These 12 men knew that Jesus was who He claimed to be—the Messiah—and without the loyalty of a handful of followers, Jesus' mission would have been severely handicapped.

The story that strikes most of us, however, is about Judas and his disloyalty. He was a person who was treated well and taught and cared for by Jesus. And yet he turned around and betrayed Him.

In stark contrast is Peter's loyalty. Even though Peter denied Jesus at the time of His crucifixion, he was extremely loyal and was transformed after Jesus' death to become a powerful, centralizing force in the establishment of Christianity.

If you look at all the remaining disciples after Judas' death, they became very bold and were very loyal to Jesus and His cause. Even though at times they had wavered and even had not understood what Jesus was all about, they became galvanized after the crucifixion and became the foundational members of the Christian church after Pentecost.

Loyalty binds people together and causes them to put others ahead of personal ambition. This is a biblical principle that God desires to see in His people. Jesus taught this powerful message of loyalty throughout His ministry and demonstrated it all the way to the Cross.

"Greater love has no one than this, that someone lay down his life for his friends." – John 15:13

Loyalty doesn't usually require that kind of sacrifice, but when God's love is the motivating factor, we will be blessed when we lead with a heart of devotion and commitment to anyone whom we have been entrusted.

In Other Words

On January 1, 1993, Florida State defeated Nebraska, 27-14, in the Orange Bowl—a game that decided the National Championships. It was a tough loss but we were proud of the team's effort and saw a lot of momentum for the future.

Not long after the season ended, Florida State head coach Bobby Bowden approached me about leaving Nebraska and joining his staff. It seemed like a good opportunity to hear him out and listen to what he had to say. Coach Bowden flew me down to Tallahassee and gave me a tour of the facilities. His program wasn't necessarily better than Nebraska's, but was certainly on the same level.

After the tour, I sat down with Coach Bowden and one of the things we talked about was my salary. He slid a piece of paper across the desk with his offer. "I kinda know what you make at Nebraska," Coach Bowden said. "I'm sure this is better than what Tom is paying you right now."

I looked at the offer and then told Coach Bowden something he wasn't expecting to hear.

"That's true except for one big difference. Coach Osborne splits his revenue from his shoe contract and his summer camps and shares it with his assistant coaches. Once you consider that income, I actually make quite a bit more at Nebraska."

Coach Bowden was dumbfounded: "Doggone that Tom Osborne! Nobody does that!"

"Well," I responded, "Coach Osborne extends loyalty to us and we give loyalty back to him."

It wasn't just about the money. It was, in fact, mostly about Coach Osborne's treatment of his coaches throughout his career. He didn't get rid of assistants when things got rocky. He didn't blame others for any issues the program might've faced. Instead, Coach Osborne approached Nebraska football as a true team effort in which loyalty was always firmly implanted in its foundation.

That's why so many spent decades coaching for him when other programs were often a revolving door. It was an uncommon level of loyalty that doesn't exist nearly as much these days, and it was something that has been embedded in my heart ever since.

~ Ron Brown, Nebraska Football Director of Player Support and Outreach, Nebraska Football Senior Offensive Analyst (2021-22), Nebraska Football Director of Player Development (2018-20), Liberty Football Associate Head Coach (2014-17), and Nebraska Football Assistant Coach (1987-2003, 2008-14)

When I think about my time at Nebraska with Coach Osborne, the first thing that comes to mind is how long his staff was together. Keeping a core group of coaches together like he did rarely happens anymore. It takes next-level loyalty to see so much consistency over a long period.

Over the past 26 years, I've tried to model the same things with my staff at Lincoln East, which has probably been together longer than any other high school program in Nebraska. Some of my coaches have been with me for 20 to 25 years. It can be done if everyone buys into what you're doing, and they buy into you like Nebraska's coaches bought into Coach Osborne. They believed in him because he did what he said. He had integrity. He took care of them. He always shouldered the heavy weight of expectation.

Coach Osborne was also loyal to his players, and they were loyal to him. Like all programs, he had players who made mistakes, and he could have easily and sometimes justifiably tossed them to the curb. But Coach went to bat for those kids. He believed it was worth the risk to try to save them. That's why he is so respected. He did things by the book, but there were times when he stepped into the gray area. There were always consequences, but he wouldn't cast anyone aside.

From a different perspective, I can relate to what it feels like for someone to stick with you during tough times. When I took over for Lee Zentic at Lincoln East, the districts were changed, and our enrollment dropped to 800. We were really a Class B school but still had to compete in Class A. That first four years, we only won a couple of games each season, and I probably should have been fired. But we worked through it, and the school stuck with us. We turned the corner and went on to make the playoffs in 15 of the next 17 seasons.

But that kind of loyalty is only earned when you do the right things, love your kids, support your coaches, and work hard. I believe in my heart that I've done it the right way. And a lot of it was what I learned from Coach Osborne over the years. He hasn't coached a game for decades, and he's showing that, regardless of age, you can still have an impact because of who you are and what you've done. For me, that impact was an invaluable lesson in creating a culture of loyalty within your team.

~ John Gingery, Head Football Coach at Lincoln East High School (1995-pres.) and Nebraska Football Player (1975)

11

~~~~~~

CHAPTER ELEVEN

LOYALTY II

THE LEGACY OF TRUST

The loyalty issue was put to the test during the 1995 season to the degree that I had not previously experienced. Just before the season began, Riley Washington, a third-team wingback, was accused of attempted murder in the shooting of an individual at a Quick Stop parking lot.

Not long after that incident, Lawrence Phillips, our starting I-back, was charged with assaulting a former girlfriend. Then, Damon Benning, our second-team I-back, was charged with assault. After that, the media really zoomed in on us. They publicized troubles that Christian Peter, one of our defensive tackles, had three years previously. For good measure, they also mentioned pending charges against cornerback Tyrone Williams who had been cited two years earlier.

I visited with Riley Washington almost daily over the 13 days he sat in a jail cell before his release on bond. At first, I didn't know what to think. The charges authorities had brought against Riley were immediate and extremely serious. Yet Riley looked me right in the eye and said he was innocent. I had not known Riley to lie to me before. As I visited with him, he continued expressing his innocence in a way that led me to believe he was telling the truth.

His attorneys at the public defender's office were able to gain information that substantiated Riley's claim of innocence. They presented their findings to Athletic Director Bill Byrne, Chancellor Joan Leitzel, faculty representative Jim O'Hanlon, Vice Chancellor for Student Affairs Jim Griessen, and myself. Those present agreed that it appeared Riley had been wrongly accused. I was given the green light to go ahead and play Riley during the season.

This decision led to a good deal of negative press. The perception was that Riley was allowed to play merely to help us win football games despite being charged with a serious crime. Since Riley was not a starter or key player, it seemed to me that the argument was rather hollow. I doubt that there were more than a handful of people in Nebraska who believed in Riley's innocence. The publicity surrounding the initial charges against him was so one-sided that most people's minds were made up before he was given his day in court.

Standing by Riley in the face of so much public condemnation was unpleasant. I believed that we had done our homework on the specifics of the case, however, and I believed in Riley. I realized that the university, the football program, and I would all come under increased criticism and derision if the facts as we understood them did not bear out.

Riley played sparingly during the last three-fourths of the season. He went to class, practice, and then to his room. The court case dragged on over the next year and a half. He became increasingly despondent and, at times, seemed to despair of ever having his name cleared.

There were many delays in the trial. The attorneys from the public defenders' office were anxious to try the case, as they were confident that Riley was innocent. Finally, more than a year and a half following the initial charges, the jury deliberated for a very brief time, and Riley was absolved of any blame.

Riley eventually decided to quit football and, after a short period of time on the track team in the spring of 1996, left athletics for good. My assessment of the situation was that Riley's discouragement reached the point where he no longer had the energy or will to compete in athletics. At one time, he was considered a top prospect for the Olympic Games as a sprinter. He also had the potential, because of his great speed, to be a receiver in the National Football League. To his credit, Riley did get his degree in four years and was eventually able to get a job.

I felt bad for Riley's mother, who lived in San Diego. Early in the legal process, she asked me to look after Riley since she was so far away. She also told me that she had lost her job as a result of the negative publicity. It had been reported in San Diego that Riley had murdered someone and was a gang member. Riley's name was also removed from the San Diego Hall of Champions.

She wrote me as follows in February 1997, after I sent her a newspaper article detailing Riley's being cleared by the jury: "Thank you so very much for standing by Riley, and thank you for the news article. You had to be searching in the sports section of the San Diego paper to find anything about the trial outcome. The TV Station that ran the information for a week when it first happened declined my request to mention his acquittal over the air. I don't think many people realize how much of his past and his future Riley lost by this ordeal. Thank you again, also to your staff and Coach Brown for having faith in my son. May God greatly bless all of you!"

It was disturbing to see what Riley and his family went through when it seemed clear that he was innocent. The prosecution's primary witness had previously been convicted of lying to police, left the state, would not appear at the trial, and changed his story, saying he did not see the shooter and had only assumed Riley had shot him. A person who had privately boasted that he had done the shooting and whose clothing matched that of the shooter (Riley's didn't) was never charged. By remaining loyal to Riley, we at least did not compound the damage done to his reputation and career.

There was also a lot of publicity about the Lawrence Phillips episode. Lawrence was charged with two misdemeanors. One was entering an apartment uninvited, and the second was for pulling his former girlfriend down some stairs. He was dismissed from the football team for six games and was required to go to counseling and attend every class. He did not start two games after rejoining the team late in the season. However, he started our final game, the Fiesta Bowl, in which we beat Florida for the national championship.

Upon initially hearing about the assault incident, I dismissed Lawrence from the team. He had not followed my instructions and had violated team policy. After learning more about the circumstances surrounding the event, however, I was not so certain that this decision would be the proper course of action.

Lawrence and the young woman in question had been dating but had a troubled relationship. I had warned Lawrence to stay away from the young woman and had told the young woman to contact me if Lawrence tried to make contact with her. If any contact occurred, it was understood that Lawrence would be dismissed from the team. Both parties agreed not to see each other.

Despite the agreement and warnings, Lawrence and the young woman continued to see each other, and Lawrence was led to believe that there was still a relationship between them. Lawrence violated my order to stay away from the young lady, and she, in turn, violated her promise to inform me if he did contact her.

When I first saw Lawrence after the incident, he was badly shaken and broke down in tears. For most people, this reaction would not be unusual given the severity of the circumstances; however, for Lawrence, it was highly unusual to show any emotion, particularly sorrow. He had grown up on the streets and had learned to protect himself by putting up a wall of invincibility and anger to keep people at a distance.

In visiting with Barbara Thomas, a counselor who worked with Lawrence since he was 12 at a group home in Los Angeles, I discovered that she had never seen him cry. She was surprised when I told her that Lawrence had broken down, as he had always been careful to avoid any display of vulnerability. I was not particularly moved by the fact that Lawrence cried; however, behind the mask, I did see a scared, hurt, and vulnerable young man. The person I caught a glimpse of was much different from the outward persona that Lawrence showed the world.

Lawrence's father abandoned him during infancy, and Lawrence and his mother parted when he was quite young. He was on his own at age 11 and adopted a tough exterior to protect himself from further rejection. I realized that he did have a reachable heart and decided that allowing him the possibility of earning his way back onto the team was the best thing I could do to turn Lawrence around. One more rejection would only harden him and make him more difficult to reach.

My faith has led me to believe that no person, including Lawrence, is beyond redemption. One of the last times I saw Lawrence, I gave him a New Testament and explained that the only solution I saw would involve a spiritual commitment. He had been scarred by his past, labeled unfit for society by the media, and would be a marked man wherever he went. A change from the inside was necessary, but only God and Lawrence could make that change.

Many claimed that Lawrence was allowed to return to the team merely to improve our chances of winning. However, Ahman Green stepped in and became a very effective I-back throughout the season.

Our talent and team chemistry was such that no one came close to beating us, our closest game was a 14-point win. We did not need Lawrence at any point to ensure victory. We were unusually deep at I back, having four players who would have started for most teams.

Many people wanted Lawrence thrown off the team permanently as an example to those who might become involved in gender violence. A university official who talked to the witnesses involved in the alleged incident told me that he had found no evidence that Lawrence hit the girl. Most media reports described the incident as a "brutal beating." Many accounts of Lawrence's behavior were either untrue or exaggerated. Our disciplining Lawrence by the facts, as described by witnesses, police reports, and the victim, was not well received.

Lawrence went on to play professional football but eventually got in trouble and was incarcerated in California. I visited him while on a recruiting trip, and he was in good spirits and very glad to see me. Not long after that visit, Lawrence was accused of misbehavior in prison, and upon having his prison time extended, he took his own life. He was never able to overcome the demons from his childhood.

Two other players were accused of assault but were never charged after police reviewed the accusations. Still, these events were lumped into the narrative that we had an undisciplined, out-of-control football team.

Loyalty Questioned

Reviewing the 1995 season and the accusations leveled at our players is painful. Even though two of the five players accused of wrongdoing were found innocent, and though the remaining three players did not do some of the things they were accused of, it still hurt to see the whole team dragged through this unpleasantness.

The reason I discuss this difficult time here is that it has to do with loyalty. Standing by the players and remaining loyal to them produced a great deal of criticism. However, in every case but one, it appears that the players' behavior after leaving Nebraska justified the trust and confidence, we showed in them.

When dealing with behavioral problems, it is hard to win every battle. Pride can be a real stumbling block. I had been proud of the fact that we maintained an excellent win-loss record over many years but had been even more proud of the fact that we had tried to do things the right way, exhibiting a positive public image.

As the 1995 season progressed, this favorable image was stripped away. People in Nebraska viewed our team with mixed emotions. They were proud of our on-the-field accomplishments but were somewhat dismayed at what was said about us off the field.

The national media was generally less kind. We were publicly ridiculed, and our image suffered greatly. This criticism was hard to accept. We had put as much effort into academic achievement and developing our players' character as we had in trying to win football games. The great majority of our players had acquitted themselves very well, yet much of what we stood for had been damaged.

Examining the situation from a spiritual perspective, I realized that wanting public approval and praise was natural but also contained unhealthy elements of pride. I spent time reviewing the scriptures concerning trials and tribulations and also explored the events challenging us in my prayer life. Unfortunately, there were no guidelines or written manuals that outlined a clear course of action. Eventually, personal instincts and a belief system had to be the foundation of decision-making.

Gaining public approval was always important to me, but so was keeping my decisions consistent with my faith. It gradually became obvious that I couldn't have both. Even though it was painful, I concluded that the most important thing was to show concern and love for the people I was responsible for and do what I felt was right in the light of my faith. The one redeeming factor through all this negative attention was that the players seemed to understand and accept what I chose to do and grew closer as a team.

The closeness and focus engendered within the difficulties we had gone through together were reflected in a greater commitment and a higher level of play on the football field. I believed that if a player was recruited to Nebraska and placed his confidence in us and the program, in return, we owed it to that player to stand behind him even when things were not going well. This does not mean that players were never dismissed from the program. We dismissed two or three players a year, on average. However, we did so in every case according to team policy and gave the player adequate chances to correct his behavior before final dismissal.

Many people do not understand that players are often far from home, and, in many cases, the coach becomes much like a parent. As John Wooden explained, "I often told my players that, next to my own flesh and blood, they were the closest to me. They were my children.... I always tried to be fair and give each player the treatment he earned and deserved."

Loyalty Rewarded

Through the turmoil of the 1995 season, our players stayed focused and committed. They knew that each player on the team was valued and would be supported. No one would be sacrificed on the altar of public opinion for the sake of appearances.

The troubled 1995 season ended with an undefeated season and a National Championship victory over unbeaten Florida in the Fiesta Bowl. The final score was 62-24 and that team has been considered the all time best by some polls. I will always remember that team's unity and commitment to excellence. The more the national media ridiculed us, the closer and the more focused the team became. The team unity and chemistry were due in large part to the loyalty the players and coaches had toward each other.

Still, the negative publicity took its toll. We were not invited to the White House as we had been the previous year. I can't think of a national champion in football since, that has not been invited.

Loyalty Returned

At the end of the 1996 season, two key players, Jason Peter, and Grant Wistrom, were eligible to enter the NFL draft after completing their junior seasons. Both were quite likely first-round picks and would have been instant millionaires, yet both chose to come back for their senior years. In today's environment, it is rare for an underclassman that is a high draft pick to return for his final year of intercollegiate competition.

We finished the 1996 season 11–2 after going undefeated and winning national championships in 1994 and 1995. However, the 11–2 finish was not good enough for Jason and Grant. They wanted to win it all one more time, and they became great leaders as we prepared for the 1997 season.

Jason and Grant led conditioning drills in January and February. They pushed their teammates during spring football and drove those around them with unusual intensity during the summer. They played great football as the season unfolded, and we ended up 13–0 and tied with Michigan for the National Championship. We would not have been able to have the year we had without them.

Many of our football coaches stayed on in the athletic department when their coaching days were over. It is sometimes hard to maintain the pace, particularly in recruiting, as the years go by. It is also very hard to get a job with another organization once a coach reaches his 50s and 60s. Nebraska took care of its people, and other coaching staffs took notice. Many coaches wanted to join the Nebraska football staff because they observed a loyalty to former coaches that was uncommon at other schools.

Loyalty served Nebraska football well for many years. If people are shown sincere interest, support, and a willingness to sacrifice for them, this expression of loyalty will often be returned. Loyalty was one quality I encountered time and again, and it was that quality that gave us unity and helped us accomplish so many of our objectives—and have fun while doing so.

In Other Words

One of the true markers of a great coach is the loyalty he shows his assistant coaches and the loyalty they show in return. There's probably no better example in college sports than Coach Osborne. Over his 25 years at Nebraska, only a handful of our coaches left for other programs. That loyalty was earned because Coach Osborne rarely let anyone go.

One of the most unique ways he showed loyalty was through his determination to give all coaches, regardless of age, experience level, or tenure, as close to equal salaries as possible. If one coach got a raise, he would do his best to ensure the other coaches got a raise.

I had some opportunities to take other jobs—usually, for a lot more money and a higher position. I always said no because I enjoyed working with Coach Osborne and appreciated the loyalty he always showed the rest of the staff and myself. It's uncommon these days to see that kind of loyalty. It certainly paid off for Nebraska football, and with a bit of foresight and a lot of patience, I believe it can still pay off for programs today.

> **~ George Darlington, Nebraska Assistant
> Football Coach (1973-2002)**

In 1968, Nebraska football coach Bob Devaney asked offensive line coach Cletus Fischer, track coach Den Brittenham, and athletic trainer George Sullivan to create a winter conditioning program to prepare his players for the 1969 season. Nebraska had gone 6-4 in the previous two seasons.

Six very demanding stations focused on agility and running drills were created. With 30 minutes of continuous work, the result was more endurance training than muscle building. In addition, there was a five-minute period with an axe handle where the players could catch their breath until it was their turn to compete one-on-one with another player. The eighth station involved lifting a barbell.

The coaches ran seven of the eight stations, but Coach Osborne, an assistant at the time, asked me if I would man the barbell station, where the players would lift a bar with 47-pound cement cans on each end. I had a general knowledge of how and why lifting weights in Schulte Fieldhouse had improved my pole vaulting, but I had no coaching experience. Coach knew that lifting weights would make a big impact on the Nebraska players. He had done some lifting while he was with the Washington Redskins.

It didn't take long for the players to see real physical development. In 1969, Coach Osborne recommended a meeting with Coach Devaney to see if he would approve of me overseeing the winter program and developing a strength program. Bob decided to give me a try but looked me in the eye and said, "If anyone gets slower, you're fired."

When Coach Devaney retired, Coach Osborne became the head coach and remained loyal to me like he was to everyone else on his staff. I am very proud and forever grateful to Tom for trusting in me and allowing me to serve as Head Strength and Conditioning Coach for the next 35 years.

> **~ Boyd Epley, Nebraska Head Strength and Conditioning Coach (1969-2004)**

PART III

~~~~~~

IMPACTFUL

OUTFLOW

12

~~~~~~~

CHAPTER TWELVE

SERVING

THE LEGACY OF PURPOSE

once had a conversation with a man who had obviously done well in the business world. I gathered that he was relatively well off financially. He told me that even though he was considered to be successful that he lacked meaning and purpose in his life. He decided that being a mentor would add a dimension of meaning.

That gentleman's story is not uncommon. In fact, many Americans report an absence of meaning and purpose in their lives. They may be happy because most of their immediate needs are satisfied, but they see no significance in their existence.

Despite the fact that so many people believe that having meaning and purpose in their lives is of great importance, far too few find it. Young people often report that they are bored. Retirees think that a life free of job responsibilities in which they can enjoy themselves in an endless round of pleasurable activities often find that retirement isn't what they thought it would be. They begin to realize that the responsibility which their jobs imposed upon them also gave them a sense of purpose, without which they began to experience a vacuum, a sense of meaninglessness. Deprived of a purpose for living, many retirees don't live the long, happy retirement they had envisioned. Instead, they often experience the many maladies of advancing age and endure premature deaths.

So what provides meaning and purpose? Author Viktor Frankl thought that one of the primary ways meaning could be found comes from loving another person. He wrote: "Love is the only way to grasp another human being in the innermost core of his personality. No one can become fully aware of the very essence of another human being unless he loves him. By his love, he is enabled to see the essential traits and features of the beloved person; and even more, by his love, the loving person enables the beloved person to actualize these potentialities. By making him aware of what he can be and of what he should become, he makes those potentialities come true."

In his book, *Man's Search for Meaning*, Frankl, a Jew, wrote that he was imprisoned by the Nazis in the late 1930s along with his wife and his parents. His wife and parents were executed in the gas chambers, but he was spared since he was a medical doctor and was of use to the

Nazis. He survived the war despite the terrible conditions. He wrote of his experience with his fellow prisoners; some descended into a self-centered brutish existence, but he also noted that there were a few who moved among them, caring for others, sometimes offering their last piece of bread. He found that those who served discovered that there could still be meaning and purpose even in Auschwitz.

There's an action attached to the concept Frankl described. It's called serving, and it's one of the most purposeful things any of us can do. Serving is also one of the most difficult things to do because it requires us to go against our human nature and put the needs of others before our own. It requires us to take time away from our lives and spend it helping people who may not be able to help themselves.

This attitude of servant leadership (whether they are part of your team or part of your community) is something everyone should aspire to have, but for the leader can be especially challenging. There are many responsibilities to balance, and it's not always easy to make time for the things that matter most.

Servant leadership, however, will often take a group further faster, and they will operate more efficiently. There will be better emotional health and a strong bond that develops between the leader and the players, employees, etc. Servant leadership creates and enhances a healthy culture. There are benefits for the giver and the one on the receiving end of that gift.

Sacrificial Serving

A study by Baumeister, Vohs, Aaker, and Garbinsky published in the Journal of Positive Psychology examined the subject of perceived happiness and meaning in the lives of 397 subjects. The study found that there was a small correlation between happiness and meaningfulness, but there were also major differences. The researchers found that happiness is mostly tied to present feelings, living in the moment, having basic needs met, and receiving benefits from others. Having enough money to purchase life's comforts was related to happiness but had little relation to purpose and meaning.

Above all, meaning was related to dedicating oneself to serving others or dedication to a cause that transcended self rather than receiving or taking from others. In other words, being happy relates to receiving, while meaning and purpose are related to giving and spending oneself on behalf of others. Having meaning and purpose in one's life tends to be enduring, while happiness is often fleeting and dependent upon feelings of satisfaction with present circumstances. Being happy and having a meaningful life are not necessarily congruent.

Serving and sacrificing for others may actually lead to increased tension and unhappiness. Devotion to family members and friends provides meaning but often involves stress and heartache as we see those we care about go through difficult times. Being a parent is often stressful and devoid of happiness, yet it is often the most meaningful experience a person can have.

These principles apply to every aspect of servant leadership. CEOs that serve their employees and staff members will inherently empathize in their moments of emotional pain or stress. Pastors that serve their congregation will share in their times of suffering and loss. Coaches that serve their players and staff will genuinely care about the everyday ups and downs that they experience.

That is one of the marks of a true servant leader. It will show up naturally in the life of a leader whose heart is filled with love, humility, and patience.

Congress

I left coaching in early 1998, spent a year teaching at the College of Business, and then noted that the congressman from the Third District of Nebraska was retiring. The Third District is a very large area, covering about 80 percent of the landmass of Nebraska. It extends all the way to the Colorado and Wyoming borders and includes 63 counties. I was born and raised in the third district, and my family came from that area. Even though I had lived many years in Lincoln, I also had a Third District home at Lake McConaughy in Western Nebraska and spent a great deal of time there.

I still had good health and energy and decided to run for Congress, representing the Third District. My grandfather was a Presbyterian minister who ran for Congress many years ago. He was defeated, and maybe his attempt to run for Congress was in the back of my mind when I decided to run. Politics had never been part of my life and was not something I had previously considered, but I thought I might make a difference in that part of the state. It was mostly rural, with a few communities having 20 to 30 thousand people. Still, there were many smaller communities that were losing population as farms got bigger and there were fewer people on the land supporting nearby communities.

I was elected and sworn in early 2000. I remember having Doug Bereuter, a longtime member of Congress, take me in to see the Speaker of the House. Doug mentioned that Nebraska had no representation on the Ways and Means Committee, one of the most powerful congressional committees, as it dealt with many areas of government spending. He asked the Speaker to consider me for that committee.

The Speaker was evasive, and I could tell from his reaction that my chances were negligible. I later learned that since my Congressional seat was considered a "safe" seat, there was little interest in appointing me to Ways and Means. Normally, those positions were reserved for those who would face significant political challenges each election cycle and also seniority was a consideration.

That interaction brought me face-to-face with Congressional realities. More prestigious committee assignments were awarded to those who might have trouble being re-elected, and length of service was also important. Those factors trumped the needs of a state or a Congressional District. However, I was not disappointed, as I served on the Agriculture, Education, and Transportation committees, which were important to my district. Still, I realized that Congress was not a meritocracy but rather a place where political expediency was often primary.

Each week, both parties held a caucus to discuss events that were of significance to that party. The chairman of the Ways and Means committee had retired, so the position was open and sought by several contenders. I recall that a congressman got up in the caucus meeting and announced that he was contributing $500,000 to the party, an obvious effort to secure the position. The next week a rival announced that he was donating $600,000 to the party, and another member submitted a contribution of $700,000 the following week.

The highest bidder got the chairmanship. The money being awarded to the party was not from the contributor's personal wealth. It was largely brought in from special interest groups attempting to gain influence with the next chairman of the Ways and Means Committee. The needs of the contributors would obviously have some preferred consideration when matters came before the committee. There was nothing illegal about the process, but it did not seem to me that it served the general electorate well.

I did not like what I saw and did not take money from special interest groups and limited contributions from individuals to small amounts. This was not popular with special interests as they felt that they had no leverage with the way that I voted. Most of my day in Washington was spent meeting with all groups, and nobody was turned away. When I traveled to the Third District, I spent my time meeting with anyone who wanted to see me. Sometimes competing groups did not like my having an open door with their opponents.

When I ran for Governor of Nebraska, I did not get the endorsement of most special interest groups even though, in most cases, I had a congressional voting record that aligned with their missions. Maybe they thought that I was a very poor candidate, but I know that the fact that they had no leverage with me since I had not accepted their money was a major reason for their lack of support. As of this writing, most polls show congressional approval rankings at historically low levels. The general public seems to believe that Congress is not performing well and that the needs of the country are often secondary to the personal ambitions of our political leaders.

I don't want to cast aspersions on all members of Congress as there are many fine people who serve, people who really do have a servant's heart and are willing to put personal ambitions below what they feel the country needs. I recall a gentleman from North Carolina who had tears in his eyes when he cast a vote, which he felt was correct but would be unpopular among the people he represented. He was defeated in his next election but did what he thought was right. Unfortunately, such acts of selflessness were not common.

Return to Serving: The 9/11 Effect

There were two places where I experienced a collegial atmosphere in Washington—the weekly Congressional Prayer Breakfast and the House gym. In those two settings, people interacted and got along irrespective of party affiliation. Unfortunately, that was often where friendships and cooperation ended.

The weekly prayer breakfast was very important to me. Each week the speaker was a member of congress. I remember one week the congressman speaking was from a prominent political family. His political views were very different than mine, but as he spoke, I sensed the anguish he had endured growing up in the spotlight. I felt for him and we became friends.

In the six months following the attack on the country, September 11, 2001, I saw Congress work together in a manner I had not seen before or since. The country was under threat, and Congress was in session when planes flew into the World Trade Center. One plane flew up the Mall in Washington DC, headed at the Capitol, and then turned and flew into the Pentagon.

I remember taking my staff to my apartment as the Capitol was locked down for fear of another plane striking the Capitol. It appears that the plane that crashed in Pennsylvania when passengers charged the cockpit was headed for the Capitol. The terrorists were apparently intent on destroying the three symbolic institutions critical to the nation, commerce (the World Trade Center), the military (the Pentagon), and the government (the United States Capitol).

I hope the same spirit of unity reemerges should the nation ever face significant peril again. As I observe the current situation, with significant threats abroad and fractures from within the country, we may be closer to a perilous state than most realize.

Many citizens have less confidence in federal agencies such as the Department of Justice, the Internal Revenue Service, and Congress.

Some question the performance of our schools, the basic tenets of Christianity, and the most basic institution of all, the family unit.

Historically great empires such as the Greek, Roman, and British have eventually failed, not from external conquest, but rather from internal decay and dysfunction. I hope we are not at that point, but there are certainly significant warning signs on the horizon.

In considering the founding fathers of our country, we see people who served the fledgling nation at great personal financial risk and even the potential loss of their lives. They came from farms and small businesses, served a few years, and then returned to their normal occupations. They set the pattern for what we now call public service.

Unfortunately, we don't see this type of selfless service as often anymore. Political priorities are to get reelected, to serve in the majority (as the minority party is relatively powerless), and then, third on the list, to serve constituents and the country. Power becomes addictive, and being addressed as Senator or Congressman often changes how people see themselves.

I have come to believe that term limits and strict campaign finance regulations would be a major improvement. I say this knowing that there would be a loss of institutional knowledge and a loss of many good people who currently serve multiple terms for the right reasons. It seems that too many people have become professional politicians rather than citizens who serve their country for a while and then return to normal activities. If this were to happen, I think that we would see more servant leadership and less pursuit of self-interest.

True Purpose

Mother Theresa once said, "Unless a life is lived for others, it is not worth living." In other words, serving gives life meaning and purpose. That sentiment should be a natural response to anyone who has read, studied, and believed the teachings found in Scripture, which contains many exemplary models of servant leadership, including:

• David: Although remembered for one notorious mistake in his life, this warrior king notably led the people of Israel with a heart of compassion and a spirit of equal justice.

• Esther: A faithful follower of God, this reluctant queen put her life on the line to save her people when she easily could have looked the other way and protected her self-interest.

• Peter and Paul: As two of the church's most influential Apostles, Peter (notoriously impetuous as a disciple) and Paul (infamously narcissistic and cruel before his conversion) were touchstones for a movement that would change the world forever, but both ultimately paid the price with their lives.

There's no question, however, that Jesus is the greatest example of servant leadership. Jesus was the Son of God, yet He sacrificed His existence in Heaven to serve humanity. He humbled Himself to be born into the world under far less than royal circumstances and then lived a nondescript life until it was time for His ministry to begin. Jesus taught Truth to those who would listen and performed miracles for those in need. Finally, He was falsely accused, sentenced to die a brutal death for our sins, and was raised back to life after three days in the grave.

That's why Jesus' words on serving are so powerful. He understood that true purpose is only found in giving yourself away for the sake of others and the greater good.

True purpose and meaning comes from serving rather than from being served. The disciples still couldn't quite understand that principle, and the concept of serving came up again when the brothers, James and John, asked who would be the greatest in Heaven, which elicited a difficult response from Jesus:

But Jesus called them to him and said, *"You know that the rulers of the Gentiles lord it over them, and their great ones exercise authority over them. It shall not be so among you. But whoever would be great among you must be your servant, and whoever would be first among you must be your slave, even as the Son of Man came not to be served but to serve, and to give his life as a ransom for many."* (Matthew 20:25-28/ESV)

The Apostle Paul, who had followed in Christ's footsteps, also had a few things to say about serving, including this encouraging teaching on the long-term benefits of putting others first:

And let us not grow weary of doing good, for in due season we will reap, if we do not give up. So then, as we have opportunity, let us do good to everyone, and especially to those who are of the household of faith. (Galatians 6:9-10/ESV)

There are certainly benefits to servant leadership—joy, contentment, fulfillment, etc. But at the end of the day, serving others is about obedience to God and bringing glory to Him.

A Blueprint for Servant Leadership

Servant leadership starts with having the right attitude and the right heart. Many of these things have been discussed in previous chapters. Still, you can't truly serve someone with pure motives if it's not an outflow of your values and a part of core character traits such as love, humility, integrity, patience, and loyalty.

Practically speaking, however, there are some key ways that you can begin (or extend) the process of serving others:

1. Give your time: Giving someone your time is your most precious gift. We can make more money, but we can't make more time. It's one of the most meaningful things a person can do. It often requires sacrifice (taking time away from work, family, fun, etc.), but there is nothing like the feeling of knowing you blessed someone with your caring, thoughtful presence.

2. Give your talent: If you're good at something or have a specific skill, find ways to use those talents and abilities in a way that might lift someone's spirits or might help an organization or cause do its beneficial work.

3. Give your treasure: Sometimes, giving money to an individual or a cause is the first thing that comes to mind and is often a great way to serve a need. Financial giving is even more meaningful when other serving aspects are attached.

4. Give your love: Words of affirmation and actions that show true care are vital to serving both those you lead and those who simply need encouragement or a boost of confidence. Serving is only as powerful as the intentional kindness and personal touch connected to it.

5. Give the truth: Timing is everything, but true servant leadership is

not devoid of saying hard things or making hard choices. As a coach, I expected my players to work hard and be well conditioned. Practices were demanding on the field and in the weight room. Part of serving them was making sure they were doing all that they were capable of doing. Sometimes people confuse servant leadership with something soft and not very realistic. I don't see it that way. I feel that there is a certain determination and willingness to go the extra mile about truly serving others.

When you lead with the end in mind, serving will become a natural practice that seamlessly fits into your workflow, family life, and community involvement. It takes sacrifice, but servant leadership is far and away the most effective and most fulfilling kind.

In Other Words

The year after my football days ended, my wife and I were at church on Easter and heard a 10-year-old boy share his testimony. His father had been killed in a horrific farming accident a year earlier. The crowd was in tears as the boy told us that he wanted to go to Heaven so he could see his dad again.

I looked at my wife, Jamie, and said, "I've got to do something for this boy."

The next day, I was working as a sales rep in a store when a customer said she thought I looked familiar. I assumed it was from Husker football. I asked her what her name was, and she said, "Jill Wolford." Turns out, she was the boy's mom! She told me that Glen was a big Husker fan, but he hadn't picked up a football or a ball glove since his dad died. I called Coach Osborne and asked if I could bring the boy to practice someday. He immediately agreed.

I'll never forget all the events that transpired that day once we arrived at the Husker stadium. Coach Osborne welcomed Glen to practice by saying to him, "Hello, you must be Glen. My name is Tom Osborne." That was the first of many surprises Glen was to experience on this special day. Coach actually had him come out to the middle of the field on the 50-yard line to observe practice with him.

After practice, he invited Glen and me up to his office, where Glen was offered an orange juice out of Coach Osborne's refrigerator. Assistant Coach, Frank Solich, walked in right on cue with both arms full of Nebraska memorabilia for Glen to take home.

Coach Osborne then started checking around his office but couldn't quite locate what he was looking for.

"Well, Glen," he said. "I had a Husker cap for you, but I can't find it, so I guess I'll just have to give you mine." Coach Osborne took the hat off his head and gave it to Glen.

He then asked Glen if he was hungry and invited us to go have some pizza. As we were sitting at our table, people came up asking Coach for his autograph. Coach said, "Glen, isn't it funny that people ask me to sign my name?"

Every instance that Coach Osborne would say something or do something for him, Glen would turn and look at me with these huge eyes like he couldn't believe it was happening.

I felt like I was sitting there watching this 10-year-old boy's joy and happiness begin to flow back into his life again. I know Glen and the Wolford family are extremely grateful for this day that Coach Osborne spent with Glen at such a difficult time in his life.

Coach Osborne has done a lot of selfless things for a lot of people. He has sacrificed so much of his personal time with his own family to help his players and people like Glen create memories they will never forget.

It was so special to witness Coach Osborne's servant leadership unfold right before my eyes with a young boy he had just met that had nothing he could possibly offer in return. The life of Coach Osborne has been a true example of a selfless, servant heart.

~ Ken Kaelin, Nebraska Football Player (1983-86)

I was playing for Nebraska when Coach Osborne started the Team-Mates Mentoring program. What really stuck out to me was how he used his influence with college athletes to impact kids that were struggling and needed some extra love and support. As I got into the car sales business, I wondered if I, too, could leverage my influence in a way that would help other people.

When I took over the dealership from my dad, I quickly felt called to take the fruits of our business and use them for good. At first, we created a non-profit organization that would allow us to funnel a portion of our profits to help people struggling with their transportation needs and spread God's Word. We eventually dissolved the non-profit and now use money directly from the company, but it's all for the same purpose and with the same heart.

Coach Osborne's servant leadership had a direct influence on my decision to have a positive impact on the community and is still evident decades later.

> ~ **Mike Anderson, Owner of Anderson Auto Group, NFL Europe Player (1993), and Nebraska Football Player (1990-93)**

At Nebraska, Coach Osborne was a true model of servant leadership. He set a strong example of serving others and making everyone feel like they were an important part of the team. He also empowered his players through many opportunities to serve in the community. Brook loved working with kids and took full advantage as his platform grew during his time in the program.

He didn't enjoy being in the limelight, but he felt a strong responsibility as a Nebraska Cornhusker to serve as a positive role model and never missed an opportunity to talk and listen to his younger fans.

There are too many stories to tell, but one that I personally observed took place in the last couple of minutes of the game against Kansas State in Manhattan, Kansas, during the 1994 season. Brook was done playing and had his helmet off. He was still engaged in the game from the sidelines as he stood by the fence in front of the 50-yard line. He turned and glanced up and smiled at us in the parents' section. His sister Drue went down to the fence to congratulate him on a good performance in the game. Some young fans took notice and began gathering around Drue. They all brought programs for Brook to sign.

There were less than two minutes of the game so he quickly grabbed and signed the first program and handed it back as he kept one eye on the game and Coach Osborne. Then he grabbed another one to sign and kept going. There was a little boy, who was smaller than the rest, and the other boys were pushing past him and blocking him from Brook's view. His dad was standing behind him and tried to help him hold his place as the son held up his program, hoping Brook would sign it.

I knew Brook was nervous about doing this even though the game was seconds away from being over. And I knew he would be able to sign nearly all of them. I kept thinking, "Brook, turn around and look at that little guy! Don't miss him!"

The buzzer went off, the game ended, and I thought, "Darn." At that very second, Brook turned around, yanked off his armband, leaned over the fence, and handed it to the little guy. Then Brook ran off to join the team. I could see the look of awe and appreciation from that little boy and his dad.

When the decision was made to play football at Nebraska, I was thankful that the fine staff inspired and molded my son into the servant leader he would become. I believe he would have enjoyed a very bright future. His continued growth in faith and character still continues to influence others today. I will always be grateful for the opportunities Coach Osborne granted and the influence he afforded Brook, which is still evident today.

~ Jan Berringer, Mother of Brook Berringer

My dad has always exemplified what it looks like to be a servant leader. He was able to do so because of some unshakable foundational values and his ability to have a clear vision of what he was called to accomplish. As a head coach, he truly felt responsible for serving the people of the state. He wanted to please them, but he would always do it the right way to please God first.

I knew how much time he put into the effort each week, all year round. In the 70s and 80s, there was relatively no limit on the number of hours you could work or the number of recruiting phone calls or visits you could make. Even at home, he'd be working or watching films after we went to bed. So, I knew the personal price he was paying to do what he did.

In 1990, we were playing Colorado at home. We were 8-0 and ranked third in the nation. Colorado was coming into its own and ranked ninth. Bill McCartney had made a big deal about circling Nebraska in red on the schedule and had been challenging us in some key recruiting battles. The Buffaloes featured Eric Bienemy and Darian Hagen, but we were pretty stout, too, with key players like Mickey Joseph and Trev Alberts.

My wife and I lived in Atlanta then and traveled back to Lincoln for the game. It was a rainy and cold October night—generally unpleasant for everyone in the stands. With a 12-10 lead heading into the fourth quarter, the crowd was in full volume, and the outlook was promising until Colorado got loose, and we made a couple of mistakes, which led to a crushing 27-12 loss.

The fans were very upset. The team was heartbroken. But no one felt worse than Dad. I was waiting for him in his locker room while he addressed the team and then answered the tough questions from the media. Dad essentially apologized to the entire state of Nebraska for coming up short.

When Dad had finished his post-game obligations, he came into the room, sat down, and quietly cried for a minute to himself. He then looked at me and said, "Mike, I'm really sorry you had to come home and see that."

That was the last thing that should have been on his mind—apologizing to his son for losing a football game for which he had spent 365 days and countless hours preparing. The least I could do was be there and support him. I knew the effort and intentions that went into every game, especially Colorado and Oklahoma. But that's just how Dad was throughout his coaching years. He had a servant mentality during the wins and the losses. He had a heartfelt desire to help people succeed and to fulfill everyone's hopes and expectations. He wanted badly to win for the state.

It all goes back to his foundational values of serving others and doing things with humility and integrity. Dad took that very seriously and never wavered in his commitment to giving his best to honor God's call on his life and to give his best to those within his sphere of influence.

~ Mike Osborne, Son of Tom Osborne

13

~~~~~~

CHAPTER THIRTEEN

MENTORING

THE LEGACY OF EXPANSION

When we dedicate ourselves to the well-being of another, someone who, on the surface of things, can do nothing for us in return, we also develop a deeper sense of purpose in our existence. In the last chapter, we talked about serving those that we lead and beyond.

One great way to do that is through mentoring, simply sharing your personal experience and wisdom with someone else. This usually takes place in one-on-one meetings but sometimes occurs within group settings. It is often done face-to-face but also can be done via phone calls, text messages, online video conferences, or other traditional means of communication.

Mentoring will entail times of happiness in which we experience moments of enjoyment in the company of the one we are mentoring; however, it will also entail times of stress and sorrow as we share in the struggles and disappointments in the life of the one being mentored. The most important thing to understand, however, is that, despite the ups and downs of any important relationship, it will nearly always result in a greater sense of meaning and purpose.

At the end of the day, however, mentoring is about serving others and embracing the legacy of expansion. Mentoring truly is a powerful way to extend your influence and all you have learned to the next generation of leaders.

Coaching

From personal experience, I can attest that coaching provides a very powerful mentoring opportunity.

John Wooden said: "While I made my living as a coach, I have lived my life to be a mentor and to be mentored! Everything in the world has been passed down. Every piece of knowledge is something that has been shared by someone else. If you understand it as I do, mentoring becomes your true legacy. It is the greatest inheritance you can give to others. It is why you get up every day—to teach and be taught."

While Coach Wooden is no longer with us, his timeless lessons continue to impact those he coached. That's why I have poured much of my life into my TeamMates Mentoring program. Wooden's true legacy was mentoring, and I believe that's true for not just every coach but every leader.

For an athlete, one season is a microcosm of a lifetime. There is a beginning with hopes, dreams, and aspirations for all the season holds. Then comes the early training camp with its physical exertion, hard knocks, and the first reality check of how one measures up against the competition.

Next, the season starts with the even greater challenge of performing against an opponent in game conditions. If your team wins and you are able to contribute to the effort, positive emotions generally result. Confidence in one's abilities and those of the team start to build. If a player is relegated to a backup role, life gets a little harder, particularly if there appears to be little chance of playing. Even then, being part of a team, something larger than oneself, can be rewarding. If the culture is sound, there is a unity of purpose among players and coaches, and one can see their efforts contributing in some way to the greater good; even a backup role can be significant.

However, things don't always go well. In a negative environment where there is disunity, little opportunity to play, and the team is obviously headed nowhere, life gets hard. Sometimes just getting through another practice is difficult.

And then there is the conclusion of the season or the end of a career. The ending is always abrupt and difficult to adjust to. The player loses his identity as a team member and loses many of the daily associations, which have become an important part of a familiar process. He relinquishes the normal routine to which he has grown accustomed; the close friendships and the flow of adrenaline competition stirs.

Because of the importance our culture puts on athletic competition and the strong emotions, which accompany sports, the coach is in a unique position of influence. The coach determines who makes the team, who plays and who doesn't, the practice routine, the strategies of the game, the team environment and culture, and many other things which affect the player's experience.

Therefore, what a coach says and does has a great deal of importance to the young people on the team. For some athletes, their coach is the most significant person in their lives.

Grant Teaff, former Executive Director of the American Football Coaches Association, once wrote: "There is an opportunity to teach life's lessons by the very nature of the game. There is no entitlement on a football field. Everything has to be earned. A coach's greatest influence is not so much in what he teaches but in how his players recognize what he teaches and how he lives his life. Coaches have a greater opportunity than ever to be positive influences in today's society. Coaches are able to use practices and games to teach values and develop positive character qualities in their players. The values and character of the teacher will validate the lessons taught."

Coaching players on the field is an obvious athletic job description, but coaching players off the field as a mentor has a much longer-lasting impact. The same is true for all leaders. While it might seem intrinsically valuable to train employees or staff how to do their job better, there is far more value and worth in mentoring them in areas of physical, emotional, mental, financial, and spiritual well-being.

TeamMates

I started coaching in 1962. I became concerned about the changes impacting young people as time went by. The drug culture emerged in the late 60s, family instability increased, and today more than half of our young people are growing up without both biological parents. Social media emerged, and young people are bombarded with unhealthy messages from the Internet, music lyrics, TV, and movies.

In 1991, I asked our football team how many would be interested in mentoring a middle school boy in Lincoln schools. Twenty-two players raised their hands, and TeamMates Mentoring began. Since that humble beginning, TeamMates has grown to more than 9,000 matches in Nebraska, Iowa, Kansas, South Dakota, and Wyoming.

Since 1991 we have mentored more than 47,000 young people without a negative incident and have graduated more than 95 percent of mentees from high school. Most of our mentees have post-secondary plans, as we want them to have marketable skills. Many of our college students continue to have TeamMates mentors. Among first-generation college students, only 65 percent of freshmen go on to their second year. Providing a mentor who has gone to college raises that percentage to over 90 percent retention.

Our research indicates that approximately 85 percent of mentees improve school attendance, have fewer disciplinary and behavioral issues, and have more hope about the future. Gallup research indicates that hope is the best indicator of future success. A mentor can help show young people that things will get better and that they are not trapped in their current circumstances. There is light at the end of the tunnel and a path to a better life.

Most of our mentors feel they benefit as much or more than their mentees. As I visit with those mentors, it is clear that giving their time and devotion to a young person adds purpose and meaning to their lives, a common hallmark of serving others.

In asking a number of mentors who had mentored for several years what they gained from the mentoring experience, I received roughly five different categories of responses, which are as follows:

1. Mentors enjoy seeing mentees mature and grow. Realizing the difference one can make in another person's life and, in turn, impacting many others is a very gratifying experience. Quite often, mentoring results in a life-long relationship in which the mentor can see the positive effects of mentoring play out over many years.

2. Mentors often report that in the process of mentoring, they find that they become better parents. Adults often assume that the world their children face is much the same as what they experienced growing up. However, technology, substance abuse, peer pressure, and altered social norms that young people face today often make the world a much different and more challenging place than what adults experienced when they were young.

3. Mentors often find that mentoring changes the complexion of their day. At TeamMates Mentoring, approximately ninety-five percent of

our mentees report that they look forward to seeing their mentors and are happy when they are with them. Seeing the response on the faces of the young people being mentored and realizing that they are appreciated is very rewarding to mentors.

4. Most mentors value the relationship they establish with their mentees. Often the relationship becomes deeper through hardship and tragedy. An important part of the relationship for most mentors is the realization that the young people being mentored implicitly trust them. This strong sense of trust helps bind the relationship. It often takes time for trust to be established, but once it is, it makes the relationship stronger and more meaningful.

5. Often, mentors report that mentoring has been educational and informative. They become more aware of some of the issues young people are dealing with, which they had not been aware of. Sometimes those issues are difficult to hear about, but the mentor's understanding of the world we live in is expanded.

Sometimes a mentor doesn't realize that small victories are really major victories in the lives of those they are mentoring. Nearly every successful person can point to at least one person (often two or three people) who has come alongside them as a mentor at a critical time and has made a major difference in their lives.

For Future Generations

Mentoring is not a modern concept. It goes back to the beginning of recorded history and is deeply rooted in God's Word. Here are just a few prime examples of mentoring in both the Old and New Testaments:

• Moses and Joshua: When Moses was overwhelmed with the responsibility of leading the Israelites, his father-in-law Jethro recommended delegating some of his roles to the people. As an extension of that plan, Moses also took a young man named Joshua under his wing. When Moses died, Joshua seamlessly stepped into leadership and became one of the Israelites' greatest military leaders.

• Eli and Samuel: As a father, Eli struggled to raise his sons in the ways of the Lord, which was ironic because his job was serving as a

Jewish priest. But when a young boy named Samuel came to live with him, Eli faithfully mentored and trained him to become one of Israel's most powerful and influential prophets. Samuel, in fact, would go on to famously anoint David to replace King Saul.

• Daniel and the Three Hebrews: After the Babylonians overtook Jerusalem, many young Israelites were returned to serve King Nebuchadnezzar. Daniel was the leader of a small group that also included Shadrach, Meshach, and Abednego. He stood up for righteousness and resisted the temptation to disobey God's commands. The three other young men followed suit. When Shadrach, Meshach, and Abednego were separated from Daniel during the king's decree to bow down to a golden statue, they stood firm and did not bow despite the consequences. Daniel was not there, yet his mentoring and guidance helped them make the right choice.

• Jesus and the Disciples: Not long after starting His ministry, Jesus selected 12 men to be His disciples. They were ordinary men from all walks of life, but Jesus knew that they had the potential to be great. He showed them how to pray, how to serve others, and how to teach Truth. Jesus mentored them through His words and His actions. When Jesus' crucifixion was imminent, He gave them instructions on how to build His Kingdom. Those men became the first Apostles and founders of the Christian Church.

The original Apostles and others that joined the cause trained others to serve in various roles at churches across the region. Priscilla and Aquila mentored Apollos; Peter mentored Cornelius; Barnabas mentored Paul; and, in one of the most documented student-teacher relationships, Paul mentored Timothy. Paul's famous letters to Timothy provide a glimpse into how mentoring should set off a chain reaction:

You then, my child, be strengthened by the grace that is in Christ Jesus, and what you have heard from me in the presence of many witnesses entrust to faithful men, who will be able to teach others also. (2 Timothy 2:1-2/ESV)

Some of the most powerful teachings on mentoring can also be found in the Book of Proverbs. King Solomon wrote advice to both mentors and mentees at all leadership levels, including within the home:

• *Let the wise hear and increase in learning, and the one who understands obtain guidance.* (Proverbs 1:9/ESV)

• *Give instruction to a wise man, and he will be still wiser; teach a righteous man, and he will increase in learning.* (Proverbs 9:9/ESV)

• *Iron sharpens iron, and one man sharpens another.* (Proverbs 27:17/ESV)

What you have as a leader is not just for you. Your wisdom, knowledge, and influence are also for future generations. Other than Jesus, the biblical leaders previously mentioned could not fully know the impact of their mentoring. Who knows what great things those that you mentor will also do?

Pass It On

If you haven't yet entered the rewarding world of mentoring, it's never too late to begin, and it's not as difficult as it may seem. There are certainly sacrifices to be made, but the rewards always outweigh the time, effort, and emotional energy required. Here are a few steps to get you started:

1. Look inside: The best place to start mentoring is at the places where you currently lead. Stay alert for opportunities with your employees and staff, within your church, and, of course, within your family.

A good succession plan is critical to the continued success of an organization. In 1972 Bob Devaney announced that this would be his last year of coaching and named me his successor. He gave me additional responsibilities and was supportive. We were very different people, but I learned a good deal from him about relating to people. In turn, I was able to name Frank Solich as Assistant Head Coach in 1997. Frank was also given added responsibilities, and knew that I had great confidence in him. Frank became Head Coach in 1998.

This line of succession resulted in 42 years of continuity, during which Nebraska had the highest football win percentages of any university during that time.

2. Look outside: As you look to expand your mentoring role, also look for opportunities with young people at places like TeamMates,

the YMCA, Boys & Girls Club, or church youth group. You can also apply your specific skill set to areas where young adults may be looking for advice as they enter their professional careers. The possibilities are limitless.

3. Be intentional: Know your strengths and decipher your best ways to serve as a mentor. If someone desires to be mentored and you're not the right fit, help them find a mentor to best meet their needs.

4. Don't spread yourself too thin: It's okay to say no when you have reached your full capacity as a mentor, but, as mentioned in the previous point, be prepared to help those that you can't personally mentor by finding them someone who can.

5. Teach others to be mentors: Encourage other leaders within your sphere of influence and those you lead to take on mentoring roles of their own. That is an incredible way to expand your reach and help more people than you could alone.

When a mentor influences a mentee, more than one mentee often benefits. If the direction of a life is altered for the better, usually the family and those close to that mentee experience better lives, and that blessing ripples on through several generations.

By loving a mentee unconditionally, determining strengths, and providing affirmation, the mentor strives to enable the mentee to become what he is capable of becoming. Interestingly, the mentee, the one being helped, also benefits the mentor significantly by helping the mentor find purpose and meaning in his own life.

You are blessed to be a leader. Don't forget that part of servant leadership is your call to pass it on and to help the next generation be ready to confidently and competently take the reigns when the time comes.

In Other Words

In 2007, when I arrived in Lincoln, I didn't know who Tom Osborne was and knew very little about Nebraska football's rich history. Growing up in California, I was much more aware of programs like USC and Cal Berkeley.

But it didn't take long to start hearing about the past greatness. Everyone was obsessed with the 1997 team, so I started watching You-

Tube videos and was introduced to Coach Osborne. You can't escape tradition, and I quickly got caught up in it and wanted to know more about him.

In the middle of my freshman season, I was born again, and my life took a radical change for the better. At the end of that year, Coach Osborne was hired as the Athletic Director, and I started seeing him around the athletic complex. I found out he was also a Christian, and my admiration for him continued to grow.

As we prepared for the 2008 season, I was looking for spiritual fathers to mentor me in my young faith and to help me navigate the college football experience. Coach Osborne was always sitting around at lunch, and one day I just decided to go sit across from him and strike up a conversation. From there, I would look for opportunities to get advice and wisdom. This also took place at practices where Coach Osborne was often present.

In my sophomore year, I started to get more playing time and wanted to learn how to mentally prepare for a big game. The night before we played Virginia Tech, I called Coach Osborne and asked him what I needed to do. I leaned on his response throughout the rest of my college and pro career:

"You prepare for every game the same," he told me. "Give your all. And then you won't rise and fall based on the opposition."

For me, that was the verification of the Bible verse that I had learned early in my Christian walk: *Work willingly at whatever you do, as though you were working for the Lord rather than for people.* (Colossians 3:23/NLT)

Coach Osborne really believed that every game was the same, and that was his approach. So instantly, I had peace going into that next game. I played well, scored a touchdown, and enjoyed every opportunity I had to be on the field.

That was the beginning of my mentoring relationship with Coach Osborne. I was like a moth to the light. He didn't intentionally come after me, but he was always available when I needed to talk to him. I saw his white hairs. He had the experience. He loved Jesus.

Fast forward to 2017: I finished my NFL career and moved back to Nebraska. Football was over. I had four kids at the time (I now have six) and I was trying to figure out what to do next. I drove to meet with him in Lincoln to ask him about the question of legacy.

"During my career as a coach or in politics, I didn't focus on my legacy," Coach Osborne said. "I focused on being faithful every day."

In that moment, I told God that whatever I chose to do next, I would be faithful in the day-to-day and trust that He would bring me to the best outcomes. So much of what led me to that conclusion was due to Coach Osborne's faithfulness to serve others as a faithful leader, mentor, and friend.

~ Roy Helu Jr. Lead Pastor of Citylight Church Bennington, NFL Player (2011-15), and Nebraska Football Player (2007-10)

Tom is the most faithful, honest, caring person I know and has gone above and beyond to really make a difference in this world. I learned so much from him over the years. He would lead by example and wouldn't ask anyone to do what he wasn't willing to do himself. One morning I had stepped out of the office, and the phone was ringing as he walked by my desk, and he stopped to answer it as he didn't want someone to not get a response. It was important for him to answer all the correspondence that came in (even after the 1984 Orange Bowl when there were hundreds of fans writing in support of his decision to go for two). He genuinely cared about everyone.

While speaking at events, Tom would reference a story that goes something like this: There was a man walking along the beach, and he stopped to pick up a starfish to throw back into the ocean to save its life. Someone asked, "There are so many starfish on the beach, why bother doing this? It won't make a difference." The man replied, "It will make a difference for this one."

I witnessed Tom be the man in this story so many times during the years I worked for him. There were so many "starfish" he saved. The TeamMates Mentoring program is a great example of one way he has touched so many lives. I was blessed to be there at the start of the program, and because of Tom and Nancy's perseverance, the program has grown to where it is today, touching thousands of lives. This program not only benefits the mentees, but I have personally witnessed how much the mentors grow as well.

Tom also mentored many players and staff members over the years. Sometimes a player or staff member would make a bad choice and would get called into the office for a discussion. Occasionally I would hear a "dadgummit," and that meant Tom was frustrated. That is as close as Tom would come to cussing. He was so well respected, and his talks would help guide those in the right direction for success. No one wanted to let him down.

I appreciated the important element of faith that he instilled in the players and staff through the chapel services that were held before games and the prayers before meals at the events we attended. The seeds that he planted during their playing days have guided many players to follow paths as pastors, spiritual mentors, and leaders, positively affecting the world and saving even more "starfish" along the way.

> ~ **Mary Lyn Kruger, Administrative Assistant**
> **to Nebraska Head Football Coach (1983-2004)**

14

~~~~~~

EMPOWERMENT

THE LEGACY OF COMMISSION

When you are in a leadership position, you have to lead those who follow you with dignity and respect, giving them the space to carry out what they are responsible to do and encouraging them on their way. It is my experience that this is done by building up others, not tearing them down. This also helps to cultivate an environment of success—where ideas are generated, objectives are carried out, confidence is built, and productivity thrives.

This principle can be best described as empowerment. It's the necessary action of commissioning or sending out people to help you do your job. Empowerment also draws employees, workers, team members, etc., into the greater good for a cause within the organization or program.

The Power of Delegation

When those you lead (people on your staff, committee, team, or even those in your family) experience the kind of leadership that is encouraging and uplifting, they feel empowered and confident about performing at a high capacity. As a congressman, it was important to me that my staff felt empowered to carry out their roles. I had to make clear that I trusted them to support me and believed that they were more than capable of executing their tasks well.

There was no way I could do my job alone. We had seven or eight staffers in Nebraska and about the same number on Capitol Hill. In the early days, it seemed they were reluctant to act on their own. If a letter was ready to be sent or if someone needed to attend a meeting, no one felt they could go ahead and do what needed to be done without clearing it through the chief of staff or me.

It was obvious that to serve 600,000 constituents, we could not have that kind of a bottleneck, so I let my staff know that I trusted them to do what needed to be done. If serving the people meant going to a meeting, writing a letter, or giving a speech, they didn't need to call the chief of staff or me to get approval. They were to just do it. They were hired because they were capable and because we trusted them to judge how things needed to be done. If someone made a mistake, I would take the heat, not that person.

It was my job to make the mission clear and trust people to accomplish it. I was fortunate to have an excellent staff of 16 people. Each person had specific areas of responsibility, and as time passed, we began to function effectively as a team.

In the same way, when I was head coach, delegation was a key component of an effective program, so I tried not to micromanage my assistants. If an offensive coach had drills that he preferred to run, great. Attending to that kind of detail was his job; he could do so with a certain level of autonomy. My job was to attend to the larger principles that would create a healthy environment for a winning football team.

Whether coaching or leading the athletic department, my goal was to make space for coaches and others to use their talents and energy to create solid, successful teams. I tried to do this by setting guidelines based on core values such as integrity, trust, respect, teamwork, and loyalty.

Creating an atmosphere where people are encouraged to give their thoughts and suggestions is essential. If a leader ignores or criticizes input from followers, it will soon shut down ideas and creativity and cause people to be less engaged and less valued.

The Dangers of Micromanagement

While I have seen the positive effects of empowerment in government office and on the football field, I have also seen the damage that can be done when the opposite happens.

Prior to my return to Nebraska as Athletic Director, a consultant from the business world was hired to evaluate the athletic department. I think the idea was to improve performance, but things didn't seem to be working out well.

Even though the consultant had been in the athletic department for only 10 weeks, he was seeking to make some major changes. He was from the business world and had no specific knowledge of athletic departments. He required administrators to report to him rather than the Athletic Director, reviewed the emails sent out to ensure they were to his liking, and had many closed-door meetings. As a result, a certain amount of mistrust had begun to pervade the department.

This consultant was in the process of setting up a system of evaluation and performance reviews, which would have taken a great deal of time to implement. The reviews would occur every 90 days, and the cost-of-living raises would be allocated based on those reviews. The only problem was that particular plan would have been contrary to university policy.

The situation became somewhat dysfunctional in that people were fearful for their jobs, and no one felt free to operate on their own initiative without first checking with the consultant. The staff fired the consultant in the time between the previous Athletic Director's dismissal and my being hired, which was a fairly good indicator of how unpopular some of his reforms had been. I did a lot of listening and encouraging.

Over time, the staff returned to an environment of mutual respect and a sense of mission. People felt much better about going to work every day.

Part of my job as Athletic Director was to help create a sound culture. I wanted to see good effort and stand-out performance. I also wanted to create an enjoyable place to work. Putting people under the gun to ratchet up their level of accomplishment from one day to the next is, in my experience, not the best way to get the best out of them. Creating a team-oriented environment that encourages collaboration is much better than excessive focus on individual performance, which fosters unhealthy competition, division, and dysfunction.

When those you lead feel cared for, empowered, and valued, you will inevitably influence their attitude, self-esteem, and performance. And when your team feels like they are part of the organization's success, it will undoubtedly create a sense of ownership and belonging.

The Great Commission

Empowerment is a biblical principle and can be clearly seen throughout both the Old and New Testaments. For instance:

• In Exodus 18, Moses was to lead the Israelites out of slavery in Egypt. It was a daunting task, and Moses did most of the work alone. After stern advice from Jethro, his father-in-law, Moses wisely delegated many responsibilities to trustworthy men within the camp. He was able to focus on the big picture while others took care of the details.

• In the Book of Acts, we find many stories of how Peter, John, Paul, and the other Apostles empowered converts to the Christian faith to take on the role and responsibilities needed to lead the churches that were sprouting up throughout the region. Paul became one of the chief delegators and encouraged others to do the same.

Within the teachings of the Apostle Paul, there is a beautiful example of empowerment found in a metaphorical explanation of the Christian church, which is also referred to as the Body of Christ:

For the body does not consist of one member but of many. If the foot should say, "Because I am not a hand, I do not belong to the body," that would not make it any less a part of the body. And if the ear should say, "Because I am not an eye, I do not belong to the body," that would not make it any less a part of the body. If the whole body were an eye, where would be the sense of hearing? If the whole body were an ear, where would be the sense of smell? But as it is, God arranged the members in the body, each one of them as he chose. If all were a single member, where would the body be? As it is, there are many parts, yet one body. (1 Corinthians 12:14-19/ESV)

Leaders should look at their team in the same way. Everyone is important, has value, and can be empowered to do something that will benefit the entire organization.

Another powerful and relevant example of empowerment can be found in the life and ministry of Jesus. He took 12 ordinary men and led them by example and edification. When the time was right, Jesus gave them the opportunity to spread their wings and act upon the training they had received (Matthew 10:5-8).

Jesus didn't stop there. After His death and resurrection, one of the last things He told His followers to do was the ultimate act of empowerment, the Great Commission, which is something Christians are still called to do today:

"Go therefore and make disciples of all nations, baptizing them in the name of the Father and of the Son and of the Holy Spirit, teaching them to observe all that I have commanded you. And behold, I am with you always, to the end of the age." (Matthew 28:19-20/ESV)

That last statement is very important and something that leaders should especially notice. Jesus made a commitment to be there for His followers until the task was complete. While He wasn't going to be with them physically, He was leaving His example, His Word, and His Spirit to guide them—just as He continues to guide His followers today.

A Leap of Trust

As a leader, it can sometimes be challenging to empower those we are leading. That's because it usually involves letting go of certain measures of comfort and control. On the other hand, holding on to all the details and micromanaging a team can lead to unnecessary anxiety and stress, and cause the leader to work harder, ultimately decreasing effectiveness and productivity.

This was the case with me in the previously related story of my trying to handle so much that I ended up having heart surgery. I learned to delegate and empower my assistants and was able to continue coaching.

If you are struggling to empower others through the mechanism of delegation, here are four things you need to do when you're ready to take that next step in your leadership journey:

1. Trust your leadership (even if you don't feel like you've taught and trained your team enough—because it will never feel like you've done enough).

2. Trust your people (even if they're not perfect—because, like you, they're not).

3. Trust the process (even if it's not perfectly smooth—because it likely won't be).

4. Trust that the principle of empowerment works (even if it's not always a perfect outcome or a little different than what you planned).

At the end of the day, if you take that leap of trust, you'll be glad you added empowerment and delegation to your leadership toolbox. It will take some of the burden from your shoulders, and it will also allow your team to grow their talents and expand their reach. And perhaps, empowerment might even result in some positive outcomes that would not have been expected otherwise.

In Other Words

I played at Nebraska during the time of the Unity Council that Coach Osborne created to help give players more of a voice within the program. We were empowered to give input into things like how practices were run, how to handle players skipping class, and even smaller issues such as the movies we would watch as a team.

But that wasn't the only way Coach exercised the principle of empowerment. Right before my senior year, I was having a hard time with someone on the staff, and it got to the point where I was planning on finishing my degree that summer and dropping out of football.

I don't know how, but Coach found out about it and pulled me into his office for a meeting. That alone was amazing, but in the meeting, he took the time to listen to my concerns and then asked if I would be willing to stay if things would change. I felt very empowered at that moment. I really had a voice, and Coach truly cared about me as a person.

I'll be darned if my senior wasn't my best year ever. My relationship with that staff member improved, and we went undefeated leading up to the 1993 National Championship Game. Even though we lost, it's hard to imagine missing out on that incredible run, and I don't think I've ever had more fun playing football.

From everything I observed and heard, Coach Osborne also empowered his assistant coaches in the same way. He sought out everyone's opinions and made sure those under his leadership felt respected and valued. The incredible loyalty he received in return was evidence of just how valuable empowerment can be.

I took that example into my business and created a leadership team I continually lean on for advice, counsel, and creative ideas. I need smart people around to help me do my best and have a better chance of success. There's strength in numbers, and things go much more smoothly when everyone pulls in the same direction. And empowering those you are leading is a surefire way to create unity and ensure long-term, meaningful impact.

~ Mike Anderson, Owner of Anderson Auto Group, NFL Europe Player (1993), and Nebraska Football Player (1990-93)

Coach Osborne always allowed me to coach in my own unique way, which was important to me. That was true for all of his coaches. He wanted us to do our best and wasn't concerned about the methods as long as we treated the players with respect and exercised integrity in everything we did.

At the end of the year, Coach would have a meeting with each coach individually. We were free to share any concerns we had with his leadership, and, in turn, he would respectfully tell us what things he would like us to do better.

Even during the season, Coach had an open door policy for us to share anything we were dealing with personally or within the team. He didn't want us trying to do our jobs if we had something we needed to get off our chests.

During spring ball, Coach also met with each player individually and encouraged the position coaches to meet with the kids they coached. Those conversations were about football-related issues—like how they were doing in the weight room and what they were doing to improve their speed—but also about how they were doing in the classroom and if they were having any challenges in their personal lives.

Tom's meetings were never one-way conversations where he was telling coaches and players what they were doing right or what they were doing wrong. Those meetings empowered all of us to take responsibility for our own development and growth. That's what made everyone around Coach Osborne get better and how the program remained solid under his leadership for all those years.

~ Charlie McBride, Nebraska Defensive Coordinator (1982-99) and Nebraska Football Assistant (1977-81)

PART IV

~~~~~~

IMPACTFUL

OUTCOMES

15

CHAPTER FIFTEEN

~~~~~

CONFIDENCE

THE LEGACY OF BELIEF

My dad went into World War II even though he didn't have to go. He was beyond draft age and volunteered. He had no prior military experience and was named company commander. My dad's professional experience was working in an automobile agency. He used that experience to recruit mechanics throughout the central part of Nebraska. Those mechanics and automotive experts became key people in his ordinance company which kept jeeps, trucks, and tanks operating on the front lines.

After five years overseas, my dad was successfully able to land in Normandy, through France, Belgium and Germany. He came out of the war as a major. I've always been very proud of his unique accomplishment. It was quite remarkable for someone that the world might otherwise deem an ordinary man.

My dad was the first person that showed me what confidence looks like. He wasn't outwardly emotive or self-centered, but he quietly exuded the definition of the word. Confidence is simply a feeling and belief that you can accomplish certain things.

It doesn't matter how big or small your leadership role might be. Confidence, that belief that you can get the job done, is going to be a vital component of your success. And if your confidence is shaken or maybe wasn't completely developed in the first place, there is still a path to restoring what you once had or building upon whatever foundation has been laid.

Cornerstones of Confidence

For most people, confidence starts early. Some believe that it has to do with birth order. For instance, I was the older of two boys, and we grew up during the tail end of the Great Depression. My dad was a traveling salesman and was gone Monday through Friday. I only saw him on the weekends. In those days, women didn't work much outside the home. My mom had been a teacher, but when she got married and started a family, she stayed at home to take care of us.

Before my younger brother came along, I got my mom's undivided attention for the first three and a half years of my life. She taught me how to read when I was three. She expected a lot of me as a very young child. Later on, as the oldest child, I was given more responsibility. That developed confidence over the years. Having said that, the war years took a toll. I was the only child in my class who did not have a dad at home, and we were always on edge concerning his safety. At times, I felt anxious and inferior.

Confidence can seem like a natural trait for some, but most likely, it is circumstantial, based on environment, or transferred through affirmation. Of course, success also breeds confidence, which, in turn, breeds more success. Unfortunately, the inverse is also true. Failure tends to make confidence a little bit wobbly. Then, the more you fail, the more prone you are to suffer from a lack of confidence. It's a vicious cycle, but one that can be avoided when you understand your true purpose and the true source of confidence.

Building Blocks of Confidence

Not everyone has the same upbringing; some may find confidence a natural extension of their character, while others may struggle with confidence because it wasn't instilled in them from a young age. The good news is that all leaders can work out their purpose in confidence. You just need to know how to use some irreplaceable building blocks along with your true purpose.

Affirmation

There's a common belief that coaching is about finding fault and pointing out things an athlete does wrong. That can be a part of it, but you need to buttress that with a fair amount of positive feedback. Otherwise, the athletes can begin to lose confidence in their abilities.

During the course of a game, a quarterback might throw an interception, a running back might fumble the ball, or a defensive lineman might miss a tackle. All of those things can seem to be catastrophic. Sometimes that player is met with a lot of verbal abuse when they get to the sideline. Nobody in the stadium feels worse than they do. They know what they did, hollering at them when they reach the sidelines doesn't help.

You can certainly point out that the fumble occurred because the player was carrying the ball loosely, or the interception occurred because the quarterback didn't read the coverage correctly. But then, you need to follow that up with some affirmation—remind them that they've performed well before and they can do it again.

Don Clifton, who founded Gallup, conducted research to back up the importance of affirmation as it relates to confidence. He found that in a business setting, positive comments should outweigh negative comments three to one. In a close interpersonal relationship, such as marriage or a close friendship, that should be five to one.

This is a good lesson, especially for those attempting to instill confidence in their employees, staff, or team members. For the leader needing confidence, however, this means finding positive affirmations from family, friends, peers, pastoral figures, and the scriptures. It's also important to avoid and reject negative internal and external commentary.

Coaching was a fishbowl occupation. Public scrutiny and comments were part of the job. I ignored it as much as possible and focused on the task.

Repetition

At Nebraska, we tried not to measure performance by the final score of a game. We had 12 offensive goals, 11 defensive goals, and seven special teams goals that measured how we did in each game. We might have won the game by 40 points, but if we only hit half of our goals, we didn't play as well as we could have. Each one of those goals had to do with how we practiced.

During practice, we had repetitions and instructions that instilled confidence in our players. To avoid fumbles, make sure that you carry the ball high and tight. To make a high percentage of your tackles, don't duck your head or close your eyes. Keep your head up, keep your eyes open, and have a certain aim point. Lock your arms and drive your feet. Those things were critical. It was a daily process. If the players did those things often enough with the right intensity, success usually followed.

When we practiced, we had two offensive stations and two defensive stations rather than the standard one station for offense and one for defense. We had twice the repetition and very few players standing idly watching. This enabled us to have better execution and fewer mistakes. It also helped us develop young players, so we had better depth, and more players felt they were contributing.

Taking that example to leadership across the board, it's important to have good training for yourself and your team. It's equally important to put that training into practice every day until it becomes a habit, eventually leading to confident action and response.

Competence

A leader might not be fully competent in all key areas of their roles and responsibilities, but certainly, there must be a certain level of know-how and skill that led to that leadership role in the first place. If you're going to lead a group of people, you have to demonstrate that you know what you're doing. That's difficult to pull off if you are unprepared or you are moving into an entirely new venue with little to no experience.

However, assuming that basic competence is in play, the aforementioned building blocks of affirmation and repetition will help strengthen the leader's confidence.

The Dangers of Insecurity

Many things can break down a leader's confidence. A coach may suffer through a difficult losing streak. A business leader may endure criticism during periods of financial setbacks and declining stock value. A parent may see a child's behavior spiral out of control despite best efforts to teach, discipline, and encourage them. A pastor may see members leave for another church or experience challenges to their spiritual authority.

Leaders are always going to face internal and external pressure. When things aren't going well, insecurity will quickly come in to replace the confidence that has been damaged in the process. Leading from a posture of shaken confidence or insecurity can create more problems than what the team or organization is already experiencing.

For example, if a coach loses a couple of games, they might be tempted to make rash decisions and start veering away from the game plan. Instead of sticking with the original design—how the offense and defense are run—the coach might throw everything out and start over in the middle of the season. But that's often a disastrous decision because there isn't enough time to effectively make those changes.

Other dangers of insecure leadership might include indecisiveness, erratic behavior, tentativeness, or paralysis. Panic is especially dangerous. It shows the team or organization that you really don't know what you're doing. Authenticity is important. People can discern fairly quickly if you're pretending or, as some people like to say, faking it until you make it.

A Fine Line

On the other end of the spectrum is overconfidence. There's a fine line between confidence and overconfidence, often leading to complacency, lax discipline, and entitlement. It usually takes place after a time of sustained success. It takes root when confidence veers into self-confidence—a belief that individual ability, talent, and effort are the primary, if not sole reason for that success.

For instance, a company might have a very good quarter and make a lot of money. Still, it may have been just some fortuitous circumstances, and it may be that the basic nuts and bolts of an effective organization were not necessarily being practiced. If the fundamentals are not sound and the proper procedures aren't being conveyed and worked on daily, the organization is being set up for failure.

In sports, if a team wins a couple of games fairly handily, it can lead to the idea that they are really good and maybe don't have to work quite as hard in practice. If the next team on the schedule has a losing record, there's no perceived need to stick to the fundamental basics. Overconfidence can cause players and coaches to think they've really arrived and now don't have to pay the same price in practice, training, or game prep.

That's why as a coach, I was consistently preaching about the team practicing hard one day at a time, working on fundamentals, and paying attention to detail. We weren't going to get too elated because we won a game. It was more about how well we really played and if we were getting better, and what things we needed to do to improve. Those are the things a leader should keep front and center in the minds of their team. Focusing on big-picture goals is critical to long-term success and can stave off overconfidence.

Truth-Based Confidence

Self-confidence and self-reliance will only take a leader so far. There is so much more we can do when we place our confidence in God, His calling on our lives, and the abilities He has given us. There are countless examples of this truth throughout the Bible. Some great stories that stand out include:

• Moses: Years after being exiled from Egypt, he lived a simple existence in the mountains. Moses lacked confidence due to a speech impediment and his fear of returning home. However, God's promise and a miraculous sign, along with assistance from his brother Aaron, gave Moses the confidence to lead the Israelites out of slavery through the parted Red Sea and on their way to the Promised Land.

• David: He was the youngest of nine brothers, which is not traditionally a strong starting point for confidence, but David grew his confidence in the shepherd's field by facing adversity (he killed a lion and a bear protecting the sheep) and by relying on God's strength and courage. That confidence led to even bigger victories against Goliath and later as king against many of the region's fiercest armies.

• Elijah: This mighty prophet was a textbook example of roller coaster confidence. He had great confidence after a big victory against the priests of Baal (calling down fire from Heaven) but was quickly shaken when Queen Jezebel placed a bounty on his head. Elijah had to spend some time in isolation and reflection to remember the miracles God had performed so his confidence could be restored.

Jesus, of course, the greatest leader our world has ever known, was supremely confident during His time on Earth. He had a clear mission and the power and authority to see it to the end through His divine connection to God the Father. Jesus never backed down from the religious leaders who questioned His teachings and ultimately paid the price through a brutal death on the cross.

We read that Jesus consistently withdrew to commune with God in prayer. It would seem that this provided greater clarity and confidence as He completed His mission.

But Jesus always knew the end of the story: He would be raised from the dead, commission His disciples to build the Church, and return to Heaven until the time of His Second Coming. His confidence was never shaken despite every evil attempt to thwart God's master plan.

Even though Jesus was the Son of God, He still relied on God the Father's strength every step of the way. As the Apostle Paul would later confer:

Not that we are sufficient in ourselves to claim anything as coming from us, but our sufficiency is from God. (2 Corinthians 3:5/ESV)

An unidentified Apostle (some believe it to be Paul) wrote likewise explaining the importance of confidence in light of the divine calling a leader may have on their life:

Therefore do not throw away your confidence, which has a great reward. For you have need of endurance, so that when you have done the will of God you may receive what is promised. (Hebrews 10:35-36/ESV)

As I've come to learn over the years, part of the Christian walk is also to learn from your failures and to have confidence in the fact that you're still loved with everlasting love, whether you win or lose.

For I am sure that neither death nor life, nor angels nor rulers, nor things present nor things to come, nor powers, nor height nor depth, nor anything else in all creation, will be able to separate us from the love of God in Christ Jesus our Lord. (Romans 8:38-39/ESV)

Rock Solid Confidence

Long-lasting and effective leadership is nearly impossible without rock-solid confidence. Whether you are building on your foundation or picking up the pieces after your confidence has taken a major blow, here are some simple steps to having that assurance and belief that you can accomplish whatever God has called you to do:

1. Get back to the basics: If you are establishing your confidence or rebuilding shaken confidence, you should first find practical ways to learn or relearn the fundamentals of your role and your responsibilities. It's important for any leader to know their stuff. Perhaps that might require going back to school, attending clinics and workshops, doing more reading and research, or getting help from peers in your field.

2. Remind yourself of past success: If you've had a discouraging setback, it's always healthy to point back to past successes. What were you doing when that happened? What did that feel like? It's a lot easier to do that if you have a storehouse full of past successes, but if you don't have a lot of success to pull from, start pointing toward positives that take place throughout the day or the week. Build on those small victories until confidence is established or restored.

3. Embrace adversity: There's a fine line between self-confidence and arrogance. I probably learned more from the games we lost than I did from the games we won. Adversity is a great teacher. It can open the door to positive change, which in turn can lead you to strategies and ideas that will help you rebuild your confidence and be stronger moving forward.

4. Shut out the noise: It's important that you know who to listen to and who not to listen to. Today, particularly with social media, you have people who have no competence in your area, and yet they'll offer an opinion. It's usually fairly uninformed. Remember that when you're tempted to pay attention to outside voices.

5. Accept wise counsel: Don't isolate yourself from constructive criticism. You want to be able to hear from people that may have some valid ideas. Make sure you're open to that kind of dialogue, and be wise enough to know what changes are doable and which are not.

6. Acknowledge the source: True confidence comes from knowing that God has called you for a purpose and equipped you for that purpose. Recognize that He is the source of your abilities and is the only one who can maximize them for the greater good.

At the end of the day, confidence is all about belief—belief in your calling, belief in your God-given abilities, belief in the relationships and resources He has provided you, and belief in the purpose that is far bigger than you can ever imagine.

In Other Words

After winning the 1994 National Championship, things were a lot different as our team pursued the difficult task of securing back-to-back titles. The previous year, Coach Osborne was the media darling and fan favorite—a legendary coach trying to break through to that elusive trophy.

But as we headed into the 1995 game against Florida, we had gone through a lot of struggles with some of our players, and we were considered the bad boys of college football. Nobody believed in us. Everybody outside of Nebraska wanted us to lose.

The afternoon of the game, right before leaving the team hotel for the stadium, Coach Osborne quietly stepped up to the podium in the conference room. The doors were locked. All eyes were on our leader as we waited for him to give his standard speech.

I looked around at the team and saw a lot of nervousness, which was unusual for a group that was otherwise known for its great confidence.

"Boy, Tom's going to have to fire them up tonight," I thought to myself.

Instead, he gave one of the most powerful game-day talks I've ever heard.

Coach Osborne pulled a small Bible out of his pocket, opened it up, and began to read 2 Timothy 1:7: "For God has not given us a spirit of fear, but of power and of love and of a sound mind."

He then proceeded to explain what that verse meant to him. Coach Osborne told the team that there was a lot of fear on this earth, but you don't have to live in fear when you decide to follow Jesus Christ. He told the team that they could have the power to rise above those things that would normally hold them down. Coach reminded them that they didn't have to be afraid of what the media had been saying, but instead, they had the power to play the very best they possibly could.

Then, he talked about the spirit of love and how it wasn't about loving a woman or loving the game of football. It was about God's love for each of them and how Jesus went to the cross for them because of that love. And how they had a special kind of love for one another that allowed them to rise above a lot of challenges.

And finally, Coach Osborne told the team that they had a sound mind. He told them they could think clearly and say yes to the things that are right and no to the things that are wrong. Coach told them that people think football players are big, dumb jocks, but that wasn't true. They were intelligent young men who could make great decisions with God's help.

That speech was given quietly and without a lot of dramatics or "rah rah" charades. Coach Osborne just read that scripture and shared it from his heart as the team listened in complete silence.

I don't know if this had anything to do with that, but we went out there with great confidence and dominated Florida all the way to a 63-24 victory and a second consecutive National Championship. But that's not why Coach Osborne gave that speech. He did it because he truly loved those players and wanted them to overcome their fear— not just in the moment but throughout the rest of their lives.

> **~ Ron Brown, Nebraska Football Director of Player Support and Outreach, Nebraska Football Senior Offensive Analyst (2021-22), Nebraska Football Director of Player Development (2018-20), Liberty Football Associate Head Coach (2014-17), and Nebraska Football Assistant Coach (1987-2003, 2008-14)**

We all have fears. Even our Bible heroes had fears—like Moses, who was afraid to speak, or Gideon, who was afraid to lead an army, or David, who was afraid of King Saul. All those men overcame their fears and became great leaders because they ultimately understood their calling and had a relationship with God, who had called them.

Some might be surprised to know that my dad once strongly feared public speaking. But because his calling compelled him, he overcame that fear and became a highly sought-after speaker because of his appealing mix of dry humor and poignant messages. When Dad gives his TeamMates speech every year at our church, it's not uncommon to see people chuckling at an anecdote or funny story and moments later wiping a tear or two from their eye drawn out by the power of the message.

Dad's fearlessness was a product of his faith. Once when driving on the highway on vacation, we came upon the site of a bad accident. There was a burning truck, and the driver was trapped in the cabin. My dad pulled to the side of the road, jumped out of the car, ran toward the truck, and pulled the driver out to safety. After ensuring the man was okay, Dad returned to the car, and we left. No one knew he had risked his own life to save another.

Dad has a quiet confidence that comes from the understanding that he was called and given everything he needed to accomplish the tasks along the path he was to travel. He knows who he intends to serve, and his unflappability comes, at least in part, from that confidence of purpose.

~ Mike Osborne, Son of Tom Osborne

16

~~~~~

UNITY

THE LEGACY OF TOGETHERNESS

Unity is something we often claim to want in our society, yet it remains one of the most elusive principles that humankind has ever known. For an effective leader, unity should manifest in the form of chemistry, cohesion, and camaraderie.

It is difficult to have true unity if there is not a high level of trust on a team. Trust starts at the top. If a coach says one thing and does another, is dishonest, and does not keep promises, there will be a lack of trust. On the other hand, if a coach is a person of integrity—tells the truth, keeps promises, and does not bend the rules—players will trust him. If the coach is trustworthy, then trust usually spreads throughout the team.

Team chemistry is critical, not just for success on the playing field, but also for personal growth in players and what they eventually get from their athletic experience. Hopefully, some of the things discussed in this book will help you develop a proper level of cohesiveness and focus on your team.

To complete your mission, there needs to be a cohesive and purposeful spirit among those following your lead. Partisanship needs to be eliminated, and you must make a point of bringing about unity within your organization, staff, team, or company. There will always be differences among people, but having a common purpose heals divisions.

At Nebraska, like most places, people like to win. They like to win football games, and they also like to win in all other sports. But our mission is not to win. The mission we developed when I was athletics director is to "serve our student-athletes, coaches, staff, and fans by displaying integrity in every decision and action; building and maintaining trust with others; giving respect to each person we encounter; pursuing unity of purpose through teamwork; and maintaining loyalty to student-athletes, coworkers, fans, and the University of Nebraska."

It might be disconcerting for many fans to hear that our mission was not to win but rather to live out certain core values that, if properly followed, will lead to effective performance. But as John Wooden pointed out, emphasizing the process rather than the score is the key to maximizing performance.

The Unity Council

I once served on the College Football Selection Committee for two years. It seemed that at the start of each season, there were 15 to 20 teams with enough talent, tradition, and coaching to end up in the four-team playoff at the end of the season. As each season wore on, there were upsets, the ball bounced in the wrong direction, or teams simply fell short of expectations. Eventually, we would end up with only five or six teams still in the hunt as the season wound down.

Some teams seemed to perform better than their talent indicated, and others underperformed. Occasionally a team exceeded the sum of its parts. Even though individual talents were limited, the team would mesh in such a way that it performed at a high level. A major factor that separated teams was team chemistry and unity of purpose. Nearly every coach recognizes unity as important but it is elusive and often difficult to create.

In 1990 we were 9-1 going into the final regular season game against Oklahoma in Norman. Our quarterback was injured badly, and we ended up having several turnovers and lost to Oklahoma 45-10, an embarrassing defeat. Then still without our starting quarterback, we lost the Citrus Bowl game to Georgia Tech 45-21. Those two season-ending losses were humiliating. Two of our three losses were to Colorado and Georgia Tech, teams who tied for the national championship that year. We ended the season 9-3, not a terrible record, but it was the low point of my coaching career.

It wasn't just the three losses; it seemed we were not a unified team with a common purpose. I discussed matters with Jack Stark, a psychologist from Omaha. Jack thought we should initiate something that he called a Unity Council. This council would be composed of players selected by the teammates from each segment of the team to represent them—two offensive linemen, two defensive linemen, two running backs, two defensive backs, and so on. This resulted in a group of 18 players chosen by the players to represent them on the Council. The coaching staff had no input on the makeup of the Unity Council; it was entirely player driven.

The charge of the Unity Council was to meet weekly, in this case on a Tuesday evening, and bring up anything they believed was getting in the way of team unity. It did not matter how trivial the issue was; it was to be brought forth and discussed. No coaches were in the room to ensure open discussion. The only staff member involved was our strength coach, Boyd Epley, who listened and recorded those things the Unity Council wanted to be brought to me. Boyd was chosen because he was not directly responsible for determining who would be on the first, second, or third team and would not have input on playing time, yet he knew the players and had their trust.

The morning after the meeting, Boyd would come to me with the list of things the players had discussed. Most of the issues were minor— the movie seen the night before the previous game, the lunch menu, a staff member being abrasive, etc. Occasionally something more serious such as wanting to wear a different shoe brand would come up.

In the team meeting later that afternoon, I would address each item. The players could choose which movie we would see that week, I would talk to the training table staff about the lunch menu, and I would visit with the staff member about toning things down. However, I would also explain that we had a shoe contract that could not be broken, therefore, we would stick with the brand we were wearing and try to get better service within the structure of the contract.

None of those matters would have come to my attention before the Unity Council was formed. Most issues were minor, but they were not left to fester and become larger. Most importantly, the players were given a voice and knew we would listen.

We also asked the players to help construct a discipline code. They realized I would have the final say on discipline, but they were involved in formulating some of the guidelines. An appearance before the Unity Council was part of the discipline process when things had gotten to a critical point with a player. Players found it was not easy to be confronted by a group of their peers. The Unity Council was not easy on those who were disruptive, and members were not shy about letting the person in front of them know they were not happy and that the transgressor better shape up.

Again, I would have the final say regarding disciplinary matters. Still, the Unity Council was involved enough in the process to understand that there was equal and fair treatment, and no one got special privileges. The perception that certain players are treated differently than others can be very damaging to team morale, and the Unity Council's involvement dispelled any such notions.

We also decided to involve the players in setting team goals. We gave each player a sheet of paper and a pencil and asked them to write down, in order of preference, the most important things for the team to accomplish that season. We then collated the responses and listed in order of importance the consensus goals of the team. In 1997, the last team I coached, the goals were as follows:

1. National Championship
2. No off-field incidents
3. Big 12 Championship
4. Unity
5. Play one game at a time
6. Be the most physically and mentally prepared team in the country
7. Team grade point average of 2.85 or higher
8. Undefeated season

We impressed upon the players that these were their goals, not the coaches' goals, but theirs. We would do everything possible to help them achieve those goals, but they had responsibility and ownership.

We achieved each one of those goals. This was rather remarkable, given how lofty those goals were. Measuring goals No. 4 through No. 6 was somewhat subjective, but that aside, there was no question we were unified, did not overlook a single opponent, and were a very physical and well-conditioned team.

Those were the 1997 team goals, however, we started letting the players list team goals five years earlier, the same time we started the Unity Council, and each year the players achieved nearly all of them. It seemed that creating a greater sense of ownership yielded remarkable results—at least during those five years.

There is a danger in having the players list team goals, as players are very optimistic, and it is possible to have them set totally unrealistic goals. If the goals are extremely high and the season starts out badly enough that most goals are unachievable by the middle of the season, this does not bode well for the rest of the season.

For many years this risk kept me from having the players set the goals. However, there is also power in having their input and ownership. Each coach will have to decide if the risk is worth it.

Focusing on the process, the daily pursuit of excellence and improvement on each facet of the game is probably more important than long-term goals, but each can play a part. If a coach can instill a sense of accountability and ownership for what happens on a team, it will make a difference.

How this is done will undoubtedly differ at the middle school, high school, and college levels. It will have to be adapted to the maturity level of the players involved, but even youth teams will value input and ownership if it is presented in a way appropriate for their age level.

The important thing to consider in the discussion of the Unity Council and goal setting is that having player involvement can be very helpful as we give our players more ownership and responsibility, and team unity and purpose improve. In the final five years I coached, after the changes were made in 1991, we won 60 games and lost three, with three undefeated teams and three National Championships.

It would be wrong to attribute all of the success those teams had to the formation of the Unity Council. We had very good players, a fine coaching staff, good administrative support, and a very loyal fan base. However, there is no question that something shifted with establishing the Unity Council and some of the changes we made. The unity of those teams was exceptional. Players policed behavior on their own and often took it upon themselves to talk to a player who was headed in a direction that was not in the best interest of the team.

Players voted to abstain from alcohol, a real problem on college campuses, and the players often enforced this rule themselves. Coaches could not be everywhere. We were shooting for the top, and we talked to the players about abstinence from alcohol, allowing us to practice a little harder during the week and perform better on Saturday than other teams. The difference might be small, but small differences are huge at the highest levels of competition, and we could not afford to settle for anything but the highest standards.

The unity and willingness to sacrifice for each other on my final five teams was exceptional. For many of those athletes, the experience has carried over throughout the rest of their lives.

On Mission

As mentioned earlier, when I returned to the athletic department in 2007, I could tell something was not right. Some people were ready to quit. Some people had quit already. The first meeting I attended on my first day on the job involved two mental health professionals offering stress management ideas to administrative staff members. I could sense that there were serious stress and morale issues and that this was more than a casual exercise.

One of my first initiatives was to get everyone together (all 240 department members) to develop a mission statement. Just as I believe a personal mission statement can be a powerful tool for making personal decisions according to one's values, I also believe the corporate or team mission statement can bring people together to achieve a common purpose.

I began by asking each person to share the core values or principles they felt were foundational to our department's success. Through a show of hands, we settled on the five core values of Nebraska's athletic program: integrity, trust, respect, teamwork, and loyalty. We wove these values into a mission statement that all the employees were encouraged to improve or alter through emails. The final product was a group effort that came from the employees. It was not imposed from the top down.

Once we had a common purpose, a mission that nearly all wanted to fulfill, I met with each division in the athletic department to brainstorm ways that our common values in a mission could be incorporated into their particular area of operation. How could the security people build and main trust? How could the food service workers pursue unity of purpose through teamwork? How could the medical staff give respect to each person they encountered? How could each sport's coaching staff display integrity in every decision in action? How could my specific area, administration, maintain loyalty to student-athletes, coworkers, fans, and the University?

I found that most people in the athletic department had never had a personal visit from the Athletic Director or had ever been in his office.

I did a lot of listening. It was important that each person in the department was given a chance to be heard and that each person knew that he or she was valued. Out of that long process, I think that healing began to occur. It wasn't overnight, but gradually people became more trusting, felt more unified, and showed more respect for each other.

Unstoppable Force

Unity is a common theme throughout the entirety of the Bible. When a group comes together for a common goal, they are a powerful force full of passion and purpose. Conversely, we see many instances where division caused a group of people meant to do great things to fall prey to the tragic consequences of disunity.

This can especially be found in the Old Testament, where the Israelites provide the perfect example of both scenarios:

The Battle of Jericho

The Israelites were undefeated when they unified behind God and the nation's chosen leader. There is no better illustration than the leadership of Joshua, who is credited with one of the Bible's most famous military victories.

Found in the sixth chapter of Joshua, the Israelites were traveling to the Promised Land but were still mourning the death of their beloved leader Moses. The newly appointed leader, Joshua, was facing the difficult task of getting his people past the heavily fortified and dangerously militarized city of Jericho.

God instructed Joshua and the people to march around the city once a day for six days. On the seventh day, they were to march around the city seven times, and then the seven priests were to blow trumpets made of rams' horns. At the sound of the trumpets, the people were to let out a great shout, and the wall of the city would fall.

Joshua obeyed and gave his people the command. For the next six days, the people marched around the city once. Then, on the seventh day, they marched around the city seven times. At the end of the march, the seven priests blew their trumpets, the people let out a shout, and lo and behold, the wall of the city fell, and the Israelites conquered the city of Jericho. Whether the walls actually disintegrated or the occupants of Jericho simply lost heart and gave up, the strategy worked.

This story is much like any great team victory. A leader has a purpose and is confident in the plan. The leader shares the plan with the team and gives them the resources to act out that plan. The team accepts their instructions and confidently plays their roles until the task is complete and the purpose has been fulfilled. Unity is a powerful thing.

A Different Take on Unity

Hundreds of years later, in New Testament times, the Jewish people were living under the harsh rule of the Roman Empire. They were looking for the promised Messiah—a Savior they hoped would rescue them and wipe out their enemies once and for all. They weren't expecting a carpenter's son from Nazareth who preached love, forgiveness, and self-sacrifice. His message of unity had a much different tone and resulted in the establishment of a much different kingdom:

The Teachings of Jesus

From a leadership perspective, Jesus taught and modeled the importance of bringing a team unit together around a common cause. However, it didn't look like the Old Testament armies, and it was built on peace and love, not violence and war. One of Jesus' more challenging parables was about the shepherd and his sheep.

"What do you think? If a man has a hundred sheep, and one of them has gone astray, does he not leave the ninety-nine on the mountains and go in search of the one that went astray? And if he finds it, truly, I say to you, he rejoices over it more than over the ninety-nine that never went astray." (Matthew 18:12-13/ESV)

Translating that into the athletic world, unity on a team can be fostered when you give the same respect and personal value to the least talented player as you do the first team player or when the student manager, janitor, bus driver, secretary, and new coach on the staff are treated well. A servant leader will do whatever they can to help that one team member, no matter who they are and what role they play.

This principle is also true in a family, in a business, in a church, in a community, and a civic organization. Everyone has worth and value, and each has a role to play, and the better each one performs that function, the better the group will perform. People need to know they are valued and appreciated and that they are performing an important function.

We honored our scout team players (primarily third and fourth team athletes) by recognizing the scout team player of the week. Our coaches appreciated these players' efforts to prepare the first team players for each game. Some former players who seldom rose above scout team status have told me that experience has been invaluable in their careers after football.

The Example of the Early Church

Unity was personified through the first believers who built the foundations of the Christian Church. Their incredible story is told in the Book of Acts, where one passage sums up their commitment to each other and their shared purpose:

And they devoted themselves to the Apostles' teaching and the fellowship, to the breaking of bread and the prayers. And awe came upon every soul, and many wonders and signs were being done through the Apostles. And all who believed were together and had all things in common, And they were selling their possessions and belongings and distributing the proceeds to all, as any had need. And day by day, attending the temple together and breaking bread in their homes, they received their food with glad and generous hearts, praising God and having favor with all the people. And the Lord added to their number day by day those who were being saved. (Acts 2:42-47/ESV)

It didn't take long for the religious leaders and government officials to take notice and oppose this movement with intense persecution. When adversity hit, the leadership stood firm, and the new Christians followed suit. They didn't splinter. They didn't turn on each other. They didn't cut and run or selfishly fend for themselves.

No, they actually got stronger and continued to grow in number.

One of their persecutors eventually came to Christ through a miraculous vision found in Acts 9. Saul, who was also known as Paul, would later write this short and simple yet powerful statement about what unity should look like:

Make my joy complete by being of the same mind, maintaining the same love, united in spirit, intent on one purpose. (Philippians 2:2/NASB)

Those are some of the most important ways a leader can encourage unity—through a message of shared vision, shared love, shared belief, and shared purpose.

Cultivating Togetherness

Unity doesn't happen overnight, but it also doesn't have to take months or years to manifest. Here are some effective ways you can cultivate an environment of togetherness among your team:

1. Communicate core values: You can't have unity if your team lacks shared values and common beliefs. Your team has to buy into your direction and the organization's foundational ideals. If possible include them in establishing core values so they have some ownership.

2. Communicate clear goals: It's difficult to have unity if your team doesn't have the same big-picture goals. Individual goals are okay if they don't detract or distract from the overall shared purpose.

3. Show genuine care for all: When you resist the natural temptation to play favorites, this will create an environment of shared love and respect, which is a key component of team cohesion and unity. The receptionist, the janitor, and the new hire should be shown appreciation for their efforts and how they contribute to the organization's success.

4. Share opportunities: When you give your team a voice and empower them to be a part of the team-building process, this will not only

inspire creativity and confidence but will also provide an invitation to take ownership of their work and their valuable contributions.

Unity starts at the top. Leadership can make or break a team's effectiveness. But it's not just about structure, organization, and administration; it's about core values, clear objective, and lots of heart and passion for those you are leading. In a time when divisiveness and disunity are far too common, servant leadership can pave the way to uncommon unity and much-needed togetherness.

In Other Words

Relationships tend to be stronger and do better when everyone involved is pulling in the same direction. For Coach Osborne, a lot of team unity was created because so many on the staff and on the team were operating from the same faith principles. He never mandated it or forced it on anyone, but there was a natural draw that brought the team together around a shared central belief.

That was especially true during the 90s when players became increasingly comfortable with approaching Coach away from the field and seeking out moments where they could learn from him and soak up his wisdom. Guys that you might not expect would hang out with Coach in the steam room or sit with him at the training table. They had the best time with Coach, and Coach enjoyed being around them away from the game.

But many people would be surprised to know that Coach Osborne had a really good sense of humor, and there was a lot of teasing and practical jokes that kept things loose and strengthened team unity even more. Coach knew I had a good relationship with the players, so I became fair game for public teasing. It always got a good laugh.

As Coach and I got closer, we began engaging in a series of practical jokes that kept getting more involved as we would try to one-up each other.

In the early 90s, a story in the newspaper revealed that Coach owed some taxes. Bill Clinton was the President at the time, so I took some cans, wrapped them in white paper, and put signs out by them around the athletic building that said, "Clinton clips Coach for a big chunk of change. Please help donate."

Coach got me back when he found a photo of me on a basketball trip to Puerto Rico. I was standing on the beach with two of the local girls. They were very tan. I was not. He had Mike Grant help him print up cardstock copies of the photo with the "Top Ten Captions" and then had them laminated and hung all around the complex.

Of course, I couldn't let it end there, so I worked with the guys at Husker Vision to take some footage I found of Coach dancing at his daughter's wedding. He wasn't slow dancing with her. He was kind of shaking it a little bit.

We took the footage and put together a hilarious video that involved, among other things, Coach dancing, Coach wearing extra short, photoshopped shorts, Mike Grant photoshopped as the Kool-Aid Man (an ode to his nickname Kool-Aid), a hilarious voiceover from Rick Allen Schwieger referencing Ron Brown's shorts and Mike's other nickname "Freaky G," an appearance from Rodney Dangerfield in "Caddy Shack," and a grand finale dance-off set to Journey's hit song "Anyway You Want It."

I held on to the video for a while until the perfect moment, which was during a practice in Lincoln leading up to the Orange Bowl. ABC was on the field getting footage of Coach as he stoically walked around observing his team warming up. Right before practice was about to start, Rick put the video on the big screen. Everyone stopped in their tracks and put their full attention on the video—everyone except Coach, who didn't even flinch.

Yes, we had the Unity Council, and that played a role in the team's success, but it was really the behind-the-scenes camaraderie and fun-loving moments between Coach and his players and staff that truly bonded us and created a sense of love and respect for one another.

~ Doak Ostergard, Nebraska Football Alumni Relations, Nebraska Head Athletic Trainer (1997-2006), and Nebraska Assistant Athletic Trainer (1989-96)

One year, Coach Osborne had a meeting with the entire athletic department. This included the night janitor, media relations, the groundskeepers, the trainers, and anyone connected to the program. Coach wanted them to report any incidents that they had with our players.

But that wasn't all; he also emphasized that they were a part of our team. It wasn't just us playing; if anything was troubling them, he wanted to know about it so it could be corrected.

I talked to one of the ladies in the ticket office, and she was so impressed after that meeting. She told me they had previously felt left out of everything but now felt like they were a part of the team. It really created a renewed sense of unity and pride within the program.

Beyond that, Coach Osborne also intentionally created unity within the family units connected to the team. He cared deeply about the coaches' wives and their children. Nancy was like the leader for the women, and she was always doing things with them to create that sense of bonding.

That was such a vital part of his leadership and had a lot to do with why everyone around the program was committed to doing their best for him and the team.

**~ Charlie McBride, Nebraska Defensive Coordinator (1982-99)
and Nebraska Football Assistant (1977-81)**

17

~~~~~~

PERSEVERANCE

THE LEGACY OF OVERCOMING ADVERSITY

One thing is certain about life; there will be adversity. Adversity presents a leader with a great opportunity to mentor and teach his team. For instance, in athletics, players will be injured, games will be lost, there may be a death in the family, or a girlfriend may decide to break up. My goal as a coach was to minimize the damage adversity caused and instead capitalize on the opportunities that adversity presented.

That's what perseverance is all about. It is simply overcoming difficult circumstances or unforeseen delays to fulfill a goal or achieve a certain measure of success.

It may be an oversimplification, but people usually handle adversity in one of three ways. They quit, they blame others or circumstances, or they see an opportunity.

From an athletic standpoint, when a person is demoted from the first team to the third team, that person may quit the team by leaving the team, or he may quit by no longer trying to improve and putting forth effort. Another player who is demoted may blame the coach who demoted him, claiming the coach plays favorites, is stupid, bears a grudge against the player, or is simply incompetent. Still, another player encountering the same fate may see his demotion as an opportunity to learn from the experience, correct some things he was doing wrong, and improve his commitment and effort.

It is obvious that quitting is not going to accomplish anything if the goal is to be a good player who gets more playing time. Blaming someone else is equally counterproductive. It may make the person feel better to blame someone else, but it doesn't improve the situation. The only response that results in a positive outcome is seeing adversity as an opportunity to improve and get better, and to learn something from the experience.

Most people can relate to experiences where a team, a business, or even a family that had an opportunity to grow and benefit from what was learned as a result of a setback, instead, unraveled and fell apart because people either quit or were consumed by finger-pointing and blaming.

Life is going to give you some pretty hard knocks. As a leader, some of those knocks come from inside the organization but can also come from the outside. If you ruminate on those things, you can become angry and resentful and build up a hostile relationship with people that you need on your side.

For me, sometimes, it was the press, and having a bad relationship wouldn't bode well in the long term because they usually have the final say. After all, they have the power of the pen. For other leaders, it might be grumbling employees, disenchanted board members, unsatisfied stockholders, or unscrupulous competitors.

Adversity can come from all sides, but perseverance—going through it until the end—is the only way to survive in one piece and reap the reward of going through the fire. Growth comes from moving through adversity; when things go smoothly, we usually stay with the status quo.

Turning Losses Into Wins

When discussing how one might deal with adversity, I often reflect on something that happened to our football team in 1996. We were coming off two consecutive unbeaten National Championship seasons in which we had won 26 straight games. We played Arizona State in Tempe, a team we had beaten badly the year before in Lincoln. It was a very bad night for the Cornhuskers. We were humiliated 19-0. We played poorly on offense, making all kinds of mistakes and committing several turnovers. Our defense wasn't that bad, but it wasn't very sharp either.

Given the fact that we had two straight undefeated seasons, had worked very hard, and were shooting for an unprecedented third consecutive National Championship, it would have been easy for the team to quit, to reflect on how hard they worked during the preceding seasons and now, with a loss and little prospect of another National Championship, to simply shut things down, go through the motions and enjoy themselves the rest of the season. It also would have been very easy to blame others.

However, we assembled the players at our normal meeting time the following Monday and informed them that even though we had not played well, the loss would be a very good thing. This would be a great learning experience since our weaknesses had been exposed. We had become complacent. We had assumed some areas of our team were good, which weren't. We would take this experience and become a great team as we worked to improve the deficiencies that had been exposed in the game. Rather than giving up or pointing the finger at others, our players began to look at that game as an opportunity to grow and get better.

One player in particular took the loss more personally than probably anyone else. Quarterback Scott Frost had replaced Husker legend Tommie Frazier and planned on helping us win another National Championship. Husker fans were upset with the loss against ASU, and as is often the case, the quarterback receives too much of the blame for a loss.

What helped him deal with the adversity was a friendship with Art Lindsay, a Lincoln man active in the Fellowship of Christian Athletes. Scott rededicated himself to his faith, and they began meeting weekly for Bible study. Eventually, he was able to see the ASU loss as something that would lead to a greater good and an opportunity to get better. Not only did he improve, but so did our team. We ran off nine straight wins and nearly got into the National Championship game for the fourth consecutive year.

This example involves losing a football game, hardly a major tragedy, although it felt like it at the time. There are many examples of a much more serious nature. I recall meeting a mother and father who experienced the devastating loss of a daughter to acute alcohol poisoning while she was in college. They resolved to make something positive of their tragedy and devoted much of their lives to speaking to young people about the dangers of alcohol abuse.

Their story was particularly impactful because they had experienced it personally, and one could sense the immense pain they felt due to the loss of a daughter. One could readily detect how difficult it was for them to relate the details leading up to their daughter's death. Still, it was also obvious that they found that by being vulnerable and reliving

the tragedy, they could impact others and possibly avert similar tragedies in the lives of other young people.

I think many of our players learned that adversity and tragedy could
be very instructional and can usually be turned into something positive if they respond in the right way—and possibly help other young
people avert similar tragedies..

The Blessing of Adversity

We tend to view adversity as something to be avoided. However, it's
almost impossible to grow in your faith or grow in your competence
unless you've been shaped by adversity.

If you go through life without adversity, there's no challenge. There's
no reason to change what you've been doing in the past. Adversity is a
great teacher and is a necessary part of the human experience.

Sometimes when a tragedy happens, or things haven't gone as
planned, people get angry with God and become disillusioned with
their spiritual walk. But when you look at the big picture—the enor-
mity of the universe, the immensity of space, and the relatively short
time that we're on the earth—it's all small and insignificant when you
compare it to eternity.

Certainly, life throws some curves. Losing a championship game
might seem like a huge loss. Not getting that big sales contract might
seem like the worst thing ever. Falling short of your annual projections
might seem like an unmitigated disaster. But looking at Scripture is a
great way to get some fresh perspective amid any especially adverse
circumstances.

Anytime I've felt like the odds were stacked against me, or when
I've faced some sort of personal adversity, I'm quickly reminded of the
Apostle Paul and everything he went through while sacrificially serv-
ing as one of the primary leaders of the fledgling Christian Church.

In his own words: *Five times I received at the hands of the Jews the
forty lashes less one. Three times I was beaten with rods. Once I was
stoned. Three times I was shipwrecked; a night and a day I was adrift
at sea; on frequent journeys, in danger from rivers, danger from robbers, danger from my own people, danger from Gentiles, danger in the*

city, danger in the wilderness, danger at sea, danger from false broth-
ers; in toil and hardship, through many a sleepless night, in hunger
and thirst, often without food, in cold and exposure. And, apart from
other things, there is the daily pressure on me of my anxiety for all the
churches. Who is weak, and I am not weak? Who is made to fall, and I
am not indignant? If I must boast, I will boast of the things that show
my weakness. (2 Corinthians 11:24-30/ESV)

Paul persevered through a tremendous amount of hardship and still
managed to spread the faith throughout the known civilized world.
It's hard to imagine how much differently the Bible would have looked
if he had given up and not written those divinely-inspired letters full
of doctrinal teaching, compassionate encouragement, and godly wisdom. Many of those books were written from a prison cell.

In that same letter, Paul talked about a metaphorical thorn in his flesh
that God would not remove to show the importance of exchanging his
weakness for God's strength. It's a difficult scripture for many Christians that don't like the idea of suffering. Who does? But it ultimately
speaks to the power of perseverance through a higher power and not
through human might.

But [God] said to me, "My grace is sufficient for you, for my power
is made perfect in weakness." Therefore I will boast all the more gladly
of my weaknesses, so that the power of Christ may rest upon me. (2
Corinthians 12:9/ESV)

There are some other challenging biblical teachings that at first might
seem counterintuitive to the human spirit but are actually quite encouraging when you take the time to let the truth of the words soak in,
such as this passage from the Apostle Paul.

Count it all joy, my brothers, when you meet trials of various kinds,
for you know that the testing of your faith produces steadfastness. And
let steadfastness have its full effect, that you may be perfect and com-
plete, lacking in nothing. (James 1:2-4/ESV)

Yes, those are difficult words indeed, but what Paul and James are
saying is that adversity isn't meant to destroy us; it's meant to make us
stronger in our faith and our character. Trials are meant to make us rely
more on God and less on ourselves. Tribulations are meant to help us

be stronger for others and have empathy when those under our leadership are suffering and need encouragement.

Paul, James, and the other Apostles and early Christians could go through persecution with such strong faith because many had seen or heard firsthand accounts of how Jesus modeled perseverance in the hours leading up to His death on the cross. The entire ordeal can be read in Matthew 27, Mark 15, Luke 23, and John 19, but here is a brief description of the awful scene:

Jesus was whipped until His muscle and bones were exposed, mocked and spat upon, given a crown of thorns that burrowed deep into his forehead and scalp, forced to carry His own cross, nailed to the cross through his hands and feet, given vinegar to drink instead of water, and positioned in a way that caused excruciating pain with every belabored breath.

Jesus didn't give up, although He had every reason to do so. In fact, He could've easily denied that He was the Messiah and escaped crucifixion. But just a few days earlier, Jesus shared a powerful statement with the disciples about how His sacrifice would empower those who trust and believe in Him to persevere through the most troubling moments of life—even when it might seem as if everyone was against them.

"I have said these things to you, that in me you may have peace. In the world you will have tribulation. But take heart; I have overcome the world." (John 16:33 / ESV)

If Jesus could persevere through those horrific atrocities on our behalf, how can we not persevere through the things we face, which are often much less significant? That's the kind of leadership our world desperately needs; leadership that doesn't shy away from difficulties but pushes through adversity until the job is done.

Better For It

Adversity is part of life. But without that, we don't grow. We will never truly become the leaders that God wants us to be if we don't experience some pain and suffering. Here are some key reminders of how you can persevere through the troubles of life and come out better for it on the other side:

1. Face it. Don't avoid it: Meet adversity head-on, and don't let it stop you from doing what you've been called to do as a leader, parent, community servant, etc. Life is too short to allow disruptions to keep you from your greater purpose.

2. Don't play the blame game: It's easy to fall into the trap of pointing fingers and looking for retribution and revenge, but that always ends up as a fruitless and shallow proposition.

3. Focus on solutions, not the problem: It's okay to recognize and acknowledge difficulties, but spending too much time on them will keep you from working through them and understanding the purpose behind them.

4. See past the problem: It's not easy to look beyond the adversity that is staring you in the face and standing in your way but pause long enough to see the purpose and the benefit in that situation for yourself and others. There is always an opportunity to grow, learn, and help someone else during and at the end of a battle.

5. Don't give up: Quitting gives adversity and those causing it an easy victory. Remember what Christ did on the cross, and know His strength is your strength.

The ultimate goal of life is to have purpose and meaning that honors and reflects well on your relationship with God. Many of those twists and turns that at one time seemed to be real disappointments and failures often turn out to be very helpful in your spiritual walk. Persevering through adversity and pain will undoubtedly will make you a better leader.

In Other Words

With the storybook 60-3 finish in the final five years of Dad's coaching career, it's easy to look past or even forget the years of striving and "nearly-but-not-quite" leading up to the big finish. Over the years throughout Nebraska and beyond, there was ever-building pressure on him to deliver Oklahoma wins, conference championships, and finally, the elusive National Championship.

Over time, some fans, boosters, and media grew restless and increasingly critical when Nebraska struggled to beat Oklahoma. Later, that discontent emanated from the desire to win a National Championship after a few close calls.

When you're part of the family, and you love each other, you feel the pressure too. We all felt the weight of not winning the "big one." We endured it together. It's hard to watch your family member be the target of criticism and scrutiny when you see first-hand the effort and sacrifices being made.

That only intensified in the 90s when a series of issues with some players brought negative attention to the program. In 1994, the national media came after Dad with some pretty harsh coverage, like the ABC ambush interview by "20/20," complete with selective edits and piercing editorials to cast the situation in as dark of a light as possible. They didn't care to understand Dad's sincere heart for helping people through difficult circumstances and instead accused him of self-serving soft treatment of players who had trouble. He was willing to take the heat and not cave into the pressure to cut players loose if he felt they deserved a chance to earn their way back onto the team.

The media looked past the fact that the players who had filled in for the troubled guys were playing at All-American levels. There was no real "need" to help the troubled guys for the sake of wins. My dad's interest was in seeing the guys make their way back and be rewarded for changing their behaviors rather than tossing them aside. Discarding a kid who would otherwise have no chance at a college education, especially when you consider the life they would return to, would not be a whimsical or light-hearted decision. And the message of the gospel was at the base of his decisions, a foundation of second chances and redemptive hope for us all. How can we not offer that to others when we have the opportunity?

The national criticism was so intense. I found it difficult to comprehend how Dad could handle the persistent negativity and scrutiny. I was angry enough to punch anybody that might want to argue about any of the situations going on. Yet my dad always personified the fact that he had a higher calling.

So when I asked him how he could stand it, he would simply tell me it was his faith. Now, I knew that already because those sustaining values had been modeled for us from the beginning. We didn't know anything else. It was like breathing air.

Dad wasn't perfect. No one is. But he has always been Kingdom-minded, and his perspective of faith enables him to endure life's tumultuous times with the same calmness you could see in him on the sidelines. Every morning he gets up, meditates, reads his Bible, and sets his mind for the day, and then he does his best and has the best intentions to obey God and walk out his calling no matter what adversity or opposition he might face. His faith has always given him the ability to persevere.

~ Mike Osborne, Son of Tom Osborne

18

~~~~~~~

EXCELLENCE

THE LEGACY OF TRUE GREATNESS

During my tenure at Nebraska, we played in a few bowl games that were ultimately for the National Championship. One of them was against Miami at the 1984 Orange Bowl. We fell behind 10-0 in the first quarter but managed to come back. At the end of the game, we went for two points and the chance to win even though we could've kicked the extra point and settled for the tie. We failed on the attempt and lost 30-31.

There was some push back from people saying we should have kicked the extra point because we would've been undefeated and still won the title, even with a tie on our record. But I felt that even though we didn't win the National Championship, we played well enough to win.

Ten years later, at the 1994 Orange Bowl, we played against Florida State, which had a great team. By many standards, we outplayed them, but we missed a field goal at the end which would have won the game. We also had a touchdown called back and recovered what appeared to be a Florida State fumble into the end zone but was ruled a touchdown. But as I walked off the field, I felt a certain satisfaction in the fact that we had played at a level where we were as good as or maybe the best team in the country.

Throughout those years, one of the knocks was that we couldn't win the big one. But even in those times we fell short, we played really well against a great opponent. I wasn't driven to distraction by the fact that we had gone a long time without a National Championship. I was always more concerned about our team's effort and attitude throughout the process.

That's what true excellence is all about. Excellence is achieving to the best of one's ability. It's doing everything you can and letting the results take care of themselves. In fact, often, there are extraneous factors that enter into the equation. The economy can shift. A leader can make a poor decision. Chance circumstances can interfere with the final result. You can't always control the outcome, but you can control your effort and dedication to a specific cause.

Faulty Measures

We often equate excellence to the accumulation of wealth, titles, recognition, popularity, influence, etc. But those aren't necessarily accurate measuring sticks. You can have all those things and still not live a life of true excellence. Excellence involves doing your best with the talent and circumstances you have been given.

Some coaches have a .500 season. They lost as many as they won, yet they might have done the best coaching job in the country. But as we all know, that usually isn't how today's world defines excellence.

Not only is excellence not necessarily about material success, excellence is also not perfection. That may be the goal; ideally, you always want to go out and play the perfect game, have the perfect sales week, or raise the perfect child. But that standard is unlikely to happen.

Excellence, however, can be measured with high standards and the belief that occasional or short-term perfection might be achieved. At Nebraska, for instance, we used measures by which we judged our team's performance—offensive numbers, turnovers, kicking game goals, etc. For example, one of our offensive goals was to average six yards per rushing attempt. In order to do this, our offensive linemen had to have good footwork, correct hand placement, and come off the ball aggressively. Receivers had to block down field every play, and the running back had to run hard and get yards after contact. Conversely, one of our defensive goal was to hold opponents to three yards per carry or less. We spelled out what defenders were to do to accomplish this.

Anything perfect is mythical and will likely never be achieved. However it gives you something to shoot for.

Therefore, material success and perfection are often faulty measures of leadership. If you make either of those things the primary goal, you will often be sorely disappointed, exhausted, and ultimately unfulfilled.

A Leader's Call to Excellence

There are two types of excellence that leaders can pursue. The first is personal excellence. Warren Buffett once said, "Invest in yourself." It's an ironic statement from a man who did very well investing in the stock market. You want to make yourself as valuable as you possibly can. That usually involves training and education or, for the athlete, time in the weight room, the playbook, and the practice field.

People often think the football season starts in late August, but it really starts in January in the weight room with conditioning, footwork, and speed drills. Athletes can make amazing physical changes with a sound conditioning regime.

The same should be true for leaders at any level and within any organization. Parents should find ways to better themselves for the benefit of their children. CEOs should find ways to invest in their intellectual and personal well-being to benefit their employees and their company. Coaches should find ways to learn new techniques or schemes for the success of their athletes and their team.

The other side of personal excellence is organizational excellence. A leader should always be asking how their organization is performing. Are individuals performing at a high level, or is there internal turmoil or apathy? A Gallup survey on employee engagement measured the involvement and enthusiasm with their work. Gallup said that 20 percent of employees worldwide are engaged. A 50 percent engagement level would be high. We were pleased to learn that 89 percent of teammates and employees were engaged with their work. When people see value in their work, are given responsibility, and are appreciated, engagement is more likely to result.

In an athletic setting, if players start or have positions of importance on that team and have not performed well in practice, then it's no longer a meritocracy where they performed better than others in their position. That mindset can quickly become contagious. All of a sudden, many people aren't willing to do their part in the weight room or conditioning and don't give great effort in practice.

Motives Matter

A leader's motives for excellence matter, and those motives are directly tied to character. A leader should have a value system. For me, that standard has come largely from my faith. I've certainly not been perfect, but most of my values have come from scripture.

You might be able to fool your employees occasionally, but being able to walk the walk consistently is important. There are other ways to do it, of course. You can be a very strong leader but not necessarily make the world a better place because of how you lead. It's less likely to have true excellence if your motives are impure or you lack integrity.

In my early days of coaching, some schools were violating NCAA rules by handing out extra benefits—cars, clothes, cash, etc. Sometimes those teams performed very well on the field. They had a lot of talent. On the other hand, the coach was teaching those players that the way to success is by cutting corners and breaking the rules. When those players left, they didn't have much of an indoctrination into personal integrity because the role modeling within the institution was built on fabrication and cheating.

True excellence involves integrity. Material success can present a facade of excellence. That might show up in the form of national championships, high stock prices in your company, or great economic benefits.

But if you're trying to measure it in terms of overall human impact and in terms of what you're teaching your employees or your players, true excellence with high standards of integrity and sound motives will set off a ripple effect that will impact each individual and ultimately influence those that they lead in their families and the community.

On the other hand, if it's all about winning at any cost, there's also a ripple effect because you've taught people a skewed way to approach life. As they deal with their families and go on to other endeavors, they will carry that with them. It might provide temporary benefit, but excellence driven solely by material success will often end up being to their detriment.

Building a Culture of Excellence

While core values such as integrity are foundational to true excellence, there are also some very important building blocks that a leader can exercise, model, and teach to create an environment of individual and institutional greatness. Here are three key character traits that I have personally observed to be invaluable to that pursuit:

Building Block One: Work Ethic

Not being located in a heavily populated state (Nebraska has approximately 1.8 million people), it was difficult to find large numbers of highly skilled quality athletes close by. Therefore it became very important for us to develop the talent we had. We were generally acknowledged to be the first university to have a full-time strength coach, and we were also recognized as having the best strength and conditioning program in the country for many years. Since our strength and conditioning program was widely recognized, our strength coach, Boyd Epley, sent over 60 assistants to other major universities and professional teams as head strength and conditioning coaches.

Boyd was a great motivator. He had records for all major weightlifting lifts, vertical jump data, agility drills, and 40-yard dash times posted in our weight room. It became a huge thing when someone broke a record. That athlete would have his record and pictures posted on the wall. We also were credited with having the first full-time nutritionist working with our student-athletes, and soon nutrition became a major emphasis for most major athletic departments.

We had one other factor working for us. Since we were the only major college football program in the state, we had large numbers of quality athletes who were willing to forgo scholarships at smaller colleges in order to walk on. Many of those players grew up wanting to play at Nebraska and were willing to pay a great price to realize their dream.

Many came from farms and small towns and had worked hard all their lives. The work ethic of these players became contagious. When some highly recruited players from other states saw how hard the walk-ons worked, they realized that if they didn't work equally hard, they could be passed up by players who may not have had as much innate ability but would pay a greater price and outwork them.

The walk-ons gave us depth, and many of them also became great players, but their greatest contribution was to the team's culture; it was truly a blue-collar team committed to outworking opponents.

We recruited walk-on players just as hard as we did scholarship players. We visited their high schools, spent time in their homes, and invited them to our home games. As previously mentioned, we saved three to four scholarships each year for walk-ons who proved their ability to contribute significantly.

Walk-ons at Nebraska, unlike many other programs, were treated the same as scholarship players. Most players did not know which of their peers were scholarship players and which were walk-ons. Things like an athlete's hometown, high school reputation, and financial aid status made no difference. Performance and hard work mattered most. And the ones who worked hardest usually had the better performance.

Probably the most memorable walk-on who demonstrated a great work ethic was Isaiah Hipp. He became interested in our program while watching the 1971 "Game of the Century." He borrowed money for a plane ticket and showed up in Lincoln waiting for a chance to play football for us in 1975. His full name was Isaiah Moses Hipp. Our sports information director referred to him by his initials, "I.M.," as in "I'm hip." I thought we should call him Isaiah, but he was fine with either, so most fans remember him by his initials.

He worked hard to earn a scholarship and rushed for 1,301 yards and 10 touchdowns during his junior year. Isaiah's hard work helped him become the most famous walk-on in our history. While he might be the most remembered walk-on, he was not alone. There were so many who followed in his footsteps during the next couple of decades. Jimmy Williams and his brother, Toby, walked on from Washington D.C. and were great players at Nebraska and later in the NFL.

It's not easy to walk-on at any football program. Only an athlete with a strong work ethic can succeed. A strong work ethic was important for the players but equally important for the coaching staff. Due to the lack of population in Nebraska, recruiting was a year-round, non-stop activity. In our recruiting efforts, we had to travel the entire nation, establish a good rapport with high school coaches in many states, evaluate thousands of players on high school films, and visit hundreds of high schools and living rooms across the nation.

We also had to be very thorough in our preparation for our opponents during the season. Our objective was to exhaustively prepare for every possible scenario that could conceivably play out on the upcoming Saturday. Details such as how we could best block a punt, get to the quarterback with a given blitz and block a certain stunt we were apt to see were examined in detail. We came in early, worked late, and usually spent 85 to 90 hours each week preparing for a game. There is no excuse for lack of preparation, and hopefully, our players saw that we were putting in the same effort they were.

Most players left our program with an appreciation for the price everyone paid to have a successful team. Many have commented to me since leaving that this has carried over to their business careers and lives after football.

Building Block Two: Consistency

Leadership fails when people don't know what to expect from the leader. One day he might come into the office, and he's the nicest guy in the world, and the next day he throws a temper tantrum. The employees might never know when they're going to be singled out for criticism just because of the boss's mood.

Leaders need to have their emotions under control and be able to be consistent and authentic day after day. Those being led should know where the leader is coming from and what to expect.

It is always disconcerting to people when their leader is erratic, up one day and down the next, constantly changing goals and plans, and treating people differently depending on how the leader feels. Nearly everyone can recall having a coach or a boss who could be one person one day and almost an entirely different person the next due to a loss or a business setback. Not knowing which person will show up keeps the whole organization on edge.

In order to create an environment of consistency, our coaching staff wrote a mission statement indicating our goals, our core values, and how people would be treated. We reviewed the mission statement at the beginning of each football season, sometimes tweaking it, but for the most part, it stayed pretty much the same. We looked at the mission statement periodically throughout the year to ensure we stayed true to its principles. Even though I was the head coach, I was not solely responsible for the mission statement. In fact, it was a document that was discussed, analyzed, and agreed upon by our entire coaching staff.

According to our mission statement, our players were to be given a place of central importance. We wanted to make sure their education came first, their health was not to be compromised, and we were not to humiliate or denigrate them, but rather we were to teach them as best we could to be good players and build their confidence whenever possible. We were to treat everyone with respect: players, coaches, support staff, the media, and the fans. We were going to be as thorough as possible in preparing for each game. Each opponent was to get our full attention.

We followed nearly the same routine each week, win or lose. We emphasized process over results. The important thing was how we played: displaying sound technique and fundamentals, team unity, exceptional effort, and self-control. We felt that if we did those things well, the final score would take care of itself. We measured performance by how well we played and how close we came to playing a perfect game, not by the final score. There were times we lost but played about as well as we could play; we recognized this with the players and complimented them on their playing at a high level. There were times we won but did not play well, and we expressed concern about the things we did not do well, as those things would eventually trip us up if we didn't address them.

It was also important to maintain a fairly even temperament throughout each game. A coach who is out of control emotionally can't help his team play well. In such cases, the team often mirrors their coach's instability and falls apart as well. The only thing that got me riled up was a lack of effort, as that is something a team is always expected to give. A player might fumble, miss a tackle or drop a pass, but nobody felt worse about the mistake than that player, so I didn't come down on them for those kinds of mistakes. Instead, I tried to encourage them. If the mistake was caused by a lack of proper technique, we would correct the mistake and express confidence in his ability to get things right the next time. Lack of effort, lack of respect for opponents, and lack of self-control were different. These things led to time on the bench.

Contrary to popular belief, games are not won because of a fiery pre-game or half-time speech or ranting and raving on the sideline. They are won by effective practice on Monday, Tuesday, Wednesday, Thursday, and Friday. It also helps if the coaches have their wits about them enough to make proper adjustments during the game itself, and a high level of emotion is often not helpful in making those adjustments.

A coach has to keep his head in the game and constantly anticipate the next move the opponent will make. I believe our players realized the importance of a steady, persistent, thorough approach to the game. Many have said they have used this approach later in their professional lives and with their families.

Building Block Three: Discipline

Tom Landry once said, "To live a disciplined life and to accept that discipline as the will of God—that is the mark of a man."

Discipline is perhaps the most important building block of excellence because it's difficult to maintain a high-capacity work ethic and daily consistency without it. In athletics, for instance, there's the discipline of going to practice every day, lifting weights, taking care of your body, and making sure you can master your assignments. Going to class, study hall, and getting proper nutrition and sleep are crucial. These things take repetition. To quote Vince Lombardi, "Discipline is not a sometime thing; it is an all the time thing!"

As coaches, we had to be willing to put in long hours, from seven in the morning until 10 or 11 at night. Those long hours were spent trying to make sure that all the bases were covered. Every week we had a routine that we went through. There weren't any shortcuts.

Our discipline was measured every week in the fall. We got a report card that was pretty stern. That's how we were evaluated in the eyes of the fans, the press, the trustees, the donors, and the administration. We might have done a great job coaching, but if the final result wasn't there, We weren't going to be around very long.

In my personal life, spiritual discipline involved a time of prayer and time in the scripture, going to church on Sunday, and participation in a weekly Bible study. As mentioned previously, we started our staff meeting each day with a short devotional time.

We were not alone; Bobby Bowden had a similar devotion at Florida State, and Vince Lombardi went to Mass every morning. I am sure that many coaching staffs recognize the importance of spiritual discipline.

True Greatness

Excellence isn't ultimately about what you do (pursuits), how you do it (values), and why you do it (motives). True excellence is about whom you did these things for as a leader. Was it for you, or was it for others? Was it for personal gain, or was it to honor God?

This is what Jesus had to say about excellence and the purpose behind the pursuit of true greatness:

"You are the salt of the earth, but if salt has lost its taste, how shall its saltiness be restored? It is no longer good for anything except to be thrown out and trampled under people's feet. You are the light of the world. A city set on a hill cannot be hidden. Nor do people light a lamp and put it under a basket, but on a stand, and it gives light to all in the house. In the same way, let your light shine before others, so that they may see your good works and give glory to your Father who is in heaven." (Matthew 5:13-16/ESV)

In this teaching, Jesus compares His followers to salt, which is known for adding flavor and for its preserving qualities. That's what excellence does. It improves things and helps get the most out of people and opportunities.

Jesus then compares His followers to light, which is an important aspect of our daily life. Light helps us see things clearly and guides our paths. Again, that's what excellence does. It gives clarity and shows our true purpose.

There are many other wise and relevant biblical teachings about excellence that any leader can glean from, including these inspiring words from Solomon:

Do you see a man skillful in his work? He will stand before kings; he will not stand before obscure men. (Proverbs 22:29 / ESV)

Hundreds of years later, the Apostle Paul, like Jesus, had some counter-cultural things to say that fly in the face of modern society's views of excellence, greatness, and the motives for such pursuits:

Whatever you do, work heartily, as for the Lord and not for men, knowing that from the Lord you will receive the inheritance as your reward. You are serving the Lord Christ. (Colossians 3:23-24 / ESV)

Paul also taught that one of the purposes of excellence is to set a standard for the world and to stave off any false accusations from any that may oppose you:

Show yourself in all respects to be a model of good works, and in your teaching show integrity, dignity, and sound speech that cannot be condemned, so that an opponent may be put to shame, having nothing evil to say about us. (Titus 2:7-8 / ESV)

At the end of the day, while altruism and serving are admirable and good, the most important "who" behind our pursuit of excellence is spiritual. If the goal is to honor God in the way we coach, treat our families, conduct our finances and our business, we will not be far from "the more excellent way."

A Culture of Excellence

Certain things can be done to promote a more excellent culture and working environment in an organization. Here are a few ways you can lead your team in the pursuit of true greatness:

1. Principled leadership: You have to let people know you care but that there are certain standards that they need to uphold. At the same time, you must also model those standards. People can perceive fairly quickly if you're genuine, walking the walk, or simply saying one thing and doing another.

2. Selfless leadership: If you don't want your team to be self-centered, you need to model selfless behavior. That means avoiding the

temptation to use your power or influence for personal aggrandizement or personal awards and achievements.

3. Consistent leadership: An effective leader will practice and model the kind of behavior they want to see in those they are leading. You can't say one thing and do another. You can't act one way today and another way tomorrow. Often, leaders are profane and abusive, this does not lead to confidence and respect for the leader.

4. Work ethic: If you want your team to work hard, you need to put in the hours and the effort so they can see that you're not coasting. The spirit of determination is contagious. It is important to know when to let up also. Before Bob Devaney came to Nebraska, football practices were sometimes as long as four hours. Bob's practices were never more than two hours, and the day before a game was only an hour. Better results were almost immediate.

5. Disciplined leadership: Personal discipline as a leader not only helps you be more effective but also sets the tone and provides an example of what you expect from your team.

Actions should fit the occasion. It makes sense to find out why the official called the penalty and which player caused the flag to be thrown; it is not helpful to throw a tantrum and draw another flag and demonstrate unbridled anger to your players.

6. Purposeful leadership: When we are more concerned about material results, there can sometimes be little to no thought about serving the greater good. But the general thrust of what we're called to do, whether we're running a construction crew, a financial service, a business, or a sports team, is to produce a net result that makes for a better environment and better people.

Ultimately, leadership focused on doing things with excellence is about setting an example for those you lead and those who might be watching from a distance. The best attitude you can have is to enjoy the journey and take satisfaction in your effort and not necessarily obsess over the immediate outcome. Sometimes outcomes depend on factors beyond your control, but consistently working hard, caring about people, and being principle-centered will yield positive results. If your goal is to honor God with what you do and how you do it, you will not miss the mark.

In Other Words

In 1986, Nebraska hosted Oklahoma in a highly anticipated, nationally televised Thanksgiving Day matchup between two of the top teams in the country. It was my senior year, and I knew I would be facing two-time Butkus Award winner Brian Bosworth. As the fullback, my main job was to block the linebacker position, so we would be getting very familiar with each other throughout the game.

All week long, Coach Osborne was suggesting to all the players not to read the newspapers. In the locker room before the game, he gave an encouraging talk saying that he not only believed that OU would not blow us out like many were saying but that we could actually win this game.

"Forget what the newspapers say," he said. "Some OU players say they know our plays, but that doesn't matter. We're gonna run right at 'em. We're gonna run pitches, traps, and isos at them all day long. It's gonna come down to the fourth quarter, but we're gonna put ourselves in a great position at the end of this game to win it."

Usually, I would play two series and then get some rest, but on that day, I played every series and was pretty beat up at the end of the game. OU was the number one defense in the nation, and it was physically the hardest game of my life.

At the end of the third quarter, we were up 17-7 and feeling pretty good about our chances to win the game. But over the last 11 minutes of the fourth quarter, Oklahoma made a comeback and tied the game up, 17-17. Then, with just six seconds remaining, OU kicked a field goal and pushed the Sooners ahead for the first time all day.

It was a gut-wrenching 20-17 loss. Win or lose, I would usually congratulate the linebackers after each game, but I wasn't terribly interested in tracking down Bosworth for one last face-to-face meeting. Instead, I decided to head straight for the locker room.

As I was walking off the field, somebody grabbed my jersey and spun me around. It was Bosworth. He had run almost the length of the field to tell me, "Way to hit out there. Great game."

Bosworth probably didn't expect much out of a no-name fullback like me, but what he didn't know was that we were never too concerned about the names on the opponents' jerseys. Coach Osborne and Coach Solich taught us the fundamentals of the game. We were instilled with the belief that no game was more important than another and excellence wasn't about a result. It was about a state of mind and playing up to our potential and leaving everything on the field.

Once in the locker room, I was exhausted, beat up, and feeling sorry for myself. That is until Coach Osborne walked in. I could tell he had given everything he could to put us in the position to win. We all knew that people would continue talking about how he couldn't beat Barry Switzer and couldn't win the big one.

We were all just waiting to hear what he was going to say. Coach Osborne looked around the completely silent room and, after a few moments, finally spoke: "Okay, fellas, let's take a knee and pray." Then he stood up and told us how proud he was that we'd given it our all, and that is all he had ever asked of us.

That is true excellence. Coach Osborne taught us to work hard. He showed us how to be consistent and disciplined. He modeled that consistency and discipline in how he lived out his life every day around us. And having done those things, Coach Osborne showed us that excellence isn't about material results. It's about giving it all you've got and trusting God for the outcome—win or lose.

~ Ken Kaelin, Nebraska Football Player (1983-86)

When I think about how I operate my business, so much of it is based on Coach Osborne's impact on me. It might surprise some people, but I don't think I ever heard the word "win" come out of his mouth. He never talked about winning. Instead, Coach spoke about the basics of what it takes to be successful.

Before each game, our team would set goals for the three key phases—offense, defense, and special teams. For instance, on special teams, we might want our average start to be on the 40-yard line and the opponent's average start to be on the 20-yard line, which would give us a significant field position advantage. Or we might have the defensive goal of a plus-two advantage in takeaways, or we might need to possess the ball on offense for a certain amount of time per series.

It was focusing on the fundamentals of the game that would help give us the best chance at success, and when we did that, we didn't have to talk about winning.

I often share that same principle with my leadership as we grow as an organization. We don't have to talk about winning. We don't have to talk about making this amount of money or selling this amount of product.

Instead, we talk about practicing our core values of integrity, teamwork, candor, humility, and drive and that we are truly here for a higher purpose. Proverbs 3:27 and 21:21 serve as our guiding principles.

Every month is like a game. When we get to the end of the month, we either win the game or we lose the game. But no matter the outcome, a new game starts the next month, and we continue to give our best effort and stay true to our core values.

There's no doubt that I learned so much of what I apply to my business leadership from Coach Osborne's steady focus on excellence, which ultimately leads to long-lasting and truly meaningful success.

~ Mike Anderson, Owner of Anderson Auto Group, NFL Europe Player (1993), and Nebraska Football Player (1990-93)

Coach Osborne has been an incredible influence on so many from the football program. I have personally been the direct beneficiary of his influence across all aspects of the business world. I wish we had a scorecard on the wealth so many of the Husker athletes have developed through the trust and respect he has had worldwide. Playing for Coach was almost an automatic trigger for anything you needed in life. The way he did everything with excellence rubbed off on us and helped pave the way to success.

My last game was the 1985 Sugar Bowl. I went to shake his hand, say goodbye, and thank him for the four and a half years of hard work and pure personal development. We all learned so many values that helped us outperform the competition.

During my goodbye, Coach asked me about my career plans. I told him I wanted to be a real estate developer. Coach introduced me to Trammell Crow, the world's largest commercial real estate developer. I drove down to Dallas and got my dream job at 22. My career was on a rocket ship. Coach had an unbelievable influence in the real estate world.

Five years later, I wanted to go to graduate school, and Coach wrote all my letters of recommendation. I was accepted into five of the top MBA programs in the world. Coach had an unbelievable influence on the academic world.

After earning my Master of Business Administration at Northwestern in Chicago, I decided I wanted to try Wall Street for a while. Hank Paulsen, who ran the Chicago office for Goldman Sachs, recruited me. He only wanted to talk about my experience with Coach Osborne and the two-point attempt in the Orange Bowl against Miami and Bernie Kosar. I got the job, and Hank became the Chairman of Goldman and U.S. Treasury Secretary under President Bush. Coach had an unbelievable influence on Wall Street.

I know my story is like many other former athletes, and we all have so much gratitude for his influence and how we leveraged our experiences at Nebraska to create significant wins in our personal lives.

Coach Osborne is a wealth creator. I owe him everything for my success, and I'm working on a $25 million donation for Coach's Team-Mates Foundation. It's the least I can do for the success he helped us all achieve.

~ Rod Yates, Owner of Nebraska Crossing Shopping Center, Owner of Fintech Company JUSTDATA, and Nebraska Football Player (1980-84)

From the moment Tom replaced Bob Devaney as head coach, he was under a great deal of pressure. Bob had won multiple National Championships and had a College Football Hall of Fame career. Tom was taking over a position at a school where everyone was used to winning—the players, the coaches, the students, the fans, the sports media, and even college fans around the country.

But Tom had a way of handling the pressure and never showing it. The players and coaches saw him as being full of confidence no matter what was going on or what was being said. Tom knew what he was doing, which fed into his success on the field.

As I was learning the college coaching business under Coach Osborne, it was clear to me that he was about the hardest working person you were going to find. When Tom would join me on the recruiting trail in New Jersey, I was always so concerned—especially at first when I didn't know the area very well. I could end up going in circles pretty easily.

I didn't want to waste any of Tom's time because I knew how precious time was to him and that he was such a hard worker. When I got to my hotel room the night before he arrived, I made sure I knew exactly where we were going the next day. I had it all planned out. Even after making my recruiting calls that evening, I would drive the route to the homes and the schools we would be visiting to ensure I could efficiently get him moving around.

Tom's work ethic stood out, and it caused his assistants and his players to follow suit. It was automatic for him, and maybe it took a little more effort for some of us to get there, but the results were clear. It's not a surprise that he was so successful in winning championships and having the record that he did.

On top of that, Tom also knew the game better than anyone else. I'm convinced he could have coached any position on the field with his brilliant mind, but he always allowed his coaches to do their jobs and never micromanaged from the lead position. In that regard, he was the complete coach, and everyone respected and appreciated him.

But it went beyond his work ethic and his impressive game knowledge. Tom Osborne always was and remains a great human being.

He's a special man. He's got a great heart. And that comes across to people. He was always so well-liked in the coaching business, and that's saying a lot because you're never going to please everyone.

~ Frank Solich, Ohio Head Football Coach (2005-20), Nebraska Head Football Coach (1998-2003), and Nebraska Assistant Football Coach (1979-97)

One of Coach Osborne's most dynamic leadership traits was consistency of message. Every single day, he would get us together before we started group work and preach the importance of having an attitude of doing your best.

Coach always used to tell us something that's stuck with me ever since: "You're either getting better or you're getting worse. There's no such thing as staying the same."

He wasn't saying we had to show huge improvements every day. Even one percent at a time meant something as long as you were moving forward. It was all about attitude, effort, and the discipline to stick to it. That message has impacted my life extraordinarily. It's still the name of the game today—do your best.

This mindset was important when we were working to get over the hump to beat Oklahoma. Coach was 0-2 against the Sooners prior to my freshman year, and we had three more in a row during my first three seasons.

Even when everyone was saying we couldn't win, Coach always gave us the gift of belief, but it wasn't just based on inspirational quotes or platitudes. There was a process in place that started in the summer, continued through fall camp, and manifested during the season.

Coach never told us what we had to do to win. He focused all his energy on what we needed to do to be our best. If we did that, the result would take care of itself. This was the coach's culture of team. It was an attitudinal approach because that was really all we could control, along with our effort. Finally, our push towards individual and collective excellence paid off in 1978 when we got Coach his first win against Oklahoma, ranked No. 1 at the time, in a 17-14 victory at Memorial Stadium in Lincoln. The Sooners were driving the field late in the game when Billy Sims coughed up the ball, and I was able to secure the fumble.

As I moved on in life, it was always great to remember that moment, but the most important thing I took away was understanding what excellence and true success are all about. It's about digging in, pushing through adversity, and giving your best to become the best you can be.

~ Jim Pillen, 41st Governor of Nebraska and
Nebraska Football Player (1975-78)

Leadership is not what people say. It's what they do. It's their actions. Lots of people do a lot of talking, but Coach Osborne made the biggest impact on me because he was willing to pay a bigger price than the other guy.

That was always his quote: "You've got to be willing to pay a bigger price than the other guy." And Coach didn't just talk about it. In terms of effort, preparation, and relational availability, he lived it out every day as Nebraska's head football coach.

We knew Coach Osborne was committed because of his physical presence. He was always here. Coach had a Ford Escort wagon with two fishing poles in the back. He parked out front on the south side of the stadium and was already there when I would get to the facilities around 8 a.m. When we all left in the evening, he would still be there.

Along with his presence, Coach also had an acute attention to detail that showed how much the program mattered to him. He was willing to do whatever it took to put his players and coaches in a position of success. It was all about work ethic, which led to excellence and some fairly significant success.

Ever since I was named Athletic Director here in Lincoln, that's what I've tried to do. It's as if Coach is right here reminding me of that all the time. I can't get it out of my mind. I get up in the morning and ask myself, "Am I willing to pay a bigger price than the next guy?"

~ Trev Alberts, Nebraska Athletic Director, NFL Player (1994-96), and Nebraska Football Player (1990-93)

19

~~~~~~~~

TRANSFORMATION

THE LEGACY OF LASTING CHANGE

F or many leaders, change is a challenging word—especially if things are going well. But the truth is, we should always be going through a process or journey that will take us beyond our limitations, out of our comfort zones, and to growth and new endeavors.

Transformational leadership has produced more positive organizational change than any other type of leadership. However, it is not the most common type of leadership.

The Three Styles of Leadership

Let's take a look at the three basic styles of leadership and discuss their varying degrees of effectiveness:

1. Laissez-faire: This style of leadership is a French term meaning "hands off." The leader doesn't want to make hard decisions or simply doesn't care about the outcomes and people they lead. They are often more concerned about doing what is popular than what is right. Politicians are often told to take a poll and find out what people want to hear. I knew members of Congress who would vote "present" rather than "yea" or "nay" if a difficult vote occurred. Sometimes coaches blame officials and businessmen blame circumstances beyond their control. Laissez-faire leadership reflects a lack of accountability and is more common than one might think.

2. Transactional: This kind of leadership is usually top-down and emphasizes reward and punishment. The leader doesn't necessarily model desired behavior but instead dictates what the behavior should be. It's "do as I say, not as I do." You can accomplish a lot in this leadership style, but there's also tension and fear of failure among followers for not measuring up.

There's often not much collaboration or feeling of mutual respect and love among the team members. There is usually a heavy emphasis on final results and the bottom line, which is usually all that matters. It can be effective for a time but often wears on both the leader and the team members, which questions its long-term effectiveness and sustainability. In military terms, there is often a good deal of collateral damage—people are expendable and are discarded when they are no longer useful.

It is impossible to coach, teach, or run a business without some element of transactional leadership. A coach has to determine who plays and who doesn't, a teacher has a grading system, and an employer has to determine who gets paid more than others. However, there is another style of leadership that differs from transactional leadership in significant ways, which can lead to optimal growth and performance within a team.

3. Transformational: Research has shown that transformational leadership is generally most effective in creating an environment where top performance occurs. Transformational leadership is also often referred to as servant leadership. The leader is not a top-down, authoritarian figure but rather one who serves those who follow. Team members are not pawns on a chessboard whose only purpose is to serve the needs of the leader. Instead, they are of central importance, and the leader seeks to ensure they are cared for, nurtured, and enabled to realize their full potential.

Transformational leadership is principle oriented. Certain core values are emphasized and considered inviolate. Even if a team's chances of winning might be jeopardized if those core values are upheld even if a business is likely to lose money if values are strictly observed, the core principles and values will be maintained. Those values are seen as guidelines, which will lead to greater long-term accomplishment if they are observed. Shortcuts and bending the rules are not tolerated.

A transformational leader leads by example. If long hours are required, the leader works even longer hours. If integrity is a core value, the leader is ethical in his behavior. If things have gone badly for the team or the organization, the leader takes responsibility. If there is personal or financial risk, the leader puts his neck on the line first. The leader does not ask anyone to do anything he himself is not willing to do.

A transformational leader listens, whereas a transactional leader often does a lot of ordering and proclaiming. The type of listening a transformational leader does is empathetic—trying to walk a mile in another's shoes, trying to understand what the person is saying and what that person is feeling and experiencing.

A transformational leader seeks to serve the best interests of those he leads. If a key player wants to transfer to another school for good reasons, and this is in the best interest of that player, the coach does not stand in the way. Suppose a key employee wants to leave the company in order to start his own business. In that case, the transformational leader helps him get started, even if that business might later be a competitor.

Often transformational leadership is seen as soft and incapable of achieving difficult goals.

This is not true. Followers feel that the leader cares about them, listens, and gives them responsibility and ownership. The end result is a culture that is unified and highly productive.

Lastly, a transformational leader focuses on the process and how things are done rather than the outcome.

Transformation Takes Time

I often found that if a player was under performing, the best thing I could do was to listen to him and try to find out what was going on in his life. The transactional approach would have been to demote him, criticize him, or punishing him by running stadium steps.

Since the need to be understood is very powerful, I often found that if a player was going through a difficult time, simply making an effort to understand what he was going through served to improve his outlook and performance. Often, I wasn't able to do anything about his problem, but the player knowing I understood and had taken the time to reach out to him, seemed to make a real difference.

Over time, adherence to principle, maximum effort, sound fundamentals, and focus on the process will more often produce the desired result than an obsession with winning. The longer I coached, the more I understood that transformational leadership principles were better for my players, my coaches, and the game itself.

Transformational leadership is more conducive to allowing leaders to be good mentors.

A leader who takes the time to instill strong discipline and a powerful work ethic in his team will have taught them that good things don't come easily and that achievement comes with a price. And finally, by recognizing that the spiritual side of human nature, that which calls us to the best and highest within us, is important and needs to be nurtured just as much as physical and mental preparation, a transformational leader can add a dimension of meaning and purpose which will last a lifetime.

The Power of Redemption

I've always believed that no one was beyond redemption. I had a former player who had been in prison three times. I had heard that he was struggling, so I wrote him a note and told him I still believed in him and cared about him. It was very simple, three or four sentences. But it hit at the right time. He had planned that day to attack one of the guards that had been harassing him, which meant he would've probably been in prison for many more years.

Instead, he got down on his knees and decided to turn things over to God. Since then, he's lived a very productive life and has become a full-time drug counselor, which is an incredible turn of events because illicit drugs had been a real problem for him.

That's why I don't think you can ever completely give up on anybody. Sometimes I got criticized for that, but if I knew a player's background, where he came from, and the things he'd gone through, I would certainly discipline him, but I didn't want to throw a person away.

Sadly, there's a great tendency today to discard people and ruin their lives over their mistakes, but that's not consistent with the scriptures and should never be the knee-jerk reaction of a transformational leader.

Radical Change

As mentioned before, true transformation starts on the inside and works its way to the outside and into a leader's everyday life. This is undoubtedly consistent with biblical teachings on the subject. The reason I believe spiritual transformation is most important is that it impacts all other areas of life— physical, mental, intellectual, emotional, relational, and financial.

For the Christian, transformation comes from recognition of sin and brokenness, belief in the sovereignty of God, confession of Christ as Savior and Lord, denial of self, and commitment to accept His calling and obey His commands.

Jesus came to be a transformational servant leader. He led by example, He loved His followers, He laid out core values, and He died on a cross, putting others ahead of Himself.

Many people were changed forever because of their encounters with him: Mary Magdalene, Zacchaeus, Bartimaeus, the Samaritan woman, the paralytic at the Pool of Bethesda, Nicodemus, Lazarus, and the Roman Centurion, to name a few listed in the Bible and not to mention the countless others not mentioned.

Of course, Jesus' disciples were also among those who went through a transformation because of their time spent with Him. Even though many were impacted instantly, it took three years of traveling with Jesus for them to be genuinely transformed. And they didn't see a complete change in their lives until after Jesus was crucified. That wouldn't take place until the events of Acts 2, where the Holy Spirit empowered them and other close followers of Christ to boldly witness to the Jews gathered in Jerusalem for the Feast of Pentecost.

Peter was one of the most powerful examples of transformation. During Jesus' ministry, he was impetuous, irritable, overly emotional, and was always asking questions. But Peter's transformation allowed him to oversee one of the most significant evangelistic events in the Church's history.

Later on in Acts 9, the most radical transformation recorded in the Bible took place when a religious zealot named Paul (also known as Saul) was traveling to Damascus on a mission to hunt down, imprison, and, if the situation warranted, kill members of the rapidly growing Christian faith. But light from Heaven blinded him, and Jesus spoke to him with an opportunity to turn from his evil ways and become an apostle of the gospel.

Paul later wrote many New Testament books in the form of letters to various churches in the region. His inspired doctrinal teachings have been read, taught, and shared globally to millions, perhaps billions, since then. Paul had a first-hand experience with transformation, which showed up in this encouraging verse:

Therefore, if anyone is in Christ, he is a new creation. The old has passed away; behold, the new has come. (2 Corinthians 5:17/ESV)

Paul also taught that transformation continues when we make a conscious effort to turn away from the world and turn toward God's ways:

Do not be conformed to this world, but be transformed by the renewal of your mind, that by testing, you may discern what is the will of God, what is good and acceptable and perfect. (Romans 12:2/ESV)

And finally, he laid out how spiritual transformation should change our thoughts, our actions, our motives, and our desires:

But now you must put them all away: anger, wrath, malice, slander, and obscene talk from your mouth. Do not lie to one another, seeing that you have put off the old self with its practices and have put on the new self, which is being renewed in knowledge after the image of its creator. (Colossians 3:8-10/ESV)

When a leader goes through a significant transformation, employees, team members, staff, etc., will notice the difference and be attracted to the positive change. That's the point. Not only is transformation necessary for the leader, but it's also beneficial for the organization and those within it.

As previously mentioned, our football staff had a voluntary short devotional to begin each day. I asked my congressional staff in Washington if they would want to do something similar, and they rejected the idea—interesting contrast.

Lasting Change

Servant leaders are rare. Not only can they get things done, but they also cause a ripple effect that influences followers' lives, which, in turn, impacts the families and acquaintances of those followers.

With that in mind, here are some ways a transformational leader can start down that path and encourage others to follow:

1. Be willing to sacrifice self-interest for the good of the group.

2. Be willing to listen empathetically to understand followers.

3. Be a role model for others and exemplify qualities that followers admire.

4. Be able to communicate and inspire others toward a shared vision.

5. Engage in actions that are rooted in principles and values rather than in external rewards.

6. Encourage growth and increased responsibilities in followers.

7. Have the organization serve others and be a constructive force in society.

8. Have exceptional awareness and vision, and be able to anticipate future trends and events.

9. Exemplify balance by being not just an inspirational or emotional leader but also a spiritual leader.

Being a transformational leader requires that one be a person of good character. Honesty, integrity, generosity, and a sense of fair play are all attributes associated with people of good character.

Unfortunately, society does not always reward those who display the qualities listed above; instead, they choose leaders who project power, promise material benefits, and are charismatic without a conscience. The result is often a good deal of pain, suffering, and disillusionment.

In Other Words

A few years ago, I sent this letter to Coach Osborne that sums up how his transformative leadership played an influential role in the life that I now enjoy:

Hey Coach, I hope this finds you, Nancy, and your family safe and well.

I saw your note to the Football Letterman's Association and thought I would send you a few thoughts as my time as a student-athlete there at Nebraska has proven to be exceptionally beneficial throughout my whole life, both personally and professionally.

Balance: This is one of my favorite words, which I feel is very important in life. While there was an overarching culture of winning, I'm certain that none of us ever felt it was "win at all costs." As athletes, you encouraged and provided tools to ensure that we were more than just good athletes but good people, husbands, citizens, and parents. You taught us that success in any one field isn't a zero-sum game. We could excel at many things at the same time.

Adapt: Just as football games don't always go as planned, neither does life, but you ensured that we were always prepared and accepted change. We were never victims. You taught us that preparation brought confidence. When faced with conflict or controversy, we simply needed to adjust quickly and audible to something more favorable. This has become a big asset for my teams and me professionally—a solutions mindset that says time is better spent solving problems instead of just identifying and complaining about them.

Lifelong Learning: Our games taught me never to give up and to learn from what we experienced. In every meeting and every film session, you showed us how to do more than just look at or feel something but to actually see it, understand it, and then take action. Regardless if it was something we needed to correct, something our opponent was doing, or just circumstances we encountered, your leadership taught us to use our experiences to grow and improve. Your ability to see what we faced and adjust quickly was amazing. Whether after a series or during halftime, we adjusted to what we were given.

Team/Alignment: I tell people often that I don't know what it is like to do something by myself. I have always been part of a team where everyone relies on others to achieve extraordinary results. You taught us that and drove that into us every day. I have always loved the sense of family that we had as a team. All of us, from many different backgrounds and learned experiences, coming together as one unit—diversity and inclusion at its very best, everyone bringing his unique skills and talents to bear. While we were talented as a team, it was this unity that I think distinguished us from others. You created a culture where we cared for one another, worked for one another, and we never wanted to let each other down. We truly were our brother's keeper. Best of all, whether a starter or a redshirt, every one of us felt that what we did mattered. We all contributed to our success. This drove a culture of excellence that I have tried to emulate personally and professionally.

Consistency: Wind sprints, weights, film sessions, QB Test, or practice, you pushed us to be the best that we could possibly be. Your instructions were always based on well-defined standards (best didn't change every week), and we understood it was never the highs and lows that would define our success but how consistent we were in executing those high standards you set for us. Whether we were ahead or behind, playing a great team or a poor team, first quarter or fourth quarter, we were evaluated against those standards. You expected nothing but the best from us no matter what the conditions. As Simon Sinek said, "Consistency counts much more than intensity in all we do."

As a husband, father, and CEO of a construction company, I've applied all these life lessons in my life and my leadership: competency, capacity, character, and consistency—four "Cs" taught and reinforced by your program.

Truly, there is no place like Nebraska.

~ Tom Sorely, President/CEO of Rosendric Electric and Nebraska Football Player (1974-79)

My son Brook was a big hunter. One day Brook went to the football department to ask permission to hunt on Coach Osborne's land. He found Tom in the weight room, and he was happy to write the note, which Brook stuck in the breast pocket of his shirt.

When Brook was leaving, one of the coaches stopped him and started a conversation. The coach noticed the paper sticking out of his pocket and grabbed it. "What is this? Your girlfriend's phone number?" The coach opened the note and read it. He looked at Brook and said, "I've been here for eight years, and I haven't gotten one of those yet!" Brook snatched the note from the coach, stuck it back in his pocket, and ran out of there.

I think that's one example of the camaraderie that developed between Brook and Coach Osborne. They had similar interests outside of football. They both liked the outdoors—hunting, fishing, flying, etc. Brook had tremendous respect for Coach Osborne. As Brook's coach and role model, he influenced Brook in so many ways besides football.

It would be impossible to know just how far-reaching Coach Osborne's impact has made in the lives of his players. That impact has traveled from his players to countless others that they have influenced. It's a beautiful thing to have role models who stand for everything that is right and good.

For Brook, those role models were Coach Osborne, Ron Brown, and Turner Gill, among others. But it was his father who instilled those core values that Brook embraced at an early age. The short time that Brook and his sisters had with their father before his battle with cancer ended when he was seven years old was instrumental in the development of traditional family values. There are so many things in our society that can pull young people away from those values. But Brook was known for his solid character because those values were strengthened throughout the years—including his formative time at Nebraska with Coach Osborne.

For instance, one thing Brook was able to do at Nebraska was keep football in perspective. Football was very important to him, but it didn't consume him. Like Coach Osborne, he had other interests that helped take away some of the pressure. He worked very hard and was always prepared because he wanted to be ready when he got an opportunity. But football wasn't more important than his family or his faith.

On the day of Brook's accident, he was supposed to speak at an FCA banquet in Lincoln. There was a lot of talk about how to handle the situation, but ultimately it was decided that Brook would want the event to continue. Of course, the tone of that gathering changed dramatically due to the circumstances.

Brook's funeral was broadcast on the radio to thousands of grieving Husker fans. Ron Brown presented the gospel and there were reports of many both at the event and through that broadcast that confessed Christ as their Lord and Savior. Just as God has used Coach Osborne to transform the lives of many, Brook included, He has also seen fit to use Brook and his testimony to transform the lives of others as well.

~ Jan Berringer, Mother of Brook Berringer

20

CHAPTER TWENTY

~~~~~~~

SUCCESS

THE LEGACY OF ETERNAL IMPACT

When I was at the University of Nebraska, there were some old trophy cases that I would occasionally walk past. Sometimes I would stop and look at those remnants of athletic accomplishment. Some of those trophies went back to the 1920s and 1930s. I was struck by the fact that I really didn't know those people, and those trophies sitting there with the passage of time had grown rather dim.

Nebraska had some pretty good football teams back then, but I don't remember those teams or those coaches. And I'm pretty old. That's how it will be for me and the players I coached one day. There will come a time, probably not too many years from now, when our achievements will become distant memories and maybe not even remembered at all.

That's the funny thing about success, that is the world's definition. You have it one day, and the next day it could be gone. Thankfully, I learned about a different kind of success that defies what modern culture has made it out to be.

I believe that success is simply getting the most out of the abilities you've been given, helping other people, and honoring God in the process. A successful life is one where you meet your responsibilities, maintain healthy relationships, and ensure those under your leadership are cared for and guided down the right path.

But success is even more than that. It's not just a here-and-now proposition. It's a here and forevermore reality. True success leaves a legacy of eternal impact.

The Daily Measure

Success often comes from daily sacrifices and doing the right thing for others. And sometimes, it's simply about routine and consistency. Throughout my professional career, I would often write down a list of things I felt needed to be accomplished in a day. If, at the end of the day, I had gotten all or most of those things finished, then I felt it was a good day.

In coaching, daily success was wrapped up in getting ready for the next game. We usually had five days to prepare. The short-term measure of success in that instance would be how well the team played. Early on, the measure was whether or not we won, but as time went on, I could detach myself from the absolute final score and focused more on how we played. Sometimes we could win a game rather handily yet not play particularly well. On the other hand, we played some games about as well as we could and didn't win.

Daily success will look different for leadership positions and professional fields of work, but other measurements can be linked to healthy relationships. If you had an unpleasant experience with somebody important to you, no matter how many items you check off your list, you probably won't feel good about the day.

However, an accomplished day with relatively positive human interaction can lead to peace of mind and the feeling of contentment with knowing that you were productive, helpful to others, consistent, and that you furthered key objectives.

A Firm Foundation

Long-term success can be hard to define. But now that I'm older, I see it through the lens of the things that matter most. I'm thankful that my children have turned out to be solid, productive individuals. They have been sources of personal satisfaction. If that had not been the case, I may have felt like a failure in that area. In that regard, our relationships have a lot to do with long-term success.

As a retired coach, I can look back and see that things didn't always go smoothly, and we didn't win every game. But overall, I hope the general experience, the body of work, and the things the players took away from their time here were beneficial. If I had to do it over again, there would certainly be minor things I might tweak, but I don't feel I totally damaged the players and coaches I worked with.

Long-term success means that you built a firm foundation within a team, business, family, church, non-profit, etc., allowing that organization to thrive and grow after you're gone. The goal is to leave something better than when you started or took it over. I hope that was the case throughout my life.

Another sign of long-term success is maintaining good relationships with most of your players, employees, or team members years after they're gone. That should be irrespective of the number of wins and losses, financial success, or public accolades and achievements. That's when you can feel like it was worth doing and was truly successful.

Collateral Damage

When I took over as head coach in 1973, I was following some good years of Nebraska football. We had won National Championships in 1970 and 1971 and, in 1972, had finished 9-2-1, including a sound defeat of Notre Dame in the Orange Bowl. That was Bob Devaney's last game. So the bar was set pretty high. I knew I wouldn't survive if we didn't win quite a few games.

We competed against a few teams with no regard for recruiting rules, creating an uneven playing field. Still, we were expected to win, so the pressure was on.

We did not deliberately break any rules, but there were so many that avoiding a transgression by mistake was hard.

I recall an incident in which Vince Ferragamo transferred to Nebraska. Vince was a great quarterback and was highly recruited. Since he had transferred, he was not eligible to play in a game for one year. We went to a bowl game that year and took Vince along as we did other team members who weren't going to play. Since Vince was not eligible to play because of the transfer, it was not permissible for us to take him on the trip. I was unaware of the rule, but ignorance is not a justification.

The NCAA infractions committee decide to make Vince ineligible for one game the following season. I told the committee that the mistake was mine, not Vince's, and if anyone was to be punished, it should be me. The committee stuck with its original ruling even though it was unfair to Vince.

I relate this incident to let readers know that we were not perfect, but there were many rules, and we did our best to keep them—it was a challenge.

From an interpersonal standpoint, a coach might win a lot of games. Still, there also might be unintended consequences if the players didn't benefit from their time in that organization or if people around the leadership felt as though they were treated poorly or unfairly.

Far too many coaches leave the profession having fostered some unhealthy relationships. There are players who finish their careers feeling like they've been used and abused. I'm sure that some among the 2,000-plus players I coached may feel that way; hopefully, they would be the exception.

To take a broader view, an owner or CEO may have had a profitable bottom line in a business, but if they didn't serve others and behave ethically, I don't think you could say that they were truly successful. For example, suppose someone is involved in the gambling industry and builds a casino that makes a lot of money; it's hard to claim true success when many people end their lives in shambles because of gambling addiction and ruined finances, which affects them and their families.

Demands of the Job

There is an inherent tension for leaders who want to focus on true long-term success but also have a responsibility to their superiors, their team members, and, as financial providers, to their families. It's that sense of urgency that comes from the demands of the job.

In business, you need to make a profit because if you don't, pretty soon, people will lose their jobs, and the banks won't give you loans. In athletics, you won't be able to coach if you haven't been fairly successful on the field. There's always that tightrope of performance you must walk while fulfilling worldly demands.

But again, the number one thing is that those you lead are valued, cared for, and treated in ways that produce growth and maintain a proper value system. How you treat people and how you go about your business should be consistent with what our faith requires.

Unfortunately, being human, none of us are where we should be in every aspect of our lives, but with God's help, we can come as close as possible. He is merciful, and He looks at your heart, and there's forgiveness when we fail. But you can't win every battle.

Losing It All

Our society has long had a wrong view of success. The overwhelming message is that achievement is for material success and self-glorification. But we also see many miserable people who have everything and yet have nothing at all.

Accolades are nice. Financial prosperity is welcomed. But in the final analysis, material things are not the true measure of a successful life. So, what does scripture say about success?

Two interesting biblical examples provide a sharp contrast on the topic of success, one from the Old Testament and one from the New Testament:

• Solomon: The heir to King David's throne, Solomon had great worldly success and access to more female companionship than any man should ever desire. God had granted him immense wisdom (in the Book of Proverbs), leading to his kingdom's exponential growth. Still, he was miserable toward the end of his life. He wrote many poignant, if not depressing, verses in the Book of Ecclesiastes about how meaningless life is when spent pursuing material wealth.

• Paul: Born into privilege and influence, Paul was a very hard charger willing to put forth great effort. He started out seeing how many Christians he could do in. And then everything shifted after his experience on the road to Damascus. He walked away from a relatively comfortable lifestyle for the sake of the gospel. Despite all the hardships he endured, Paul just kept coming. He experienced a great deal of rejection and physical damage, yet he had a tremendous impact.

Like 10 of the original 12 disciples, Paul died a martyr for spreading the Gospel of Jesus Christ. In the world's eyes, dying for a fledgling cause that seemed to have all the odds stacked against it wouldn't be a good example of success or winning. But because of their work, the Christian church was galvanized. The Christian faith grew from something that was almost a tiny seed, and now there are nearly 2.5 billion

Christians around the world. That was all done with a price. The level of commitment was remarkable.

Jesus was the inspiration for that commitment. He came to show us the true definition of success and the dangers of pursuing worldly success.

True success is being willing to lose everything for eternal reward. It is embedded in the belief that only what is done for God will last and that there is another life to come that will be far greater than anything known to humankind.

For this world is not our home; we are looking forward to our everlasting home in heaven. (Hebrews 13:14/TLB)

Legacy is about planting spiritual seeds. It leaves people with the truth of what purpose is all about. And the ultimate life of success is hearing God say, "Well done, my good and faithful servant."

Eternal Impact

I don't know that God is fully concerned about whether you won or lost a particular game, whether or not your business was the top earner in your field, or whether or not your church had the biggest attendance and served the most people. I think He is more concerned with the process and the procedures and how you relate to people.

Are the people you're leading better off for being under your leadership and your program, or are they worse off? Did they see a consistent faith through your words and actions, or were you hypocritical, self-serving, and lacking in moral character? Those are the things that are important in the long term. Those are the things that have a lasting, eternal impact and are, in my estimation, the measure of true success.

The final analysis isn't the trophies, the rings, the watches, and all the material things we think are so important. None of those things add up to anything of great significance. The older I get, the more I can see that truth. I'm not disappointed that we didn't win more National Championships, although I certainly would not have turned them down if they had come our way.

I want to end by relating a story about a successful life that was lived long ago and was probably not seen as highly successful then.

My dad always signed important papers as Charles C. Osborne. I asked him what the C stood for, and he would never tell me. I learned from an uncle that the C stood for "Currens." Some research indicated that Reverend Currens was an itinerant preacher who had ridden in a horse and buggy, starting churches in Western Nebraska, Eastern Wyoming, and Western South Dakota. He is credited with starting more than sixty churches in the 1880s and 1890s in that newly settled region.

On one occasion, Currens attended an event where Tom Osborne, my grandfather, spoke. He was still in elementary school but impressed Currens with his speech. Currens complimented my grandfather and told him that he thought my grandfather could be a fine preacher. Every time he went through that little town, Bayard, Nebraska, he would visit with my grandfather and encourage him to consider the ministry. He became my grandfather's mentor.

My grandfather graduated from the seventh grade, the last year of schooling in Bayard. Nearly all young people went to work after the seventh grade in those frontier towns. Currens encouraged my grandfather to continue his education at Crawford Normal, located one hundred miles away in the northwest corner of Nebraska. Very few people in Western Nebraska went on to high school. However, my grandfather went to Crawford Normal. Whenever Currens was near Crawford, he would visit my grandfather and encourage him to think about going to Hastings College to prepare for the ministry.

Because of Currens, my grandfather enrolled at Hastings. He would go to college for a year, then work for a year as an irrigation ditch rider or sheepherder to have enough money to pay for school., He was the football team captain, and married my grandmother. They graduated together and were one-half of the graduating class of four in 1900.

My grandfather went into the ministry, served many churches in Western Nebraska, and served in the Nebraska State Legislature. When his first son, my dad, was born, he named him after Currens. My grandfather realized that without Currens' influence, he would have ended his education after seventh grade and never gone to high school, college, or into the ministry.

So why do I write this story at the end of a chapter dedicated to "Success?"

Was Currens a success? He made little money and traveled many lonely miles riding in a horse-drawn buggy. He received little recognition and was undoubtedly not famous, yet a baby born on a homestead in Western Nebraska was given his name. The sixty churches he started were often the first and only churches in those small towns. Currens mentored my grandfather and many others.

He spread the Gospel in an area where it had not been preached, only sporadically, inspiring many to become people of faith, like my grandfather.

He started a ripple effect in my grandfather's family as all five of his children graduated from Hastings College during the Great Depression and lived lives of service.

Currens also impacted my life as I always looked up to my grandfather and hoped I would measure up to his faith and example.

The influence does not stop there, as I am certain that my children would not have become who they are had it not been for Currens.

So, again, was Currens a success? In a worldly sense, probably not, but measured in terms of transforming lives, the answer is undoubtedly yes. There are thousands of people living in that Western region whose lives are different because of a man they likely had never heard of. It is hard to determine impact and success unless it is examined through the lens of time.

Currens was to Western Nebraska, South Dakota, and Wyoming as the Apostle Paul was to most of the Roman Empire. The influence of Currens and Paul rippled down through generations. We are called, in our own way, to do the same.

In Other Words

I didn't usually go into the locker room when Tom gave his pregame speech to the team. But one day during the 1977 season, I decided to experience what a Coach Osborne motivational talk was about—and it was like nothing I'd ever heard.

"We don't have to win this game," he said.

That took me back a little bit. I wondered, "So what am I doing here?" Then he continued: "What we do have to do is play as hard as we can on each play. If we do that, the score will take care of itself. Should we lose, you have nothing to be ashamed of, we got beat by a better team."

When you think about it, that almost makes too much sense, but that made Tom different from so many coaches. He emphasized effort over results. He placed a higher value on the process than the outcome. And in the end, Coach Osborne knew that true success was a lot bigger than anything that happened on the playing field.

~ Charlie McBride, Nebraska Defensive Coordinator (1982-99) and Nebraska Football Assistant (1977-81)

My dad's success as a leader emanates from the simple decision to be obedient to the calling of his faith. Everything else unfolded from there. It all goes back to when he found himself at the foot of the Cross and accepted Christ at age 20.

So, when winning seasons and bowl games weren't enough for the media and some of the fans, Dad didn't change his view of success, and he certainly didn't change his approach to his life in general, which was doing things the right way and trusting God for the right outcomes.

A powerful and somewhat counter-cultural example of Dad's perspective of success can be found in his approach to material wealth. There are many references in the Bible about serving God or serving money. Although Dad was well compensated, he could have made a lot more money than he did. He always held to the principle that the football coach should never make more money than the highest-paid academic position at the school. So he refused to take a raise beyond that. When he retired, Bill Byrne, the Athletic Director at the time, offered Dad an annual payment based on his final salary, but he declined.

Dad understood that everything in this life is short-lived and that there's a greater future beyond the here and now. We should be more concerned about eternity in Heaven than the temporary things we can gain here on Earth. Dad was comfortable with the idea that success has more to do with doing your best and your motivations than the results. As long as you've given a sincere effort, done your best, and had pure intentions, what more can anyone ask?

That's the Christian perspective. God sees the heart even when people don't. My dad's life is indicative of a person whose motivation is a concern for what God wants from us and for us. Nothing more.

~ Mike Osborne, Son of Tom Osborne

Contributor's Index

Chad Bonham is CEO and co-founder of 51 West Entertainment and has been working as a creative media specialist for 33 years. Chad has authored or co-authored more than 40 books, including *Husker Legacy, 3D Coach, Sports Parables, Faith In The Fast Lane, Life In The Fairway,* and Kingdom Sports' *Doing Sports God's Way* series. Chad is also a producer and filmmaker who has worked on six documentaries along with several screenplays and film treatments. He serves on the Board of his wife Amy's non-profit, A Special Purpose, which benefits families caring for special needs kids.

BIBLE STUDY
EDITION

Chapter 1 - ACCOUNTABILITY

1. In this chapter, Coach Osborne shares a story about his first experience with accountability. Can you recall a time early in your life when you were first held accountable for your actions?

2. Who are some of the people you have been and are currently accountable to, and how has that impacted your life?

3. Has there been a time when you lacked accountability in an area of your life? If so, what were some of the long-term consequences you eventually faced?

4. How have you found accountability to be helpful in keeping you on the right path?

5. In what ways do you believe a greater sense of accountability would be helpful for today's leaders?

6. What are your thoughts on the concept of submission to authority? Is this something you've found easy or difficult to do in various stages of your life?

7. Read Matthew 25:14-30. How does this parable speak to you and your current state of accountability?

8. Read James 5:16 and Hebrews 13:17. How do those passages challenge you regarding communal and spiritual accountability?

9. Read 2 Corinthians 5:10. What weight or heaviness of responsibility to your actions do you feel when you read this passage? Explain.

10. Of the items listed to help you lead with greater accountability, which ones have you struggled to implement and maintain? What must you do to follow those suggestions and become a leader who understands being accountable to God, others, and yourself?

Chapter 2 - PRIORITIES

1. How would you define priorities and why every leader should have them?

2. What are some of your current priorities as a leader at work, at home, in church, and in the community?

3. How important of a priority is physical discipline? What are some specific ways you order that area of your life?

4. How important of a priority is intellectual discipline? What are some specific ways you order that area of your life?

5. How important of a priority is spiritual discipline? What are some specific ways you order that area of your life?

6. Considering your responsibilities to God, your job, and yourself, what are you doing to keep your family on your priority list? What are some challenges that work against your efforts in that area of your life?

7. Think back to a time when you weren't good with priorities versus a time when you were. Compare and contrast what your life looked like (health, finances, spiritual walk, etc.) in those two seasons (e.g., order vs. disorder, peace vs. chaos, etc.).

8. Read through the scriptures on various aspects of priorities. Which ones do you find to be the most challenging? Explain.

9. If you're struggling with priorities (making them and keeping them), what can you start doing today to help you get back on track?

10. If you're not struggling with priorities, what can you do to ensure you stay on track and not get distracted away from what's truly important in life?

Chapter 3 - STRATEGY

1. How important is the concept of strategy as a leader, and why?

2. What does short-term strategy or planning usually look like for you?

3. How much does long-term strategy play into your preparation and planning?

4. Where do you usually get inspiration for short-term and long-term strategies?

5. What are the solid foundations necessary for short-term and long-term strategies?

6. What factors may cause you to consider tweaking or changing your strategy? Has this happened to you in the past, and if so, what was the outcome of your decision to either stick with the plan or reverse course?

7. How often do you consider looking to the Bible or going to prayer as you devise your leadership plans? If you have done that, does it help? If you haven't done that, what has kept you from implementing spiritual guidance when putting together your strategies?

8. Read through the scriptures given that discuss biblical approaches to strategy. Which of those have you tried, and how did they impact your planning? Which of those have you not tried, and how might following their instructions make a difference?

9. Read Ephesians 2:10. What does that passage say about the importance of preparation and planning within your leadership role?

10. Read through the five key elements of strategy. Which of those concepts have you struggled with as a leader, and how might consistently applying them to your preparation and planning help you improve your short-term and long-term strategies?

Chapter 4 - VALUES and VISION

1. How often do you reflect upon or evaluate the foundational beliefs that create the basis for your leadership model?

2. What would you say are some of your core values?

3. Where and how did you learn those values?

4. What are some of your core values that have come under attack or that perhaps you've even questioned at times? How did those challenges impact your ability to remain consistent and firm in your leadership?

5. Read Matthew 7:24-27. In what ways can you relate to that parable?

6. As a leader, how often do you think about the importance of vision (having a long-term goal, seeing the big picture, etc.)?

7. Read Proverbs 29:19. What is your interpretation of that passage? How have you seen that play out in your life or those around you?

8. Do you ever think about the end of your life and the impact you hope to have made as a leader? If so, how does that impact how you approach your daily life? If not, how do you think beginning with the end in mind might change the way you are currently approaching your leadership?

9. How do you think values and vision work together? What are some things that can happen when they aren't fully aligned?

10. What are some things you can begin doing today to help you better define your values and ensure they match your vision for the future?

Chapter 5 - LOVE

1. What are your initial thoughts about the phrase "leading with love?"

2. How often do you think about what spiritual, emotional, physical, and material outcomes you want to see in the lives of those you lead?

3. Read John 15:13 and Romans 5:8. True love requires selflessness and, sometimes, great sacrifice. What are some areas of your leadership where you could improve on being more selfless?

4. Is positive affirmation usually easy or difficult for you to give others? Explain.

5. How can you intentionally affirm those under your leadership?

6. Read 1 Corinthians 13:4-7. How would you define unconditional love in the context of leadership?

7. What might tough love look like in your specific role as a leader?

8. How might you need to speak truth in love to those you lead?

9. What might you expect to change in your relationship with those you lead as you begin leading more holistically with selfless, sacrificial, affirming, and truth-based love?

10. What are some specific ways you can begin to allow love to dictate your actions, decisions, interactions, and motives?

Chapter 6 - INTEGRITY

1. In this chapter, Coach Osborne talks about his earliest exposure to integrity through his parents. Who are some people that have demonstrated integrity in your life?

2. How did those examples of integrity impact how you lead today?

3. What has been one of the more difficult instances where your integrity was tested? How did you respond, and what was the result of your actions?

4. Can you think of a time when acting with integrity cost you something? Do you feel like you were ultimately rewarded in the long run, or do you think your integrity still puts you at a disadvantage?

5. Is integrity ultimately worth it in every situation? Explain.

6. When has someone been dishonest to you or shown a lack of integrity in some other way? How did you deal with that experience? How did it impact your commitment to maintain your integrity within your relationships?

7. What stands out the most when you read about how Jesus showed integrity? How difficult would it be to live with integrity if you knew your life was on the line?

8. Take some time to read, ponder, and discuss the following passages: Proverbs 10:9, Proverbs 11:3, Proverbs 28:6, Luke 16:10, and 2 Corinthians 4:2.

9. What are some areas of your life where you could improve your integrity? What steps can you take today toward that effort?

10. How can you fight the temptation to be dishonest or cut corners in a way that would undermine your character and integrity? What steps can you take today toward that effort?

Chapter 7 - HUMILITY

1. What is your definition of the word "humility?"

2. Who has modeled humility to you, and what impact did it have?

3. Is humility something you have found to be an easy or difficult character trait to exhibit as a leader? Explain. What are some things that make humility challenging?

4. What circumstances have humbled you, and how did that change how you approached leadership moving forward?

5. How have you tried to model humility for those you lead? What have been the challenges to making those gestures of humility authentic and consistent?

6. Read Matthew 16:24-25. Which of the three parts of this passage is most difficult (denying self, picking up the cross, or following Jesus)? Explain.

7. Read Matthew 10:35-45. What aspect of this story stands out most regarding the battle between humility and pride? How does it speak to your current approach to leadership?

8. Read Philippians 2:3-8. How does this powerful passage about Jesus' humility challenge you to be a more humble and selfless leader?

9. Read Romans 12:3. How do you interpret this passage, and how might you apply it to your life?

10. Read over the five keys to leading with humility. Which ones are you currently struggling to implement? How might applying those principles change the way you lead?

Chapter 8 - PATIENCE

1. On a scale of 1 to 10 (1 being not patient at all, 10 being extremely patient), how would you rate your patience as a leader? Are you more patient in some situations but not as patient in others? Explain.

2. What are some things in your leadership role that try your patience and why?

3. Who are some people that have modeled patience for you? What specific things have you learned from them that have helped you be a more patient leader?

4. What does "impatience wants next, but patience wants best" mean to you personally?

5. Can you think about a time when impatience caused you trouble as a leader or in another area of your life? What were the ramifications of your impatience?

6. Can you think about a time when patience helped you make a better decision as a leader? What was the ultimate result of your patience?

7. What does it mean to have a long view, and how should that impact your patience? Where does trust factor into having that mindset?

8. Think back to the two Bible stories referenced in this chapter (Joseph, and Jesus and Peter). What are some truths from those stories that resonate with you as a leader or in your personal life?

9. Of the four keys to being a more patient leader, which are challenging to you and why? How might applying them more consistently help you be more patient?

10. What is the one thing you need to do today to begin following a more patient path as a leader?

Chapter 9 - SELF CONTROL

1. Who in your life have you seen model self-control? How have you been able to apply that example as a leader?

2. How easy or difficult do you find it to control the things you see and hear that create a thought pattern in your mind? Explain.

3. How well do you generally keep your emotions in check? What are some circumstances that make that incredibly challenging?

4. In what ways have you seen your thoughts and emotions lead to self-control issues with your words?

5. In what ways have you seen your thoughts and emotions lead to self-control issues with your actions?

6. Give an example in general or in your own life of how negative inputs produce negative outputs (a lack of self-control). Now, do the reverse and share how positive inputs have led to positive outputs (a display of self-control).

7. Which of the three temptations (lust of the eyes, lust of the flesh, pride of life) do you struggle with most?

8. How can Christ's three examples of self-control in Matthew 4:1-11 help you overcome the same issues you face?

9. Read Ephesians 4:26-27, Proverbs 18:21, and Philippians 4:8. How do these passages show the biblical path to overcoming common issues of self-control?

10. Of the seven keys to self-control, which do you most need to activate? What would your life as a leader and in general look like if you consistently did so?

Chapter 10 - LOYALTY I

1. In this chapter, Coach Osborne talks about his earliest exposure to loyalty (his father and Bob Devaney). Who are some people that have demonstrated loyalty in your life?

2. How did those loyalty examples impact how you lead today?

3. Can you think of a time when your loyalty cost you something?

4. Do you feel like you were ultimately rewarded in the long run, or do you feel like your loyalty still puts you at a disadvantage?

5. Is loyalty ultimately worth it in every situation? Explain.

6. When has someone been disloyal to you? How did you deal with that experience? How did it impact your commitment to be loyal to others?

7. When you read about Jesus' disciples and those who founded the Christian church, how do their loyalty to God and the mission of the gospel challenge you to be more loyal in your personal life?

8. Take some time to read and discuss the following passages: Proverbs 18:24, John 15:13, and 1 Corinthians 16:13-14.

9. What are some areas of your life where you could improve your loyalty? What steps can you take today toward that effort?

10. What are some ways that you can fight the temptation to be disloyal? What steps can you take today toward that effort?

Chapter 11 - LOYALTY II

1. What has been one of the more difficult instances where your loyalty was tested (tempted to be disloyal, etc.)? How did you respond in that situation, and what resulted from your actions?

2. What would be an instance where you felt like your loyalty was being questioned? How did you respond in that situation, and what resulted from your actions?

3. Have you ever been given an opportunity to return loyalty to someone loyal to you? If so, what was your response?

4. Has someone ever returned loyalty to you? If so, how did that make you feel, and how did it impact your future decisions?

5. Have you ever been on the wrong side of disloyalty? If so, how did you respond to such hurtful actions?

6. Read Proverbs 17:17 and Proverbs 21:21. What are some lessons about loyalty that you can take away from these passages?

7. Read Matthew 7:12. How might living out this teaching impact your approach to loyalty?

8. What might "next-level loyalty" look like in your life?

9. How would you expect increased loyalty within your team or organization to impact on daily operations and long-term outcomes?

10. What are some things you need to do as a leader and within your organization to help you achieve that loyalty throughout?

Chapter 12 - SERVING

1. Why do you think many people lack meaning and purpose today? Has that ever been something you have experienced? Explain.

2. How would you define the term "servant leadership?" In what ways have you tried to implement this concept in your own life?

3. Who are some people in your life that have modeled servant leadership? What lessons have your learned from them that you have been able to apply to your role as a leader?

4. How have you tried to guard against the temptation to serve others for disingenuous or prideful reasons?

5. How would you say serving others is connected to true purpose? How do you balance the difficult aspects of caring for people's needs with understanding the purpose?

6. What inspiration do you take from those biblical servant leaders (David, Esther, Peter and Paul) referenced in this chapter? Who are some other biblical figures that have inspired you to serve others?

7. Read Matthew 20:25-28. What is the contrast between the examples Jesus set as a servant leader versus the typical leadership we see in today's world?

8. Read Galatians 6:9-10. What specific encouragement do you receive from this teaching from Paul?

9. Of the five keys to serving listed in this chapter, which ones have you struggled to walk out as a leader and in your personal life? Explain.

10. What steps can you take today to help you become a more holistic servant leader?

Chapter 13 - MENTORING

1. What is your experience with mentoring (have been mentored, currently mentoring someone, or have no previous experience)?

2. If you have been mentored or are currently being mentored, how has that relationship helped your personal, professional, and spiritual development?

3. Have you ever mentored someone? If so, what was that experience like? If not, why haven't you entered the world of mentoring?

4. In what ways might an increase in mentoring positively impact our world?

5. What hindrances might leaders face if they consider becoming a mentor? Have you personally faced those hindrances, and if so, how have you overcome them?

6. Where are some places that you might be able to be a mentor if you aren't already or if you're looking to expand your reach?

7. Looking back at the biblical examples referenced, what things stand out to you regarding the benefits of mentoring (e.g., preparing the next generation, empowering others to do greater things, etc.)?

8. Read 2 Timothy 2:1-2 and discuss how mentoring can have a ripple effect. What might that look like for you as a leader at work, home, church, community, etc.?

9. Read through the Proverbs shared in this chapter. What are some of the most relevant pieces of advice that you can use in your mentoring journey?

10. Of the five steps to get started as a mentor, which ones have you struggled to implement? How might taking those steps impact your ability to expand your reach and impact future generations?

Chapter 14 - EMPOWERMENT

1. Can you think of a time when a leader empowered you and allowed you to take personal responsibility for your job or role within a family, team, or organization? How did that help improve your confidence?

2. Do you generally find it easy or hard to give away responsibility? Explain.

3. Do you utilize the tool of delegation? If so, do you find yourself taking responsibility back quickly, or do you tend to leave that responsibility in others' hands for as long as possible?

4. When are you tempted to micromanage your team, and what does that typically look like? Is this an effective method? Explain.

5. Go back and look at the three biblical examples of empowerment. What are some inspirational or challenging takeaways from those stories?

6. Read 1 Corinthians 12:14-19. How might embracing the concept of the Body of Christ help you be more intentional about engaging in empowering leadership?

7. Read Matthew 10:5-8. How does this story exemplify empowerment? How does it inspire you to give people more freedom to once they have the tools to do their jobs?

8. Read Matthew 28:19-20. In what ways is Jesus' command to the disciples the ultimate example of empowerment?

9. Of the four steps to empowering others, which ones do you struggle with the most and why? How might implementing those principles help you become a more confident and empowering leader?

10. What is the one thing you need to do today that will help you take that leap of trust into empowering leadership?

Chapter 15 - CONFIDENCE

1. What is your definition of the word "confidence?" Where do you think confidence comes from?

2. On a scale of 1 to 10 (1 = no confidence at all, 10 = extremely confident), how would you rate your confidence as a person in general and as a leader?

3. Who is someone you believe has a lot of confidence? What other traits have they exhibited that helped you make that determination?

4. What are some things that build your confidence and why? How important is belief in that equation, and where does that belief typically come from?

5. How do the cornerstones of confidence (affirmation, repetition, and competence) impact your confidence and the confidence of those whom you are called to lead?

6. What things tend to erode your confidence or create insecurity in your role as a leader and in your personal life?

7. Have you ever become overconfident? If so, what were the ramifications of that mindset?

8. Look back at the Bible stories referenced in this chapter. What were some of the key actions and circumstances that gave them the confidence to do great things?

9. Read 2 Corinthians 3:5, Hebrews 10:35-36, and Romans 8:38-39. What are some ways the Bible tells us we can gain true confidence (not self-confidence) through a relationship with God?

10. Of the six steps listed to building or restoring confidence, which ones have you struggled to follow in your leadership journey? How might embracing those principles help you avoid insecurity and overconfidence and become the confident leader God wants you to be?

Chapter 16 - UNITY

1. What is your definition of the word "unity?"

2. How would you describe the state of unity in our world today? Why do you think unity has been such an elusive principle throughout humankind?

3. From your experience and understanding of history, what things tend to unite a group? What are some things that tend to break down or destroy unity?

4. Is unity something your team or organization finds easy or difficult? Why is that so?

5. What usually happens when there is unity within a team, organization, community, nation, etc.? What usually happens if there is disunity? Provide some examples for both.

6. Compare and contrast the two Old Testament stories shared in this chapter. How did the concept of unity factor into the outcome?

7. How can favoritism or a lack of respect for all team members affect the greater organization? How does Jesus' parable in Matthew 18:12-13 provide a different take on unity?

8. Read Acts 2:42-47. In what ways did the early Christians model unity? What inspiration can you take from their story?

9. Of the four ways listed to cultivate unity, which ones have you struggled to implement from your leadership position and why? How might putting those strategies in play more authentically and consistently change the outlook of your organization's unity?

10. What do you need to start doing today that will help you end any divisiveness within your team and bring forth a spirit of true unity and togetherness?

Chapter 17 - PERSEVERANCE

1. What is the most challenging thing you've experienced as a leader? In that circumstance, did you quit, blame someone or something else, or look at it as an opportunity? Explain.

2. Why do people tend to avoid adversity at all costs? Have you ever done this, and if so, what was the outcome of your story?

3. Do you agree or disagree that adversity can be a blessing? If you agree, have you experienced this in your life, and how did that situation work out for your good? If you disagree, will you consider that your story may not be over?

4. Can you think of a time when a tragedy or disappointment seemed terrible at first but turned out to be not as bad and possibly turned out to be a good thing? Explain.

5. Read through 2 Corinthians 11:24-30. What do you think gave Paul the ability to persevere through such adverse circumstances?

6. Read James 1:2-4. In what ways have you seen adversity develop moral character and endurance in your life?

7. Read 2 Corinthians 12:9 and John 16:33. How should those passages embolden and strengthen you to get through even the most difficult circumstances?

8. Of the five key reminders on how to persevere through life's troubles, which ones do you struggle to act on the most?

9. How might embracing those principles help you better face adversity?

10. What one thing do you need to do today to develop your perseverance further and lead with unshakable strength in Christ?

Chapter 18 - EXCELLENCE

1. What is your definition of excellence?

2. Do you think it's possible to achieve excellence but not necessarily achieve the highest awards, accolades, or material benefits? If so, what might be an example that illustrates that point?

3. Can you pursue excellence with impure motives? If so, how might that impact the actions attached to that pursuit?

4. What are some of the dangers of mediocrity? How have you personally fought against mediocrity in your own life?

5. Of the three building blocks of excellence (work ethic, consistency, and discipline), which are the most important and why? Which of them do you struggle with the most, and how has that impacted your pursuit of excellence?

6. How would you describe your attempt to balance the pursuit of excellence against your personal values and inner motives?

7. Read Matthew 5:13-16. What are some ways that you can be salt and light as a leader?

8. Read Colossians 3:23-24 and Titus 2:7-8. How do you think pursuing excellence for God's glory might impact your daily actions as you lead others?

9. Of the six ways to pursue true greatness given in this chapter, which ones do you struggle to implement in your daily life? How might embracing those principles fully impact your approach to excellence?

10. What is the one thing you can start doing today that will jump-start a deeper pursuit of excellent leadership?

Chapter 19 - TRANSFORMATION

1. How would you differentiate between the word "change" and the word "transformation?"

2. As a leader, what are some ways that you feel like you should be transforming over time? How do you hope to see your team members transform over time?

3. How do you define transactional leadership? How do you define transformational leadership?

4. Do you ever feel the tension between the practical necessities for transactional leadership versus the long-term impact you hope to have through transformational leadership? If so, is it possible to utilize elements of the former while primarily focusing on the latter, and what is the proper balance?

5. What are some markings of a transformational leader? Have you experienced this personally? Explain.

6. In what ways were Jesus' life and ministry examples of transformational leadership?

7. How does Paul's conversion story impact your view of what positive radical change can look like? Have you ever seen anything like that in your personal or professional life?

8. Read 2 Corinthians 5:17, Romans 12:2, and Colossians 3:8-10. What are some of the markings of a transformed life that jump out at you through these passages?

9. Of the nine attributes of a transformational leader listed in this chapter, which ones do you struggle with the most in your leadership role and why?

10. What steps do you need to take today that will help you get started down the path toward transformational leadership?

Chapter 20 - SUCCESS

1. What are some past awards or accolades that are a part of your past and how often do you dwell on them?

2. What is your definition of success? How much would you say your definition of success matches up with or differs from modern culture's definition?

3. What does short-term success look like for you as a leader, and how do you measure it?

4. How much thought do you put into long-term success? What are some big-picture goals that you are pursuing?

5. What does the phrase "collateral damage" mean to you as a leader or someone who has been an employee or team member? Have you ever caused collateral damage or been caught up in someone else's? If so, what lessons did you learn from that experience?

6. How do you balance the demand for material success (financial gains, wins, losses, etc.) with a desire to pursue lasting spiritual and eternal success?

7. What inspiration do you take from Paul's story of having everything and then walking away to pursue the biblical definition of success? Why do you think he would do that?

8. Read Hebrews 13:14. What does that passages tell you about the meaning of eternal success? How much do you think about the next life and whether or not material success truly matters?

9. Read Matthew 6:19-21. What does this passage tell you about the importance of material success versus eternal success?

10. What's one thing you need to do today that will help you shift your mindset away from material success toward spiritual and eternal success?